THE LAST BEST
ADVENTURE

Howard L. Smith

ISBN: 0615503659
ISBN-13: 978-0615503653

Acknowledgements

The front cover of this book is graced by a copyrighted inspiration from Ward Hooper of Ward Hooper Gallery in Boise, Idaho (wardhooper.com; 208-287-8150). An immensely talented artist, Ward is renowned throughout the Northwest for his iconic historic and vintage renditions. Thank you Ward for capturing the very essence of *The Last Best Adventure* in a single memorable image.

Lesley Van Foster's considerable creative talents assisted in the production of this book. Without her collegiality, joie de vivre, capacity for spirited thinking, commitment to action, and enthusiastic encouragement, these pages would merely exist as an electronic file. Thank you Lesley for making such a difference.

Boise State University supported the creation of this book through a sabbatical in academic year 2011-2012.

A portion of "The End of Adventure" (Chapter I) was adapted and extended for an academic audience and appeared in the *International Journal of Wilderness* in 2011.

Finally deepest appreciation is reserved for my wife, Valerie, who enjoyed, and sometimes endured, my quest for backcountry revelations. Over the years we have discovered that love is truly the best epiphany of all.

THE LAST BEST ADVENTURE
Chapter Outline

Page

Shaping Identity

Venerating the Ineffable

I

The End of Adventure

Turn out the lights, the party's over.
Adventure is dead.

Kaput. Over. Fini.

Game-set-and-match.

It's a wrap.

Earth-based journeys into the unknown are sliding toward an inevitable endgame. Few places on this magnificent planet have escaped explorers' snowboards, footsteps, parachutes, paddles, skis, or knobby bike tires. Supremely remote enclaves that haven't been touched are squarely in the sights of determined adventurers armed with satellite maps, GPS and assorted technological accoutrements. They are on a mad rush to chalk up remaining "firsts;" the last exploration trophies left to conquer.

Adventure aficionados the world over have their work cut out for them. Although all 8,000+ meter peaks have fallen, there remain plenty of virgin 7,000+ meter peaks. Untold tributaries spilling into the world's major rivers remain inviolate for that courageous first run. Zillions of cliffs, bridges, towers and buildings call to the BASE jumping community. Mountain bikers, skiers and snowboarders can forge new track down slopes previously considered not run-able; possibilities are limited only by imagination. Countless acres of jungle, tundra and forest have never known the weight of a human being.

In this sense adventure isn't truly dead; it has swaggered into a definitive lingering phase of glowing twilight years. Those who live for interminable physical battering, carousing through uncharted territory and enduring mental sufferfests still have sufficient reason to be very optimistic.

Another interesting twist also shapes adventure's future. Even decades ago as Mt. Everest, deepest Africa, and the Arctic ice cap fell to victors' flag-planting; adventure was undergoing a transformation, a redefinition. An expansive new horizon was unfolding as thrilling possibilities bubbled up.

One of adventure's most respected multi-sport prodigies, Mark Jenkins, couches the end of an era this way, "Striving for superlatives is part of human nature – the highest, the longest, and the deepest. But now that many of these goals have been reached, the future of adventure lies in more subtle, more discriminating endeavors….*Adventure will be less about simply surviving and more about performing with grace and virtuosity. More personal, more internal, just you and your dream*" (Italics added).

Jenkins reached this revelation after a failed summit attempt with his partner on 20,059-foot Nyambo Konka in the far eastern edge of the Tibetan plateau. Back at base camp he searches in vain for another option up this impressive unclimbed peak — another "first" to be notched on his ice tools, this time one where he will solo. Unfortunately no probable line surfaces that's even remotely safe; all have risks outweighing the value of reaching the summit.

Jenkins retreats; confident of the correctness of his decision but wondering what it all means.

Another legendary mountaineer getting old?

Perhaps.

On the other hand, Jenkins is at the height of his game on Nyambo Konka. The weather is accommodating if breathtakingly windy. He has dealt with gnarly ice, rotten rock and cleaving crevasses on countless other expeditions. Everything points to a climb of heroic proportions. However, this time something deep within Jenkins, an awakening, argues vehemently to forego the insanity of a summit bid.

Jenkins' introspective weighing of odds for achieving the summit versus risk of not making it back to his wife and daughters illustrate both his maturation as an adventurer and attainment of another elusive level in mountaineering. He realizes that adventure is more than chalking up another superficial "first;" it is about intensifying one's personal understanding through discovery. Jenkins' moment is akin to that plaguing countless explorers before him when they discern something vitally mental, emotional or spiritual beyond the joy of being first or exceeding the bliss of having survived physically.

Jenkins admits that a decade earlier he would not have hesitated to try one of the calamity-infested routes offering access to Nyambo. But his scruples have little to do with age since he is at the physical and mental peak of adventuring. Mark Jenkins' hesitancy primarily reflects his expanding personal horizon of why and how he climbs mountains. Such a transformation can occur at any point in a lifetime of passionately pursuing adventure; it's not the sole purview of over-the-hill mountaineers.

Startling parallels are evident between Jenkins' reflection and that of another renowned adventurer, Richard Bangs. A former

Colorado River guide gone ballistic on world-wide adventure, Bangs can be credited with commoditizing life-challenging experiences through his firm Sobek Expeditions. Bangs launched commercial adventure travel bereft of fundamental hardship. Sobek clients could do it all: smell the stink of high-tech petrochemical gear after multi-day trekking, taste fear's brittle metallic flavor, listen as potentially deadly conditions closed in on them, feel the shiver of danger, and see big-time adventure unfold on a personal plasma full-screen, while at the same time being pampered by cushy support — comparatively sumptuous lodging, gourmet meals and effortless customer-centered service.

There is a downside. Clients who partake in this genre of adventure usually miss out on the magic — persevering through grueling and deplorable circumstances. Risk is carefully managed while comfort waits until clients survive harrowing and occasionally life-threatening escapades.

Thirty years after launching Sobek, Bangs observes that commoditized adventure often approximates authentic experiences, but it seldom leads to *"...the epiphany that came with a special effort, time and place."* Like Jenkins, Bangs is referring to that unique moment when adventure attains a higher level of meaning because someone has a gripping revelation, discovery, epiphany, paradigm shift, or other soul-altering realization; they transcend being first on an ice-throttled peak or first at careening down a raging river.

Yvon Chouinard, founder of Chouinard Equipment (later reinvented as Black Diamond Ltd.) and Patagonia, Inc., experienced a similar transformation as Jenkins and Bangs. However, Chouinard's moment didn't happen in the field on some distant mountain or in a river but rather on the business-side of outdoor equipment. In his book *Let My People Go Surfing* Chouinard recounts the crisis Patagonia reached on July 31, 1991 when recession fueled a

20 percent shortfall in sales. Chouinard terminated 20 percent of Patagonia's workforce in order to save his business. It was a watershed moment.

Terminating 120 employees who had grown into family members sparked an epiphany for Chouinard: Patagonia, Inc. was irrevocably addicted to growth. From that moment forward Patagonia assumed more responsibility for living within resources and constraints. This epiphany-moment spun off a continuing search for goals and strategies that fit consistently with an earth-friendly philosophy of sustainability rather than economic growth for the sake of monetary gain.

As these illustrations suggest, the future of adventure isn't solely about being there first, achieving the most massively gigantic goal (whether in the outdoors or in business), or physically surviving extreme conditions at the edge. It's also about cultivating personal discoveries that lead to uniquely insightful epiphanies or revelations – *the last best adventure*.

For many adrenaline-crazed outdoor enthusiasts, the testaments of Jenkins, Bangs, and Chouinard may seem a bit heretical. After all, the common metrics outdoor devotees use to assess adventure typically are peaks bagged, thousands of vertical feet skied, trail miles covered, pounds carried, buildings scaled, hours of air time, or any of the hundreds of super-human goals associated with ragged-edge physical exertion. Conquering some near-8,000-meter peak in the Himalayas, kayaking a narrow Peruvian defile sloshing with wildly agitated whitewater, or paragliding over Kabul (and living to tell about it) are passé.

Times have changed.

For that reason, the manner in which outdoor exploits is measured will inevitably undergo redefinition. The last best adventure is as much if not more about mental, emotional and spiritual discovery when journeying through wild lands as it is physically surviving an outing. It's not exclusively the goal of being first in the world, but also taking self to a new level (a different kind of "first") in mental, spiritual and emotional development. Adventure's next frontier will be found in essentially subtle, discriminating discovery rather than physical one-upmanship.

The Last Best Adventure focuses squarely on epiphanies I learned during various explorations of wild country. When using the term "epiphany" I'm referring to an attention-grabbing revelation or vigorous insight into how and why I pursue outdoor adventure.

This book argues for the inestimable value gained from adventure beyond mere physical accomplishments. Physical challenges are very important in shaping informed understanding. However, when looking over the totality of adventures I've enjoyed, those of greatest value are soul-altering experiences rather than heroic physical conquests. As Jenkins, Bangs, Chouinard and other savvy outdoors addicts have discovered, this personal epiphany-side is adventure's future. We strive to get past glorifying physical accomplishments which exclude more primordial, spiritual, and emotional realms.

Each of the following chapters replays a compelling revelation (or revelations) I had in the course of various outdoor quests ranging from snowshoeing to rafting; from accumulating gear to enjoying wildlife encounters. Not surprisingly the magical epiphanies I've experienced tend to share common denominators and so have been loosely grouped together in this book.

Occasionally visceral eye-openers arise after bumping into something totally unexpected such as grizzly bear #399 and her 3 cubs in Grand Teton National Park. These collisions invigorate life and inject a healthy dose of fascinating thrill into backcountry travels. Surely many people discover, like me, that passion for adventure in the outdoors is fundamentally about living a big, richly invigorated life where the unanticipated inevitably intercedes.

I have also learned from disparate adventures that there is enormous worth in overcoming primal challenges and tackling rather hairy stretch goals. Confidence grows upon reaching remote alpine lakes; surviving Class IV+ rivers; battling snow storms; walking among dangerous predators and overcoming the entire litany of outdoor tests. In this sense physical prowess enhances personal independence. But, this doesn't have to translate into a continual grab for elusive "firsts." One-upmanship is pretty shallow compared to the comforting knowledge that I know my way around wild country and even wilder animals.

Exceptional individual-shaping moments in wild country have proven valuable in defining who I am as well as in shaping how I think, particularly about our natural environment. Chasing after adventure has taught me perspective and personal understanding. This is precisely what Mark Jenkins realized on looking at Nyambo. He finally achieved equilibrium between his family and his adventurous pursuits. One more "first" wasn't worth dying for. Jenkins had crossed that threshold from physical to psychic adventure.

Last but not least, I have become intensely sensitive to the spiritual overtones of wild country when tramping through knock-dead-gorgeous places and even rather mundane territory. I am continually reminded that there is something far more enduring at play in the wild than our human imprint. Accordingly, insightful discoveries associated with outdoor adventures enable a consciousness for, and commitment to, honoring sacred ground.

This set of epiphanies isn't exhaustive — that's the intriguing aspect of adventure's future frontier. By opening our minds to a broader, more full-bodied, definition of adventure the possibilities seem virtually endless. In the course of hunting adventure it's rather intriguing to see what revelations wait around the next grotto, over a stunning alpine pass, or through a patch of old-growth. This is all part and parcel of living a vibrantly vital life outdoors; something certainly worth striving to achieve.

Like an old dog worrying a rank T-bone, *The Last Best Adventure* mulls over ways to make old-school adventure more personally rewarding. In many respects the tales that follow serve as a how-to manual for enriching adventurous travels – focusing on how-to-find and how-to-enjoy soul-stirring discoveries. Through the epiphanies I've experienced fellow mountaineers, hikers, rafters and other outdoor fans may begin to see their personal adventures – past, present and future – in an entirely new and satisfying light. These revelations can help them shift their paradigm of thinking about adventure in a shrinking world beset with a plethora of harsh realities and depressing environmental implications.

Undoubtedly a decreasing cross-section of today's adventure buffs will continue clinging to traditional one-dimensional images. It isn't really adventure unless they vicariously brave the Sahara by camel, sleep close to alpha predators in the Rift Valley, or nearly freeze to death in the Arctic. Sadly this myopic view fails to do justice to the more robust spiritual, emotional and visceral sides of adventure. And, it fails to acknowledge what is becoming widely recognized in the adventuring community. Our pervasive human footprint has penetrated so deeply that few places are able to maintain pristine wildness. Animal species that are not yet extinct are either depleted or habituated and as a result only mimic their former wild selves.

These new realities argue vehemently for an enlightened world adventure ethos. If everyone flocks in a big panic to see the last polar bear or gorilla, we certainly won't save those species. Consider the environmental degradation that has resulted from commoditizing Everest Base Camp, Patagonia, Bhutan or any other popular destination made famous in trendy adventure media like *Outside* or the defunct *National Geographic Adventure.* There are simply too many people and too little wilderness with too little indigenous flora and fauna.

Those who are so obsessed with a one-dimensional love for adventure that they can't contemplate a more robust notion replete with mental, emotional, spiritual and intuitive overtones are encouraged to pause and reconsider why and how they look for adventure. Such questioning may in and of itself stimulate a revelation (or revelations) that lead to a more progressive, and sustainable, passion.

It's time we opened our minds, hearts and spirits to the next best adventure: discovering wild epiphanies.

Adventure as Epiphany

2

First Tastes of Epiphany

Wild-eyed Valkyrie goddesses with golden tresses flailing in the wind and festooned in gossamer burgundy tunics wheel erratically across the sky on flaming chariots. It's basically that kind of invigorating day; bruise-colored clouds fight a sparkling lemon sun for dominance. Swooshing frigid gales from the north are waging a wonderfully theatric battle against a Pineapple Express over Los Angeles. No sooner is daylight obscured and temperatures plummet, then whirlwinds swirl away cloud cover and radiant life returns; warmth penetrates to the core.

Driving from my low-rent Brentwood flat to Pasadena where a trail runs up Arroyo Seco Canyon behind Jet Propulsion Laboratory, I have no intention of getting very far into the San Gabriel Wilderness today. Solitude and exercise are all I seek; a reprieve from raucous car exhausts, slamming doors, loud radios blaring staccato rap beats across the neighborhood, snarling barking dogs defending apartment balconies, and boisterous arguments among loving partners.

I'm searching for a connection back to wild lands where L.A's overbearing urbanization evaporates like a bad dream. But, there is no way of anticipating that today's modest San Gabriel adventure will open my mind to an entirely new way of looking at hiking. A fundamental shift in thinking about the outdoors – a revelation – lays waiting beyond Arroyo Seco Canyon's trailhead.

Mid-afternoon traffic is semi-heavy, what other cities might call an inextricable traffic-jam, as throngs of cars clog the Ventura Freeway – what a lousy way to live, chained to impassable thoroughfares. By the time Pasadena's exit creeps up I'm ready to dump Los Angeles: too many people; too many cars; life has to be better than this. A trail guide suggests parking by the Laboratory, but this easily accessible lot immediately conjures anxious thoughts. Are unattended cars convenient targets for thieves? Which desperados are watching the lot this very minute?

Welcome to Los Angeles.

Following my trail guide's detailed instructions; I'm walking briskly north from the lot. Passing a Laboratory guard on duty, I expect to be vigorously interrogated at length about my intentions. Surprise! He pays absolutely no interest as I skirt a crusty galvanized chain-link fence and enter jungle-like growth of dense avocado-colored willows, variegated bamboo and washed-out chaparral shrubs. Jet Propulsion Laboratory's fortress looms in the west; hovering over this trail and raising skepticism about whether my travel effort is worth it – worth the hassle of fighting freeway traffic to get here. Paralleling the fence a trail hunts through thick vegetation that screens hush-hush, foreboding ambitions at the Lab.

A trickle of water is audible….

The rich smell of wet earth, damp growth and verdant life, abruptly overwhelms my senses.

Enchantment time…

This trail follows what amounts to a very decent little stream fresh with scurrying water pushing bits of white-silver-black-gray gravel along a serpentine canyon floor. Near-vertical walls laced with granite boulders like ancient faded Galapagos tortoise shells rise rapidly above this enchanting streambed, embracing it protectively from urban shock just yards away. Hillsides are covered in low-lying brush; dense, gray-brown and dry — perfect fodder for wildfire. From down in the canyon it is difficult to see what these cliffs rise toward. The ravine deepens and Arroyo Seco's trail dives for this streambed with its persistently steady flow, murmuring contentedly.

On reaching streamside a thrilling thought floods my mind. Here I am no more than one-quarter mile beyond the Jet Propulsion Laboratory compound and yet I have crossed a definable threshold into wilderness. I cannot see, hear or smell the Lab, but it's back there a few hundred yards, make no mistake about that. Wildness and solitude fill Arroyo Seco Canyon. It harbors almost nothing in the way of visible human touch and encroaching insidious civilization will be left far behind after leaping across these flowing waters.

Arroyo Seco's stream is richly swollen with fresh runoff from previous spring storms — they have been an abundant blessing to this otherwise desiccated watershed. This mini-torrent seems to possess a slightly wild character coursing down-canyon laden with bits of decomposed granite. In drier times the stream is undoubtedly more tranquil, perhaps only flowing beneath a sandy surface. My trail curves around a rocky corner to the left, but given impenetrable brush, it's impossible to see what lies ahead.

Puma? Bears? Rattlesnakes? What waits upstream in the very dark recesses of this remote and seldom used arroyo? To find out all I have to do is jump over the stream and keep going for several miles. It's not any more complex than that.

Preparing to take the leap I have a gnawing intuitive feel that something far more magnificent waits up canyon. With limited time to explore, it'll be impossible to fully capture this unknown gift, but instinctively I know wild adventure is there – the thrill of uncharted feral territory.

That's when an epiphany unfurls.

I've come to Arroyo Seco seeking peace and exercise as a tonic. That's it: all I want is a modest workout and time away from other people.

Instead there is more waiting for me; much more than I ever thought possible.

That Arroyo Seco insight became a personal image for the topsy-turvy mosaic associated with wild country: risk from the unknown; solitude, even lonesomeness, from humanity's oppressive presence; magnificence of natural lands untouched; the physical and mental challenges of negotiating raw wilderness; and the entire kaleidoscope of emotions and experiences accompanying adventure beyond civilization's boundaries.

After Arroyo Seco I will forever look at trailheads with a different set of spectacles. Launch point for a multi-day raft trip down the Deschutes River; Indian Creek's trailhead in the Glacier Peak Wilderness; an unnamed river landing for a float plane in Katmai National Park; and thousands of other portals to backcountry explorations have become symbolic of wildness itself – special doorways to that other side of adventure where wild epiphanies wait.

Poised to jump across Arroyo Seco's stream I achieve a level of fulfillment that makes further exploration up the canyon unnecessary. I'm fully content with this merry stream flowing raucously at my side. Birds are calling and flitting about in an impenetrable mass of willows. Scents of life waft over me, heady with bouquet reeking of fecund earth and unimaginable possibilities of nature gone wild.

The visual peace of a canyon driven by the perfect interplay of rock, greenery and upslope surround this little enclave. The sound of wilderness settles in the canyon bereft of the city's hum, but yards distant.

I leap over the stream, part the veil of wildness and begin the quest. Catamounts, bears, magnificent tranquil pools, rattlesnakes, showy wildflowers, secret forested glens – does anyone truly know what waits ahead? That's the delight of wilderness – you never know what to expect down these backcountry paths.

Mostly it is the unpredicted that materializes. Seek bears; find waterfall. Search for wildflowers; discover a colossal river of boulders. Hunt for an inspirational viewpoint; sight a red-tail hawk gliding effortlessly on the wind. Come to think of it, perhaps the anticipated aspects of wilderness are merely an excuse to find magical epiphanies and to wallow deeply in their embrace.

A life dedicated to outdoor adventure has to begin somewhere and for me that moment and place was Arroyo Seco's canyon. I fell passionately head-over-heels into backcountry adventuring; hiking, backpacking, rafting, snowshoeing, camping and the myriad other activities centered on wild places.

As these adventures accumulated I began to notice a distinctive pattern. Like many outdoor followers I first focused on peak bagging, trail mileage milestones, surviving brutally gruesome conditions, and related adrenaline-laced goals. Epic slogs through incredibly rough country and despicable weather were all fundamental prerequisites of rugged outdoors-craft. I took great pride in assembling heroic accomplishments.

Nonetheless, it wasn't gallant macho deeds that ultimately grabbed my attention, although these were important in punching my card as a bona fide adventurer. What continually held sway and mattered most were the consistent subtle, but meaning-laden, discoveries materializing without warning; insights of astonishing understanding surfacing when I least expected them.

* * *

Exuberant from my little foray to Arroyo Seco, it was time to try my hand at peak bagging. I set my sights on conquering Strawberry Peak; a hike that requires a modicum of confidence and dexterity to successfully scramble the Peak's steep upper ramparts.

Strawberry Peak is a siren spire named by late Nineteenth Century adventurers reposing at Switzer's Camp along Arroyo Seco River. To them this looming peak looked exactly like a gigantic strawberry as it captured a day's last sunny rays before nightfall, radiating alpenglow. Down there in the massive umbrella-shaped sycamores, impenetrable willows, and stringy alders where mere mortals played, this peak was a beneficent beacon calling them to higher explorations.

Like those adventurous predecessors I too felt Strawberry Peak's weight when I first explored Arroyo Seco with its prancing waters, plush vegetation, and infamous Switzer Falls. Commodore Switzer Camp was beyond charming due to its effusive greenness among these normally parched San Gabriel and San Bernardino mountains. But, Strawberry Peak served as a continual reminder that the true throne of the mountain gods waited 3,254 feet higher in rarified air; a colossal granite buttress where even the holiest of angels dared to tread lightly, genuflecting as visitors to this grand and glorious citadel.

I pull into the nearly vacant parking lot at Red Box Ranger Station a dozen-plus-miles above the up-scale community of La Cañada where every teen is above average and drives only the finest imported metal. A man on a mission, I have my game face on and set to go. Strawberry Peak will be mine today after tackling it the hard way – not along some easy ridge walk, but straight up the near-vertical northern backside groping my way through a boulder minefield.

Bona fide wilderness rests below Strawberry Peak's edifice. With this 6,164-foot peak standing guard overlooking the San Fernando Valley, its northeastern backside enjoys a bountiful blessing of shade. As is so often the case, this huge summit blocks California's penetrating sunny rays during the heat of the afternoon. This spells a completely different microclimate than the western face. And what a staggering dissimilarity it is. Instead of waist-high scrub, a captivating meadow in the peak's silhouette is fringed by healthy chaparral leading into dense copses of pines and occasional spruce.

Unlike other San Gabriel trails which struggle through crisp-fried grass, chaparral bordering my trail is almost as grossly bountiful as the matted shaggy mane of an ancient lion. Live oak dimple the grassy bowl and with it a vibrant community of red-limbed manzanita, brittle scrub oak and always optimistic mountain mahogany. However, this relatively verdant under-story cannot hold a candle to luxurious forest anchoring the mountain slopes. Regal Jeffrey and Coulter pine discovered sound purchase on Strawberry's underbelly and enough nutrients and moisture to flourish. There's nothing like a good bit of healthy forest in Southern California to make one feel as though wildness is at hand.

Reaching this paradise will be easy. All I have to do is plod along a fire road for a couple miles and drop down into the sylvan bowl. I have become accustomed to hiking through chaparral's necessary monotony. It isn't necessarily displeasing to look at; dryness is the disturbing factor. One match, one little spark, and it is evident for all to see that this stuff can blow into a conflagration that only an endless procession of slurry bombers can ever contain after thousands of acres have been charred and untold little critters turned into toast.

A barely detectable chill hangs in the air. Goodness, it is uplifting to begin these forays early in the morning. Up out of the grimy brown poisonous smog suffocating Los Angeles' lowlands, a semblance of normal air waits above on these higher peaks. It is almost foreign to not have my eyes stinging and watering; to exit that noxious haze continually slamming me in the face and drowning my lungs in toxic vapors.

Equally fortifying is the sense of moisture mixed with coolness. Chaparral communities thrive in otherwise impossibly dry conditions because of summer's fog, a brief respite that nourishes until winter's snows or rains return proper amounts of life-giving water to the land. Visualize what it's like to go from breathing acrid smog to suddenly walking with your nostrils refreshingly attuned to a calliope of scents woven within a melody of invigorating humidity. In the first twenty yards after setting foot on the trail my senses blossom with an elixir of life.

A little saddle connects Mt. Lawlor and Strawberry Peak; it's the critical decision point for me and a crucial descent toward Strawberry Spring. One always has to be cautious about these abrupt changes in the landscape. I don't want to be needlessly hiking back up this trail because I went the wrong way only to lose the ability to reach my target. But, the way seems clear and shortly the path bounces in-and-out of forest as I swing toward the tantalizing prospect of running water.

Approximately one-mile later I reach Strawberry Peak's grass-filled meadow and realization that wildness surrounds me. To this point I've been semi-waltzing along without any deep cares in the world. It's a nice morning and I'm relishing the press of fresh mountain air and rich scents. Feels great to be out in lonesome country – I've not seen a single soul since beginning this escapade.

What transforms this hike is more than the sum of solitude, clean air, and near-forest vegetation. *Silence* commandeers this backside of Strawberry Peak. I can't hear Los Angeles' continuous din anymore. On west slopes a persistent hum rises from millions of souls going about their lives. Mainly I mentally block out this pollution; my ears have become so accustomed to it that it doesn't exist. Moments like this reinforce how oppressive living in a huge metropolis is compared to distant backcountry.

As I pause at a little gully to get my bearings, I have one of those epitome moments. There's still a hint of chill in the air and an effervescent sun bores right through to the bones – seemingly bypassing any intervening flesh – but not making it seem overly hot. My nose informs me about a distinctively warm-chaparral aroma that hovers over this meadow. Occasion zephyrs bring a tangy perfume of pine drilling through musty chaparral. Spruce and pine bracketing this meadow are fighting for control. I'm searching for the bouquet of damp earth and water – telltale signs of Strawberry Spring's life-giving fount. I'm anxious to check out any tracks to see if puma or bear have been frequenting this oasis.

Spinning a slow-motion 360 degrees, I soak in all of this goodness and begin to meld with the land. But, I can't quite overcome my astonishment at the vacuum of noise. It's so perfectly silent that my ears almost hurt. There's not even a methodic pattern of airplanes passing overhead destined for one of a zillion airports in Los Angeles' massive catchment area.

Not a single human sound is discernible.

A fly buzzing me sounds like a helicopter.

A slight breeze blowing through the Jeffrey pines swish for a moment before becoming still.

Grass bends in a faint slump across this meadow emitting an infinitesimally soft sigh carried to my ears in a most delicate way. Three live oak leaves fall to the forest floor in a muted crinkle.

I am as intimate with Strawberry Peak as a person can possibly be without living in this place.

Which way to go?

Clearly I don't want to follow the trail down the gully – that leads to Colby Ranch. I'm looking for red arrows painted on rocks that stretch toward the massive cliff rising directly overhead, and I'm still searching for the proverbial spring. Where is it in this maze of vegetation?

Scrambling up beneath a dowager live oak, watching every step I take for fear of rattlesnakes, I see a toaster-sized moss-covered granite-gray rock with a faded swatch of red paint. Here's the trail, at last. I was getting a bit nervous about finding this needle in a haystack and the prospect of retracing my steps loomed as a distinct probability if I didn't ferret-out some sort of marker before very long. One little niggling problem persists – I still haven't found the doggone spring. There's not a clue from this perspective looking out across the meadow: no bright green plants; no healthier looking shrubs; and certainly not a channel of damp earth.

I focus on finding the next virtually hidden marker, another rather pocket-sized stone almost forty feet directly overhead – straight-up above me. To get there I have to balance on a marble-field of unstable rocks looking like they'll cascade down into the meadow at any moment. And, much to my annoyance, this isn't some trail, but a pick-your-way around shrubs and deadfall from the surrounding live oaks and pines.

The decision is made. I want to stay on-track inside this cool canopy that is at least twenty degrees cooler than out in the meadow. No wonder this miniature forest is thriving so well. Strawberry

Peak more than adequately shelters the entire north face from too much sun. Conditions also suggest a perfect setting for snakes. With all of the rocks there are plenty of places to crawl into and the spring likely brings a wonderful smorgasbord of birds, rabbits, squirrels and crawling things to quench a viper's gnawing craving. Given how well camouflaged most snakes are, this is a perfect place to grab onto one as I pull myself up the 50+ degree hillside, or to unwittingly step on one as I try to make progress upward.

Totally concentrating, I'm drilling down into the moment. All my senses are in play as I try to locate the next little zig or zag up this mountain, and to make progress without doing something stupid such as falling on my butt or becoming a snake's worst friend. I'm so focused that it becomes an immense adventure. And, there's this rising feeling of confidence in what I can do, and not do, alone out in the wilderness.

Halfway up the peak I stop and pull out a sesame-honey bar for more energy. A long sip of water drains my bottle to half-full. I'm beginning to realize that I need to carry more fluid and snacks since I'm going to continue tackling physical challenges of this heft. If this route were in the direct sun I'd be hard-pressed for water right now. I chew on this thought for a few more seconds as heaving breaths subside.

Eventually I haul my body up an increasingly vertical draw of slippery rocks and gravel weaving among large boulders and diminishing tree cover. I can see a gradual flattening toward a ridge – hopefully a shoulder of Strawberry Peak from which the final scramble will ensue. I'm beginning to discern more boot-beaten track so I'm confident that I must be going in the right direction. That's when I hit this modest ridge and a final, much more vertical, path to the summit.

I drain half of what's remaining in my bottle. I now know that I'll make it since even in this mid-day sun there is nowhere to go but down once I peak-out. Slinging my pack back in place, I continue to grab for handholds, test my footing, and sash shay around shrubs as the peak comes into view.

I'm there.

What a climb that was. Twirling a full circle I cop a stupendous view of the San Gabriel's and what appear to be the far northern reaches of the San Bernardino's. I can even see the Pacific Ocean and the Brentwood/Santa Monica area where my little abode lies. How exhilarating this day has been up a Class-three scramble.

As I look north toward lonesome high desert country an older fellow comes crawling up the last thirty feet, picking his way carefully from rock to rock. He's effusive on topping out and I can relate to his joy in having made it this far. I'm especially impressed because he is no spring chicken.

He blows out for a few minutes, takes in the view and then sits down.

Next thing I know he's striking up a conversation. Now, I didn't come to the wilderness seeking people; but I have to admit that I'm intrigued about what makes a fellow his age — perhaps mid 60s — decide to risk life and limb climbing a mountain. "What do you do down in the city?" he asks.

"I'm a full-time graduate student, and you?"

"Well…I used to be an architect. But, I retired and quit my firm back in February. Now I've got plenty of time to go hiking."

"How often do you hike?"

"Forty years ago I made a decision to hike one major trail every week of my life. I've lived up to that commitment for the most part when I gave up smoking. I needed something to replace that lethal urge. It's pretty obvious to me that hiking has saved my life."

I had to admit that he wasn't pudgy in the slightest. He radiated health and a deeper spiritual well-being.

"Here's one of my former business cards. Give me a call if you want to go hiking someday."

With a sincere goodbye I start down ridge toward the saddle I crossed a couple hours earlier. It was a different hiker who cleaved that saddle early in the morning – one who was still learning his way about the details of walking in wilderness. I was so focused on the actual doing of it that I didn't have time to reflect on the bigger picture. That all has changed.

Certainly the technical lessons of scrambling Strawberry Peak were a concrete take-away from my morning's investment. I was more confident about my ability to handle the physical challenges. I still needed to make some refinements in what I carried. I was less hesitant about leaving a clearly-marked trail for a route that might grow obscure.

Even the visceral pleasure of becoming one with a wild spot in the mountains was *not* part of the most monumental revelation I had. Those rare moments in the meadows below Strawberry Peak continued to hold sway in my mind as truly distinctive and symbolic of what I would henceforth chase in each and every hike. But, that magic of wildness did not compare with a larger epiphany that dominated my mind.

I was returning redefined; committed to getting out in the backcountry as often as I possibly could. Forty-plus years from now I want to be like that former architect. Did he have any idea about how he influenced my thinking on a magical spire? He helped launch me on a quest for wildness. I looked forward to accumulating as many forays into wild country as I could possibly assemble over the course of my life. I envisioned myself forty years later as fit and trim as he – with clarity in my eyes equal to that in his.

Decades after that fortunate meeting I still wonder whether it was a real person that I met on Strawberry Peak or some sort of angelic apparition. In my mind's eye I can make out his athletic build, albeit in a 60-something husk of a man; his short cropped gray hair bristling around a bald dome; wiry glasses, white t-shirt and navy blue shorts; and a most remarkable twinkle in his eye.

* * *

First tastes of epiphany – everyone who becomes captivated by wilderness eventually confronts these rites of passage head-on. These initial experiences embody the depth and breadth of revelations that, for me, were refined in subsequent tramps through supremely wild country. Wilderness, I discovered, is a gateway to adventure and so much more: a vibrantly rich mosaic of physical and mental challenges; a restorative tonic of serenity, silence, solitude and mystery; and, a setting for honing gritty details about gear and technique that makes such explorations possible.

In the final analysis one revelation embodied by a retired architect (or possibly a guardian spirit) stands head and shoulders above the rest: a life lived for wildness is a life more likely to be lived long and deeply rich.

3

A Diminutive Mountain Lake

Auntie issued a very prophetic warning as we chatted about my impending move to Washington from rain-starved Southern California. *"Trees are thicker than bloated fleas on a mangy dog's hide. They're so dense that it looks like they'll grow right up out of the asphalt."* This was an eye-opening prophesy since only once – one time – in two decades-plus had I seen snow fall in Southern California. I never owned a coat with any hint of honest-to-goodness insulation until I was twenty-something-plus.

California's Mediterranean anchor was about to be blown to smithereens. The Northwest delivers huge swings in temperature, rain and snow compared to southern climes. But that wasn't the primary point of Auntie's not-so-subtle prediction. It's what precipitation creates in the way of luxuriant vegetation and seemingly endless trees – infinite green, green, green foliage dominating the land; Douglas fir, maples, western red cedar, alders and hemlock forming forests with chokingly dark claustrophobia and smothering emerald canopies.

Those who have visited the Northwest know the feeling of slap-happy anticipation. It's a supernatural land with vastly entertaining and highly civilized cities such as Portland and Seattle. The Northwest is where Starbucks, Nike, Microsoft, and thousands of other chic firms matured from infancy to household brands. Fresh seafood, a stellar cup of coffee, crummy weather, endless trees, unsullied lakes, stunning spring-time blooms, and many other powerful portraits embody the Northwest. However, all of these beloved characteristics are surpassed by an even more dominant feature – wildness. *Wildness.* As Auntie said about the trees, "…it looks like they'll grow right up out of the asphalt."

In truth, the Northwest's inescapable wildness indelibly alters life whether in the megalopolises or rural burgs. People are never very far from wildness even though they may try to deny its reach. Like most pilgrims to the Northwest, wilderness grabbed me when I was least expecting it…during a final exam. And, little did I know that my most important learning wasn't going to be in a classroom. Out in the backcountry of Mt. Rainier National Park a diminutive mountain lake would lay this legendary peak low and in the process unveil a truly epic epiphany about wildness.

* * *

"*I'm toast!*"

On the face of it Professor King's remaining test question seemed easy enough: "Compare and contrast the advantages and disadvantages of the Tukey, Scheffé and Bonferroni simultaneous equation methodologies for analyzing multiple factor levels." However, looks can be deceiving. What little wrinkle is Professor King trying to catch us on? That's the real question.

This test has turned out to be a gruesome nightmare. The "official" exam period ended 15 minutes ago and kindly old Professor King announced that we only have 30 minutes left to finish. His statistics class has been more than a match for me. Despite hundreds of hours poring over the text and working complex mathematical problems, statistical mumbo-jumbo remains mysterious magic performed amid clouds of swirling vapors.

The quandary is primarily one of intention. Professor King went about his august course as though we would someday teach statistics. Little did he know that our collective goal is radically different. At least three-quarters of us only need the tools to complete our research – not qualify as statistical theorists. We merely want to know which statistics to use, why, when and how. Our real interest dwells on interpreting findings *after* all of the statistical sleight of hand is finished. Yet here we sit my colleagues and me, anguishing over the most dismal of sciences.

At least I learned about the bell-shaped curve, and I now know without a shadow of doubt that I will be representing the bottom-end of all students taking his test. Having resigned myself to this calamitous eventuality, I manage to project a swarthy bit of blooming pride. My countenance is almost regal. Not everyone can be last on the grading curve – I know this unequivocally from sitting through statistics.

I glance longingly out Balmer Hall's grime-stained windows searching desperately for a sign. Wouldn't you know it, this beautiful May afternoon radiates sunny optimism. Why does it have to be so nice on such a rotten day? Only thirty minutes and then I will be free to fight Seattle's rush hour traffic racing toward the Hood Canal Bridge. On reaching the Olympic Peninsula I'll be emancipated from statistics' stranglehold. A liberated man, I can then wander Olympic National Park's Elwha River Valley where sanity and nature reign. Let Tukey, Scheffé and Bonferroni come along to find out how life really should be lived – to suck the marrow of resplendent days in a dazzling semi-rainforest and to live a larger-than-imaginable, honest-to-goodness existence in wilderness.

A beatific smile gradually spreads over my anxiety-dry lips, erasing a knitted frown and desperate blank stare. Here in my darkest hour going through the motions of scoring pathetically on a very important test, all I can think about is living for backcountry adventures. "What's wrong with me?" I ponder. I'm not taking this seriously enough. I'd much rather watch sunlight filter through western red cedar, hemlock and Douglas fir gracing the spectacular University of Washington campus.

Only 30 more minutes of captivity and then I can go heal my bruised and battered mind and perhaps have a bit of adventure as a soothing tonic. Capitulating, my pen begins to write impressive words that come from somewhere deep in my brain. I will soon forget the test, but not the sight of that gorgeous sunlight sifting through delicate boughs.

* * *

How many others love the wild and endure agonizing moments – such as intricate statistics tests – in order to soar when set free? There is no sure-fire method for estimating the number comprising the ranks of the faithful. But, if someone would rather spend New Year's Day outdoors in some sweat-drenched activity like cross-country skiing, snowshoeing or post-holing through two-feet-plus of snow instead of watching an obscure and soon-to-be forgotten football game, then we share a common bond.

Being infatuated with the wild means exactly that: at any moment I have a greater statistical probability (thank you Professor

King) of thinking about something related to nature and wildness. I am more likely to end up choosing a vocation, partner, place to live, vehicle, lifestyle, education, friends, enemies, or fashion sense that reinforces my love for the wild. I can't help thinking about wilderness – its challenge, beauty, serenity, and distance – during daily lulls. And, after finally setting foot on wild land, I come vibrantly alive in the fullest sense – physically, spiritually, emotionally and intellectually.

Life is fundamentally different when beyond the boundaries of urban and suburban communities. This distinctiveness exerts an often unrelenting magnetic pull on individuals who value wildness; a tugging that can only be satisfied by being in wild places. I am more likely to hear celestial music when urban distractions are at a minimum and survival is a primal concern; a way of living each-and-every-second.

Excitement about possible danger and the unknown heightens immersion in wildness. It's not so much that threatening events or perilous moments actually occur, as the *prospect* of them occurring – that at any moment the predictable evaporates, replaced by conditions and trials beyond control. An unanticipated and obscured thunderstorm racing over a saw-tooth ridge; a rattlesnake curled beneath a fallen log obstructing the trail; or, a caribou materializing from a clump of arctic willows – these and similar surprises add zest to life and deepen our appreciation of wildness.

Let's embark on a bit of backcountry adventure to see how everyday wilderness jaunts many of us enjoy are more than mere walks in the woods. In my mind these seemingly simple explorations are vibrantly rich with opportunities for discovering wild epiphanies.

* * *

Mt. Rainier is pretty high up there on the adventure cachet scale. This is a world-class mountain by virtually any criterion whether vertical rise from a near sea-level base; amount of precipitation falling as snow on upper reaches and rain below 5,000 feet; or, diversity of topography and geology. Add to this an abundance of plant and animal life; trail challenges from glaciers, perpetual snowfields and rollicking streams; and, the unknown. Weather can change very rapidly on Mt. Rainier turning a tranquil morning into an afternoon's downpour or blizzard. With all that snow and ice hanging above tree line, it's not uncommon for stream levels to rise dramatically. The mountain tends to create its own weather further complicating any semblance of what might be construed as "normal" conditions.

Mt. Rainier's vagaries drew me to the Carbon River and a lengthy day hike to one of the world's ultimate visual feasts – Moraine Park. This was also one of those rare opportunities to hike from semi-rainforest past a glacier to sub-alpine forest and meadows and finally up to the finest alpine country conceivable. The mountain is beginning to surface from winter's embrace. It's early July which translates into negotiating plenty of rotten snow the higher I travel. This is a perfect recipe for adventure – distance, elevation, swollen glacier-fed river, route-finding, and disintegrating snow-covered trails.

Mt. Rainier tops out at 14,410 feet which means that storms are forced to ride upward to overcome this physical barrier. The result is heavy precipitation. Only 100 miles from the Pacific Ocean, it experiences the full brunt of storms barreling down from the Gulf of Alaska leading to extraordinary snowfall. The Paradise Ranger Station located at 5,400 feet on the mountain recorded an annual high of 1,122 inches or 93.5 feet of snow in 1971-1972 and 1,070 feet in 1973-1974. In 1998-1999 snowfall totaled

1,032.5 inches. The lowest amount of snowfall, 313 inches or 26 feet, fell during 1939-1940.

From October through April the average daily high temperature at Paradise Ranger Station is below 50 degrees. The highest average daily low temperature occurs in June and July at 44 degrees. These statistics underscore how cool the environment is near the alpine/sub-alpine transition zone. Above 5,000 feet trees encounter extremely harsh growing conditions.

Geologists estimate that half a million years ago Mt. Rainer was created through a series of violent eruptions that may have produced a summit 16,000 feet high. Steam vents on the crest attest to the fact that Mt. Rainier is a live volcano. Some sixty miles south, Mt. St. Helens offers compelling testimony about how quickly a dormant volcano can be transfigured. Further confirmation of Mt. Rainier's volcanic potential occurred in 1963 when a huge rockslide estimated at 14 million cubic yards peeled off of Tahoma Glacier due to a steam explosion.

Mt. Rainier encompasses 235,625 acres most of which are designated wilderness. Four distinct life zones are found on the mountain: lowland forest zone (2,000-2,900 feet) characterized by western red cedar, Douglas fir and western hemlock that reach 250 feet high; Pacific silver fir zone (2,900-4,500 feet) dominated by Pacific silver fir, noble fir, western white pine and trees from the lowland zone; sub-alpine zone (4,500-6,000 feet) with copses of white bark pine, mountain hemlock, Alaska cedar and Engelmann spruce; and alpine zone (above 6,000 feet) where perpetual snowfields and glaciers thrive.

A slow two-hour drive from Seattle to the Carbon River Entrance unfolds along country lanes and past several small towns. These obstacles are beneficial because they force me to slow down and enjoy transitions to inland old-growth forest; at least what's left after mining and clear-cutting. On reaching Wilkeson some 50 miles from Seattle, what lies ahead – a massive snow-covered upside-down strawberry – is very apparent if it's a sunny day. Odds generally favor that the peak will be cloaked in clouds or wearing a concave cloud-cap signaling deteriorating weather.

If it is sunny, proceed with all due haste because you are in for one monstrously awesome experience. If you can while driving along the road, overlook slash piles, eroded hillsides and missing thousand-year old Douglas fir. Virgin forest remains within the National Park boundary. And, if the Carbon River hasn't ripped out the rising and falling two-lane blacktop (which it did in November 2006), you might just make it to Ipsut Campground. The road has been destroyed so many times that a new campground above flood stage replaces the existing site converting it to backcountry status accessible only by foot and bike.

My little foray into backcountry adventuring is taking place on a Tuesday so when pulling up to the trailhead at 7:30 a.m. there isn't a lot of competition for parking spots. Even Ipsut Campground has a few empty spaces. What a world of difference a couple of hours and a latté make. From Seattle's hyper-congested freeways to ancient forest, the metamorphosis is startling. An early departure was selfishly strategic. I didn't want to spend time fighting others to get nowhere in town, and I have big mileage and thousands of feet – 3,500 or so – to climb.

Despite some fog, misty-drizzle and low-hanging clouds in Seattle, it's all sun and good tidings at Ipsut Creek. Mt. Rainier wears a modest cap of clouds that rise and fall like cotton candy being blown to-and-fro. It's not raining so I'll be able to revel in wonderful sunshine. And, there's really nothing quite as thrilling as a sunny day in the Pacific Northwest; absolutely nothing can hold a candle to these bellwether days.

Day pack lying on the gravel parking lot, I'm tying my boot laces when a Park Ranger sidles up to give me the once-over.

"Where are you headed?" he asks.

"Up to Moraine Park if all goes well," I reply, uncertain of where this interrogation is going.

"That's a long way to go. You by yourself?"

I pause a moment, exasperated by the implication that officially they don't like that sort of thing happening. "Yep, all by myself."

He ponders a minute, looks at my well-worn boots and pack, and then says, "Be careful." It's not that I'm disrespectful, just seasoned – no reply given.

Up an old gravel road bordered by an almost impenetrable forest the trail winds beside the Carbon River. From here it all rises toward Columbia Crest at 14,408 feet. To my right is a steep hill with ferns liberally sprinkled among downed Douglas fir – nurse logs for an ensuing generation. Washtubs of rain kindle life-gone-wild and turn the forest floor into a fluffy sponge of gray moss, rust-brown fir needles and green-gray toppled giants. But, like many dense forests, eventually its perfection becomes monotonous and my attention drifts to the raging Carbon River.

Only a couple of miles south to its source of origin, the Carbon Glacier, this river runs milky-white to gray-white depending on sediment and sunlight's reflection. Today the Carbon River seems relatively tame, perhaps the legacy of several cloudy days and cooler temperatures. Still it has enough punch to press down to the lowlands as boulders rolling downstream, intermittently clacking into each other, testify. I've seen many days where the river was at least twice as wide from days of heavy rain. Those moments are a bit terrifying watching a first-rate mountain shed huge amounts of accumulated precipitation.

An incessant breeze blows downstream over Carbon River as frigid air sinks in the early morning hours. Once the sun gains some purchase this will moderate, but for now it's pretty cool, actually refreshing, especially along sunny stretches of this persistently climbing path. Sometimes it's pleasant to warm up to a wilderness adventure rather than being immediately thrust headlong into a difficult challenge. That's the beauty of this trail, I'm easing into things. It wasn't but a quarter-of-a-mile from leaving the trailhead that I entered a wilderness state of mind.

Since I'm out here alone my sense of solitude is heightened; this is why I came in the first place. It's not lonesomeness, but the simple pleasure of being unaccompanied and enjoying a full day in wilderness. At the same time I'm alert; not in the sense of being anxious or afraid, but attentive to the world around me. It's a form of deliberate subconscious focusing. I'm continually taking a reading on the changing weather – sun's intensity, temperature's moderation in the shade, status of the swirling cloud cap – while scanning Carbon River trail ahead – its rise and fall, a protruding fir, or a slight creek cutting its path. All signs shout keep going.

Eventually my trail rounds a ridge. East across the Carbon River is Alice Falls whose source is Crescent Lake at 5,500+ feet in a rocky cirque. I drift back to an early October day when my friend Jim and I hiked a trail to Crescent Lake via Windy Pass. We were bound for a forested hollow holding – appropriately named – Lake James. It was a brooding day with descending dull gray clouds and a looming storm, the type that would close Windy Pass for the rest of the season.

Flashing back to the present, a few more steps and around the corner is a perfect view up to Carbon Glacier and thence to Mt. Rainier's north face – Willis Wall.

It's one of the most spectacular scenes imaginable.

This single moment makes the effort of driving two hours worthwhile and epitomizes backcountry adventuring. I'm both deep in wilderness (though not that far in mileage from Ipsut Campground) *and* connected to the wild. Some would characterize this as "being in the moment." I'm as much a part of Carbon Glacier, the steep forest rising above me, chattering river, and sunny interlude as a person can be. In almost all respects I have blended with Mt. Rainier – it's hard to tell where it begins and where I end.

Turning back to hiking, aptly named Cataract Creek splashes headlong into the Carbon River after falling from Mist and Spray Parks – cold alpine country north of Flett and Russell Glaciers. I'm watching for a hanging bridge over Carbon River just shy of the glacier's snout. It's only yards away hidden behind a copse of trees and close to a junction with the Wonderland Trail.

What better way to intimately know the 378 square miles comprising Mount Rainier National Park than to circumambulate the mountain via the Wonderland Trail? That's not a challenge that most of the two million plus annual visitors to the park choose to take on. However, it is one of the supreme outdoor adventures waiting for the bold and determined. This is not one of those long lazy trails that invite sauntering. This is a rugged test in pristine wilderness with weather that can vary from the sublime to full-on raging blizzard in short order.

Estimates indicate that the Wonderland Trail is 93 miles long. Big mileage is the least of a backpacker's worries. Hikers routinely climb up a ridge gaining 3,500 feet or so and then immediately drop back down an equal measure into a glacial valley bisected by a freezing milk-colored river. It is not uncommon to experience all of the major life zones found in the park over the course of a day in navigating from one glacial valley to the next.

Sounds easy doesn't it — easy *until a frigid rain begins to fall that doesn't let up for a couple days.*

Most who decide to hike the Wonderland Trail plan on taking 7-10 days to complete the squishy circle. Officially one person completed the entire trail in less than 28 hours back in 1991, but rumors exist that this record has since been broken. Such an effort almost seems sacrilegious. The backcountry of Mt. Rainier contains incredible flower gardens, expansive vistas, roaring rivers, creaking glaciers, dancing streams and deep wilderness solitude seldom available in the United States.

Ten miles a day means almost a week outdoors with little else except what's carried in a backpack. Many hikers plan on at least one food re-supply — typically at Longmire, Sunrise or Mowich Lake — to make their burden lighter. However, if a spell of wet weather falls over the park, expect to carry more weight as gear has a tendency to accumulate moisture.

Balanced against sore muscles, bruised and battered feet, dirt, grease, grime, and hunger for fresh food are the almost other-worldly experiences of raw mountain moments. To complete the circuit is to make a definitive statement about physical conditioning. But, this achievement brings so much more to those who persevere. The fortunate who make it through this hike know the sublimity of a magic mountain that is a rare gem among the very best this world has to offer.

The swinging bridge at Cataract Creek is another metaphor for backcountry adventuring. You never know when Mt. Rainier will wipe out these audaciously puny structures with a massive rush of snowmelt. And, no matter how many times I've been over it — with companions and without — there's a distinct taste of danger. One slip and you would fall twenty feet into raging glacial melt. Although the river is relatively low today, there's never a soft landing on those bowling ball boulders channeling Carbon River. That's what backcountry adventuring is all about – the X-factor. There's no way of telling what the water level will be or whether the bridge will still be standing.

Tenaciously clutching dual wire ropes serving as handrails, I quickly walk across the jouncing swaying bridge, stopping briefly in the middle to tempt fate. On the other side a steep climb begins through flourishing Alaskan Cedars and rocky cliffs toward Moraine Park. A thousand feet in elevation have been gained in reaching this point; another two-thousand feet or so remain.

Carbon Glacier draws my attention like a moth to a flame. The trail climbs along its leading edge offering a great view of a thick debris mantle on top and rushing river pouring from its stubby snout. Small boulders roll into the violent river or onto lateral moraines while the air is awash with cracking, creaking and groaning as the glacier grinds to its death. Carbon is a perfect name for this particular glacier due to soot-colored dust blown onto the ice and black rock cascading off Willis Wall. Being this close to a living glacier gives perspective on enormous snowstorms that batter Mt. Rainier, coalescing into ice, and then falling to the base of Willis Wall at 10,000 feet.

After about a mile of steady climbing, a broad scree pile signals an important change in the topography: the beginning of Moraine Park, a mile long meadow that is spectacular with wildflowers toward the end of summer and rife with marmots. Passing a camp with two tents, I run into several backpackers who are fussing with breakfast – they're the only people I'll see until back at Ipsut Campground.

The rest of the way it's inexplicably magnificent and once again I'm in the moment. My trail is skirting Moraine Park's massive meadows at the edge of sub-alpine country. I'm walking in a trail trough – a semi-riverbed awash with snowmelt – through copses of stunted fir no taller than fifteen or twenty feet. Glacier lilies – mostly brilliant white, but occasionally a field of delicate yellow – blanket the trail's shoulders. Moraine Park will progressively warm over summer and transform from glacier lilies and marsh marigolds into heather and lupine.

Willis Wall begins to take center stage as the trail reaches a pass just shy of 6,000 feet.

And then, there's no farther to go.

I follow a boot-beaten path southwest along several small tarns to a jumbled heap of rocks before taking a seat in full sun. Thin misty clouds swirl at the top of Mt. Rainier 8,500+ feet almost directly above me. A few mosquitoes buzz over for a snack until a slight wind blowing off Mt. Rainier washes them away. Sun bores through my dark-green Pendleton shirt and my mind empties except for thoughts about this spectacularly wild mountain.

With the enormity of avalanche-raked Willis Wall looming overhead I'm trying to comprehend the scale. It's simply dominating and a bit intimidating being this close to such massive rock and ice falls. There are few comparable references to understand a vertical four-to-five-thousand-foot wall swathed in ice that seldom sees a ray of sun. Liberty Cap sits atop with blue-white ice hundreds of feet thick poised to fall to the huge Carbon Glacier. Further east, Winthrop and Emmons Glaciers flow in enormous brilliant white tongues off Columbia Crest.

Like many extraordinary sights, it takes time to appreciate what you're seeing. I have a bit of early lunch, a swig of water and stretch my muscles. For a good half hour I've had almost no thoughts whatsoever, merely existing in concert with a mountain and a fantastic day. A distinct spirit is detectable – the spirit of wildness and untamable lands – and it is good; very good.

Eventually realizing that my adventure is only half over, I rise to go. I still have to safely negotiate 7-8 miles back to the trail-head. Having melded with wildness, it isn't finished until I reach the beginning, returning ablaze and refreshed. Make no mistake about it; I'm confident that my travel will be safe. However, a niggling bit of anxiousness keeps me honest – it's the razor edge of adventure calling.

* * *

Some might see this as merely a day hike up-and-back to a remote corner of Mt. Rainier National Park. I didn't forge a new path in the wilderness. I didn't go where no one has ever gone before. Lots of people routinely backpack the Wonderland Trail and in so doing pass through Moraine Park. Others take a day, or several, to walk these miles and enjoy moments of wildness and adventure. A very few encounter more than they anticipated – extreme weather, falling rocks, washed-out trails, snow-covered scree, run-ins with black bears, and unexpected swims in powerful mountain streams. Disasters happen.

This is the tantalizing reality that brings us back for more. Although I am not the first to discover Moraine Park; even though others camped along Curtis Ridge last night while I only visited for a day; and despite the fact that the Park Service has made certain that I can cross Carbon River on a shaky swinging bridge; these facts do not lessen the rigor or authenticity of adventure.

What happens when people begin to string together a series of adventures; a life-time of wilderness explorations? Eventually they are reshaped. Backcountry adventuring becomes their persona and dramatically affects how and what they think and why. It's no longer fundamentally about notching another exploit on a trekking pole, canoe paddle or handlebars. Instead, they begin to crave wilderness — an obsession that permeates their very souls.

Adventuring isn't solely about thrilling exploits out in wilderness. It's also about the people we hang with and how we relate to wild lands. It's about the diverse literature we read and the media we watch. It's about the funky clothes we wear and the high-tech gear we fantasize about. It's about how we spend our time and what captures our minds when we can't be out in the wilderness. In short, it's all about knowing that deep in our hearts we cannot get enough of those crazy trips beyond civilization's veil.

A little day hike to the far reaches of Mt. Rainier National Park only partially exemplifies what it means to vigorously pursue wilderness adventure. As it eventually turned out, the real discovery of the day was *not* Moraine Park. Despite all of that incredible beauty on Curtis Ridge below Willis Wall, today's highpoint of adventure was yet to come. Imagine; perfection wasn't quite achieved on this most wonderful of wonderful days.

The personification of a broadly-defined understanding of wilderness travel came *after* I reached Ipsut Campground trailhead.

No, I didn't run into any natural catastrophe along the way back. A mountain lion didn't come bounding off a steep hillside. I didn't get pulled into a frantic rescue effort of pilgrims who had fallen into the Carbon River. The weather didn't shift from sunny to sleet in a matter of hours. None of these events happened that might have ramped up the extreme adventure quotient many so-called authorities would use in assessing my little sojourn.

After arriving at the trailhead in early afternoon I was still aglow with the good fortune of a fantastic day. Despite covering fifteen or so miles and gaining some 3,500 feet in elevation, I wasn't the least bit physically tired. Thus, as I walked by a nondescript trailhead to Green Lake, a thought occurred — here's an opportunity that can't be passed up. Green Lake beckoned with an alluring song about adventure and beckoning waters I'd never seen.

Two miles seemed a small price to pay so I emptied trash from my pack, reloaded with water and headed up a precipitous trail through old-growth Douglas fir forest. It was akin to climbing a staircase of roots for almost 1,000 feet straight-up, but this wasn't unpleasant work. Other than the roots, Green Lake's trail was smothered in duff from fir and hemlock needles floating off huge trees towering 150 feet plus overhead. It gave a spongy spring to my step after the trek to Moraine Park. It was refreshingly cool; a dark forest was precisely what I needed since the day was growing warm. It was also a perfect counterpoint to Moraine Park's wide alpine vistas and Carbon River Valley's vast openness.

Only a few folks were returning down the trail paralleling Ranger Creek and by the time I broached Green Lake's outlet, the entire bowl into which it was tucked became mine, and mine alone. I wandered over gnarly burnt-brown roots toward the southwestern shore and nestled in a sharp shoreline cleft. Anyone who came to the lake would have to negotiate these pesky roots to invade my little space. Satisfied that I was hidden from view, I made myself comfortable and slipped off day pack followed by boots.

It was startlingly quiet on Green Lake – even the sound of Ranger Creek falling to the Carbon River was muffled. This made me realize how constantly noise accompanied me while walking along the Carbon River. Only Moraine Park was relatively silent except for an occasional breath of wind and sharp crack or two from avalanches high on Mt. Rainier. Not only was it quiet at Green Lake, but stillness held sway. Nothing moved except the sun as it tracked high overhead.

There was no unexpected physical challenge in reaching Green Lake, nor did the lake possess extraordinary beauty. It was fundamentally a little forest lake completely surrounded by steep tree-covered mountainsides radiating an inordinate measure of peace. Once again I was having difficulty delineating where the lake began and I ended while sitting quietly on the shore innocently looking, listening and emptying my mind of any thoughts. This hour was perhaps one of the most refreshing that I have ever enjoyed on any wilderness foray.

It was the epitome of a wild epiphany.

I marveled at how sunlight played on the lake's surface and a thousand shades of green swirled across the water. Various insects flitted above the water doing their dance of life while silver-black trout cruised just below, waiting for the unwary. I could easily see the little drama unfolding at my feet. Sunlight's softness filtering through fir boughs was exquisite, a gauzy mix of light and shade. It seemed as though time had decided to stand absolutely still and with it a command was ushered for no human intrusion. Silence was beyond deafening except for the tiniest of trickles to the west where snow melt was finding its way toward the sea.

What a surprise.

What sheer unadulterated wildness!!

I had planned a full day of backcountry exploration to arguably one of the Pacific Northwest's ultimate wilderness destinations. My expectations were entirely fulfilled and then some as I ventured alone to a remote ridge over which Mt. Rainier's enormous summit towered. My thirst for adventure had been slaked by incredible weather, numerous wilderness challenges, stunning natural beauty and distance sheltered from civilization.

Rewards from this trek to Moraine Park were plentiful, but they couldn't match an unforeseen little side trip to a diminutive forest lake. That's what wild epiphanies are all about – unanticipated surprises and heaping platefuls of unbridled wildness. Green Lake was totally unexpected and it was this sort of adventure that feeds a wild obsession for more. As I rose to head home, a vibrant connection between Mt. Rainier and me was broken. It would come again to be certain – at another time; another place. That's the promise, and the gift, from being addicted to backcountry adventure; from living for wildness.

* * *

A love for wildness is embodied by explorations to inaccessible nooks and crannies along crenellated high country ridges, to frighteningly wild and scenic rivers, to bone-dry desert wilderness laced with intriguing side-canyons, and to far flung estuaries where glacial streams return merrily to their origins. However, craving wildness and adventure isn't just about the doing of it; it's about the entire ensemble – of developing an appreciation for being immersed in wild country, of walking in primal ways, and of fashioning our lives around wildness in the type of people with whom we interact and the paraphernalia we buy to support our outdoors-centered habits.

Outdoors recreation is a simile for my life. It helps remind me about how important wilderness is in the face of modern society that works actively and aggressively, even if unthinkingly, to extinguish it all – to drill for oil in pristine wildlife refuges, to carve up seamless habitat for a few trophy homes and ranchettes, to remove protections for endangered species, and to destroy old-growth forest for a few more two-by-fours.

At the end of a dozen hours at Mt. Rainier, my biggest adventure wasn't a physical rush due to slogging long miles solo fashion. It was an unexpected *revelation* about wildness, and how easily accessible wilderness is if I only change my mind set. That's a life-altering shift in thinking, but an important perceptual shift that others might benefit from contemplating. In a world of radically changing realities I, we, need such transformations in order to keep alive a spirit of adventure and love for wildness.

Invigorating Life

4

They're in There Somewhere

After spending an inordinate amount of time in the woods, it appears to me that unanticipated adventures – both small and large – seemingly materialize when least expected. Not every afternoon saunter, day-long hike, river rafted or mountain biked leads to a refreshing escapade. In fact most of my backcountry excursions play out pretty much like I anticipate them to without any dramatic parting of the heavens or life-threatening theatrics.

Nonetheless, every so often a trip to wild country leads to an experience that leaves me ringing like a bell, tingling with joy. These soul-shaking dramas whet my appetite for more. I view them as life-invigorating moments – those astonishing times when I am specially blessed. Bundled into the experience is a distinct consciousness that for whatever reason I have been specifically selected for a unique and, clearly, an extraordinary event.

Life-invigorating moments from backcountry adventuring are so gratifying that I try to increase the odds of them happening. And, few places offer higher probabilities for these incidents than the enormous ecosystem clinching Grand Teton and Yellowstone

National Parks. Thus, it's not surprising that when the parks first open each year in May, I'm right there knocking on the door….

Grand Tetons in majestic snow-covered splendor.

One-thirty a.m. on May 22.

It's so frigidly cold that my bulging nose is clogged with massive icy stalactites and stalagmites, aching beyond belief. Some masochistic bully is pinching the tip, refusing to let go. Eerily, a pitch-black blanket smothers Colter Bay. There's virtually no light except a lamppost's feeble overhead beam muted from soft-white snow and hidden by a dense copse of stark black lodgepole pine and Engelmann spruce.

That's when an eerie wail darts through the forest sending a shiver down my spine.

What am I doing out here exposed to forest gnomes and starving critters on the loose? It's time to hustle back to my cabin's blessed comfort before freezing to death or ending up under some predator's pile of decaying pine needles, frosty earth, limp weeds and sweet-smelling sage.

Welcome to springtime in Grand Teton National Park.

Yesterday was a jumbled collage of dismal weather; about par for the course. River valleys received a sporadic but intense onslaught of sleet and rain. It was either full on, or off – nothing in between. No gentle showers; no light dusting of snow – completely full-on or totally full-off. When sleet came it hammered the countryside threatening to tear tender willow and black cottonwood leaves right off their stems. Rain poured from purple-tinged clouds. A huge car wash was sweeping over the land – one minute drenched in moisture and the next everything sparkling with wet diamonds as sun reclaimed a sodden land.

Snow fell intermittently a couple hundred feet above the National Elk Refuge in Jackson Hole, but the signature spires of this fabled park – Tweeinot, Mt. Owen, Grand Teton, Middle Teton and Nez Perce – were really blasted. They're robed in pristine white – testimony to how long winter remains rooted in the Northern Rockies. With such heavy snow comes cold flowing down from sky-high spires and plateaus. A gigantic refrigerator clinches Jackson Hole to north of Yellowstone Park.

This is precisely what I've counted on. All that snow coupled with bitter temperatures will keep tourists at bay for another couple weeks. Except for a few other hardy souls, the Grand Tetons are all mine. I'm willing to pay the price for minor discomfort while accepting the possibility that I'll have to hole up for several lay-over days while a storm passes through.

The reward?

Spring is an absolutely fantastic time to see wildlife. Elk and moose drop calves like a Toyota assembly-line at full throttle. Bears are out roaming looking for a tasty mammal tidbit or two while harvesting lush meadow pastures. Bison trundle across ever greener plains, targeting roadside grass banquets. Asphalt soaks up solar radiation warming roadside soil and stimulating a flourishing abundance of new growth. Add in road salt and you have the perfect recipe for hungry ungulates anxious to stoke their internal fires.

We've come to Colter Bay northwest of Moran Junction for a little springtime adventure. It's our annual May ritual for celebrating the return of warmer temperatures. This year the weather forecast is dismally marginal but my wife, Valerie, and I are determined to keep our string of visits intact. Bailey, legendary trail dog, doesn't care about any records; she just wants to get out and luxuriate in all of those tantalizing smells.

Dusk is edging to night when we check into our decrepit cabin. It's a rustic two bedroom affair with a crude bathroom. A good six inches of fresh snow covers the surrounding woods and an equivalent amount lingers on the cabin's rooftop. Bitingly sharp breezes course through the stunted lodgepoles as a final spring storm exits toward vast plains of eastern Wyoming.

Pathetic electric wall heaters can't keep up with the descending temperatures. It's so uncomfortably cold in the room that there's only one place to head – under a massive down comforter that we've brought along due to the vagaries of these Teton Mountains. Then – lights out and Colter Bay's embracing ambience floods over the cabin. We're deep asleep.

That is; until Bailey decides she needs to go out at 1:30 a.m. She pounces on the bedside giving a little shake to grab our attention. Valerie simply rolls over on her side. Message conveyed – I'm the pathetic sucker who will supervise Bailey's potty break.

I'm not going outside unprepared. Dressing for Colter Bay's smothering arctic cold doesn't take rocket science – only persistence. On go long underwear top and bottom; followed by wool pants and a fleece top. Add fleece vest, gloves and hat before topping off with a massive down parka. I can't move, but at least I'm somewhat warm while fumbling into my boots.

With dog on leash we step outside to a sharp slap in the face. It's in the high teens and darker than Lechuguilla. Bailey tugs at the lead eager to chase down alluring aromas pressed against the ground by heavy cold. At moments like this terrier instinct takes command, rendering her brain to mush. If I drop her tether there's no guarantee that she'll respond to voice commands.

We skirt along brooding pines with her sensitive black nose on high sniff. Coursing in a zigzag pattern, she's trying to read what's been out here. It's probably nothing more than chipmunk squatters who over-winter around the cabins. However, I don't like Bailey's body language – tail down and ears perked forward. Something bigger is at play.

She darts back and forth while I mutter a silent prayer for her to get on with it. Meanwhile I glance up to the cabin's roof. It's still covered with five-and-a-half inches of snow. Melting has stopped despite the heat we've been generating inside. Above the roof a massive hole in the clouds materializes; stars explode with scintillating light as a luminous Milky Way wheels overhead. The entire universe seems to be looking down upon the Tetons, flooding over distant peaks and across sage infested hills.

Head tilted back I'm slowly spinning a tight circle relishing the spectacle above while Bailey does her stuff. Then....

Ooowwhhhoo.

OOooooowwwwhhhhhooooo.

Ooooooooooolllll.

At first I think it's a solitary coyote yapping at the star-studded night. Then in quick succession a chorus of howls and wails fill the distant air. This isn't coyote yipping by any means. A wolf pack is hunting out there somewhere exchanging a bit of news.

Bailey's head cocks to one side as she tries to read the howls. If she only knew that these big dogs have something on their minds other than sniffing rear-ends. Playing it safe, she keeps her tail tucked and edges a couple steps nearer to me. Terrier bravado vanishes when she senses that danger lurks out there.

Elated at the show – a stunningly vivid cosmos spinning above lighting the snow muffled forest in muted softness plus a melodiously plaintive wolf symphony – I'm richly rewarded for making the effort to get out of the sack. But, that doesn't make it any warmer. Time to head back inside.

As I scramble back under the covers a question comes to mind: exactly what are wolves trying to communicate when they howl? This seemingly simple query has sparked considerable research over the years and in turn has led naturalists and others to several definitive conclusions. Howling is very strong glue that keeps wolf packs together. Wolves are highly social animals with distinctive social structures. Howling generally reinforces the social connections wolves have with each other in a pack.

A pack's howling is an effective way to define territory and send a message to other packs or individual wolves that a pack has strength. Arguably the larger the number of wolves in a pack that howl, the louder and more intimidating is their message to potential interlopers. In this regard howling can function as a form of safety valve that prevents outright physical conflict because invaders may decide to avoid confrontation. This sort of preventive howling is frequently used by alpha males as a threat display to trespassers.

Modulating variations in howling echoing off cliffs, other rocky terrain or hard surfaces tends to amplify the volume of their efforts. This can mask the actual number of wolves contributing to a group howl. It fools potential intruders about a pack's strength and may prevent combat. Some experts dispute whether wolves intentionally use modulating howling to disguise pack size. Less subject to question is the fact that larger packs tend to howl more because they are confident in their ability to defend their territory.

Howling is an excellent way for wolves to remain in contact when they are far a- field and physically distant from each other. Their howls communicate location – physical presence – and sensitize them to becoming disconnected from their pack. As the elasticity of this relationship eventually breaks, disconnected wolves may initiate repeated howling in an effort to reestablish location and reunion.

Common folklore suggests that wolves are especially predisposed to howl at a full moon. In reality wolves howl anytime. A howl typically lasts anywhere from ½ second to 11 seconds and usually carries 1 mile. Authorities suggest that howling can be heard over 10 miles distance from the perpetrator.

The scientifics about wolves and their howling are engaging, but I'm more smitten by the sacredness of it all. In my mind howling wolves equates with wildness. That's why I'm here in the Grand Tetons freezing my butt off.

* * *

Hours pass until a hint of sunlight breaks through the trees — *it's* bear patrol time along Jackson Lake. Eastern slopes of the Teton Range soak up first light which creates a comfortable magnet for large mammals such as elk and bear. East-facing foothills nourish abundant growth since they're first to receive sun and at the same time are shaded from afternoon's harshly hot conditions.

Dodging the Visitors Center and ambling toward the lake we overhear a backcountry ranger admonishing a guest to be careful about walking around Colter Bay and adjoining Swan Lake.

"*A grizzly has been frequenting this area!*" warns the ranger.

That certainly piques my interest. Funny, when we checked into our cabin the staff issued no warning about a grizzly wandering through the campground.

Our day is lost in preternaturally aborted trips stopped by lingering snow or gi-normous run-off. A visit to Pilgrim Creek turns up a frothing river unlike the genteel creek of summer after Yellowstone's high country empties of snow. Pacific Creek is also roaring next to a pot-holed gravel road leading deep into the Teton Wilderness. Even Cache Creek down in Jackson Hole has been bloated by the recent weather but at least it offers a chance to stretch out along a boulevard trail shared by horses, mountain bikes, runners, hikers and a gangly mix of mutts.

When evening settles over the Tetons we take up a familiar post at Jackson Lake Lodge overlooking broad willow flats. The Grand Tetons' most beguiling moments occur at dusk when a radiant orange-red sun settles gradually among layers of diaphanous clouds. Almost immediately the atmosphere changes in dramatic ways with a biting freshness and caressing zephyrs – chilly air dropping from the Yellowstone Plateau. All manner of creatures suddenly materialize, especially within the relative safety of willow flats. The world takes on a mellow, almost alpenglow, blush. Looking west from the venerable Jackson Lake Lodge, this is one of the grandest sights our national parks offer.

It was only eight decades ago that the foundation was laid for Grand Teton National Park in June 1923. At that time a number of Jackson Hole community leaders gathered to examine the feasibility of establishing a national park. Horace Albright, 33 years old at the time, was an integral part of this movement. At the time Albright was serving as Stephen Mather's assistant. Mather was the first director of our National Park Service.

Albright became the second director of the National Park Service in 1929, the same year that President Hoover signed a bill creating Grand Teton National Park. At that time the park included the northern portion of the Teton Range and lakes at the base. John D. Rockefeller, Jr., who had established the Snake River Land Company as a means to anonymously acquire Teton Valley acreage, would later donate significant property to expand the fledgling park.

Rockefeller also created the Grand Teton Lodge and Transportation Company in 1952 with the intention of increasing visitation to the park. The company invested $6 million toward a new lodge that officially opened on June 11, 1952. Fifty-one years later Jackson Lake Lodge was listed as a National Historic Landmark on the National Register of Historic Places.

Today Jackson Lake Lodge has 348 guest cottage rooms – essentially motel accommodations – located on the north and south ends of the main building as well as 37 guest rooms in the main lodge itself. Conference facilities are available for 700 people with 17 breakout rooms and 17,000 square feet of meeting space. The lodge's lobby has spectacular 60 foot picture windows offering an expansive view of the Teton Range. The Mural Room provides fine dining for breakfast, lunch and dinner. The room's 100 feet of windows capture scenic views, but the walls behind the windows also flourish with 80 feet of murals by master painter Carl Roters illustrating scenes from 19th century Jackson Hole.

It is the youthful Grand Dame of this park – not a group of rustic cabins like Colter Bay. Gentility smothers this signature building with a bluff-high commanding view toward the saw-tooth Teton crest – an enclave for those who only want to stick their big toe into wildness.

In grungy outdoor clothing, Valerie and I sneak around the north side of the lodge with Bailey in tow passing through a half-empty parking lot of bug splattered SUV's and grimy sedans from surrounding states.

In another couple weeks park roads will be clogged with folks driving from grass-green willow copses to meandering oxbow river bends craning their necks like Great Blue Herons to see something – moose, elk, bison, bears, foxes, swans, otters, coyotes or anything in between. We're no different except we've honed a predictably successful strategy. By starting the evening at Jackson Lake Lodge, probabilities are extremely high that we'll spy several moose or elk. Once we've notched that onto our binoculars, we relax several grades and drive around much less anxiously hunting for other wildlife.

Target destination for tonight is beneath towering dark green firs that partially block the lodge's imposing brown façade. A weathered post-fence keeps visitors from falling off the high bluff and creates a perfect platform to steady binoculars. We scan left-to-right looking for movement or an incongruous black-brown lump against vivid lime – young willow leaves stretching toward sun and a new year. This time we're in luck; moose and elk are rampant among the bushes.

A dark brown cow moose is 75 yards dead straight west, lying in a shrubby copse of wintergreen willow. She's partially obscured by branches, but we can see her gently nibbling willow leaves. Other than a moose chewing its cud, there's not much action so I swing due south where 100 to 150 yards away the broad back of another cow moose appears and disappears among the greenery. Almost 20 yards closer to us a cow elk is meandering in a meadow that's no larger than a living room.

It's when I'm focusing on the elk that springtime magic floods over Jackson Lake's willow flats.

On spindly golf club legs a newborn elk calf takes tentative steps around the meadow. It can't be more than 48 hours old given its totally uncoordinated movements. Mom is keeping a sharp eye out for lurking predators while the calf attempts to nurse. She is especially wary of the cow moose wandering her way. Shuffling her legs to accommodate her calf, she twists 90 degrees to face the moose head-on. A few seconds later she takes a few steps to the east behind a bush, effectively blocking our sight.

Without warning the moose spins 180 degrees and gradually begins migrating away from the frustrated elk. Five minutes later she steps out from behind the tallest willows and there at her side is an equally wobbly young one, perhaps less than a day old. Her calf is almost totally charcoal black with a monstrous head waving in front of a pint-sized body. Its herky-jerky walk is more reminiscent of a spider than a moose. They disappear behind more shrubs and the cow elk goes off full alert.

As springtime hits the Tetons, a deluge of new life bursts forth. Most prominent are a spate of moose and elk calves that appear in May. Since moose and elk browse woody shrubs in winter while feasting on leaves in summer, they tend to birth their calves in habitats that are in near proximity to their summer seasonal areas. In the Tetons these calving rituals translate into great concentrations of moose, and to a lesser extent elk, around Jackson Lake Lodge.

Moose and elk use Jackson Lake Lodge's willow flats as a gigantic nursery. In May unusually high concentrations of moose and elk seek out these flats to deliver their young and give them a head start on a threat-prone life. At first glance this tendency to congregate around people by habitually reclusive mammals appears to be inimical to their solitary lives, but scientists suggest that moose and elk may be strategizing. These ungulates suffer the close proximity of people during calving because people tend to keep predators away.

Moose in the Anchorage, Eagle River and Homer areas of Alaska have developed a tendency to calve close to cities and towns. It is hypothesized that these people-prone sites are valuable because wolves and bears avoid them despite the bounty of delectable young calves. The same phenomenon may be occurring beneath the expansive windows of Jackson Lake Lodge. People keep the predators at bay.

For elk and moose in the Tetons, this safety valve is especially important. It is only within the last decade or so that grizzly bear and wolves migrated down from Yellowstone and expanded their range within the Teton Range and Valley. The first predators arriving found easy pickings because moose and elk tended to view wolves as simply large coyotes – not something to react to with great fear when contact occurred. The ungulates had lost their predator avoidance behavior.

Joel Berger with the Wildlife Conservation Society of New York has studied the effects of a 50-year lull in the grizzly bear and wolf populations within the Grand Tetons. Berger tested wolf howls, wolf urine and raven calls (the latter warning signals and communication about the presence of a predator that might translate into a quick meal) on moose in the Teton Valley. At first Teton moose showed no reaction to these stimuli, unlike their brethren in Alaska that initiated anxious predator-avoidance behaviors.

Gradually Teton moose are becoming more responsive to ravens' cues about traditional predators as their mortality increases. Berger notes that "Teton moose are regaining their astuteness with surprising speed." It only takes a loss of one calf to predation for mothers to regain their sensitivity. He concludes that instinct explains why prey populations do not crash with the reintroduction of predator species.

As elk and moose dance about in the willows a middle-aged woman in creased denim jeans, purple fleece top and black leather vest joins us at the rail fence. Just what I didn't want – company during quality time. She makes a few disgusting cooing noises to Bailey before ending my lonesome reverie.

"See any moose?"

"There's several out there including one elk; all have calves at their sides," I add in a neighborly manner while maintaining the Swarovskis at eye level. I scan to the right away from her hoping that our new best friend will magically disappear. I'm not in the mood to share this particular pair of binoculars tonight.

"Cute little dog you've got there."

Ah yes. That's what everyone thinks about Bailey the white West Highland terrier. She's an attention magnet. Should have owned one back when I was single. I mutter, "Thanks."

Bailey sits on her haunches and prepares to dish out a few licks. Life's tough for a princess turned trail dog.

"Wouldn't need those binoculars last night at Colter Bay's gas station when that mother grizzly walked by with her three cubs."

Whoa.

That got my attention.

I drop the binoculars like a hot rock and then look her straight in the eye trying to determine whether this is a bunch of bull or smidgen of truth.

"What happened?" I inquire a bit too anxiously letting her know that I'm all hers to play with. Looking deeply into her eyes searching for the story, there's no depth, no connection other than a fact-filled description of her encounter.

"It was after 8:30 last night when we pulled in for gas. The sun had almost set below the trees. I was waiting in the passenger's seat looking toward the main park road when a huge brown bear stepped tentatively out of the forest onto the asphalt. Head swaying side-to-side she hesitated slightly before taking another step. Three cubs materialized behind her. They all looked real nervous. Finally the four of them walked slowly between the cars and headed south into the trees."

"Everyone stopped pumping gas and watched in disbelief. I had to pinch myself to make certain that I wasn't dreaming."

"Oh look. Is that a moose out there?"

I turn back to the binoculars and focus on the moose and calf. But, I'm not really seeing them. All I can think about is hustling back toward Colter Bay at the earliest possible moment.

Fifteen minutes later while driving slowly past Colter Bay's service station I know the chances of seeing bears in the same locale 24 hours later are next to nil. But, if we don't make the effort to look, we'll never see them. Passing the station we creep toward the cabin area scanning frantically for furry monsters out on the hunt. Intuition tells me the truth – these bears have already gone to ground.

Ensconced in our cozy cabin, every so often I glance out the window hoping to catch a glimpse of ghost grizzlies. Despite straining my eyeballs, nothing is out there except Wyoming's cold dark night. Seeking solace in a good book I tumble toward deep sleep.

Hours pass, and then….

What's that?

Swimming out of a deep dream I slowly gain consciousness in the rocking bed. Bailey is once again trying to capture our attention. I check my watch – 2:00 a.m. – while Valerie rolls on her side and lets out an enormously loud sigh. Looks like I'm the dedicated dupe to take Bailey out again.

Going through the same motions as last night, this time it's colder and Bailey doesn't appear too eager to leave the cabin. On leash, I tug her pass the door. It closes with a wooden "thunk" leaving us shivering in the pitch-dark night.

"Come on Squirt, get it over with."

Bailey hunkers down, head low and shoulders hunched while I pull extra hard on her leash almost ripping it over her head. Stubborn little cuss, she's made up her mind to stay right where she is. No problem. I'll try reverse psychology.

Starring at the glorious cosmic light show peeking through claustrophobic trees I blot Bailey out of mind. Another magnificent star display is pasted overhead. It's a startling portal to another dimension.

If there's one thing Bailey can't stand, it's her Dad ignoring her. She scrambles back to her feet and begins sniffing the air while cautiously stepping three feet out in front of me. Glancing down, there's an alarming news flash to be read. Her posture speaks a thousand words. She's ready for battle: tail straight down covering her furry white butt; rose tinged ears perked forward scoping out sounds whose minute frequencies elude my ears; crinkled nose twitching at vaporous scents; head waving back and forth like radar on a battleship; and a body rigid as a young Arnold Schwarzenegger's set of abs.

A little shiver courses through my body as I realize what's happening. Bailey is catching a distinct scent of something BIG, furry and threatening. Moose? Elk? Wolf? Or…grizzly? There's no way of knowing precisely what she reads on the wind; but, it's definitely there somewhere waiting in the dark.

A few puffs of my breath rise like steam from a geyser, vanishing into the limitless black hole overhead. Seconds later I decide enough is enough. Dog has done her duty by marking our presence; we retreat into the cabin locking out wandering apparitions who know the Tetons as home.

* * *

As springs morphs into summer, and summer slides toward fall, four months later we have a brief Labor Day window to revisit the park. Our target this trip is Pilgrim Creek. This significant stream drops down from the far reaches of the Teton Wilderness and Yellowstone plateau. Although only three gravel-road-miles from the main park highway, most visitors never make the effort to see where this rough washboard leads. Those that do find a rutted, washboard mess that kicks up plenty of dust.

From the highway the nondescript turnoff has all the appearances of a good route for viewing elk and moose during the evening hours. A few adventurous types may explore, but somehow it never does deliver fantasized possibilities except for a solitary elk or two. Pilgrim Creek runs on the far southern shoulder of a little valley carrying this stream. For the most part all you find along the road other than choking clouds of dust are dried out sage and a braided plain of river rocks attesting to the creek's formidable spring runoff. We passed one truck and a fly fisher a half-mile back. But, other than this it looks like we'll have the trail all to ourselves.

Bailey takes the lead checking sign. That's when our fascination with grizzlies in early spring is reconciled in a magnified way.

Grizzly bear tracks!

It's virtually impossible to walk down the trail without stepping on cub prints. I scan them carefully taking measure of the arch among toes and length of claw extensions to verify that these are indeed grizzly rather than black bear prints. Valerie looks up with bug eyes while I call Bailey in. The trail is literally littered with tracks.

We've hardly walked more than twenty yards and already we're reaching for pepper spray. Safeties will stay on but these cans aren't going to leave our hands. I've also extricated the air horn from my pack. We're locked and loaded – ready, if that's possible – for bear.

Next challenge is crossing Pilgrim Creek. We find a wide spot and hop clumsily across usually. The air temperature may be warm, but this stream is freezing. Bailey slips and slides on the rocks; she's only half drenched after crossing and ready to go, waiting on the opposite shore with nose up testing for scent. Yes, we sense it too — the palpable presence of something magnificently wild wafting out of a crazy mosaic of willows.

I've got goose bumps and it's not from our frigid river crossing. Intuition warns us about imminent danger ahead. My heart beat raises several notches and my mouth cotton balls with adrenaline. I'm looking everywhere, scanning the willows; peering through the forest, trying to drill down while looking for trouble on four legs.

We enter a copse of black cottonwood, spruce and pine. Val is coughing loudly. I chide her a bit knowing what she's up to — hoping her noise will scare the bear(s?) off. Part of me wants to tease her and the other half wants to join in.

It's creepy in here.

Quiet floods over the forest and Pilgrim Creek silently trickles to our left lost in a maze of brown-green willows. A little breeze blows toward us laden with frigid air trapped by Pilgrim Creek's petite canyon and lush vegetation.

Another fifty feet and we finally spot an adult-sized print. A BIG adult-sized print. By now interpretation is virtually assured. There's a female grizz in here with at least two cubs. The prints are so fresh, so precisely sharp in wispy dust, that no mistake is possible. These prints were made sometime late last night or very early this morning. If they had been made prior to that, the prints' demarcation would be compromised by sand blowing back into each depression.

Safeties off on the pepper spray.

Both Val and I are calling to keep Bailey corralled with us. It's another ploy to warn the bears. I'm whistling every couple of seconds to keep Bailey near and bear(s) far while feeling around in my pack for the dog leash — time to rein puppy in before she unceremoniously brings grizzly hell down upon us. Our pace slows to a crawl as we live totally in the moment; as alert as it is humanly possible to be.

Winding between copses of trees we enter the canyon in which Pilgrim Creek calls home.

Ssssnnnaaaapppp.

Pppllloooooooppp.

Ccruunch.

Ssnaapp.

We freeze and aim our pepper spray at the trees wildly searching for? Bear? Moose? Elk? Most likely it's bear or bears, but there's no way of being sure until whatever it is runs us over. I've got spray in one hand and the air horn in the other both aimed directly at the trees. We're only 25 yards away but we can't confirm what biomass is making the commotion.

Make no mistake; *they're in there — somewhere.*

Val has had enough. She quickly retreats a good 40 yards at a fast paced walk — probably too fast given the conditions. Bailey is stuck between; uncertain of which instinct to follow. She's scared and wants to run away with Mom, but she doesn't want to leave her Dad.

Sssnnaaapppp.

Ccrunncchhh.

Rruusstttllee.

At first it seemed to me that the culprit has left but now I steel myself — we're about to be spanked big time.

For the very first time in my life I actually believe I'm about to be charged by a bear. My gut tells me we've gone too far this time; pressed the matter beyond a bear's comfort level.

There's a little hollowness in my stomach now in addition to all of the other symptoms of fright. Shoulders hunched, I expect to be trampled at any second.

Then….thirty seconds of nothing.

I straighten up and look over to Valerie and Bailey. They've both got saucer eyes.

Now another loud *SSSSSnnnnnaaapppppppp!!!!!* echoes from the trees fifty-or-so yards to our right. We still can't see anything.

Bailey turns 90 degrees and then eventually 180 leaving her facing directly down trail. Her ears are twitching like radar receptors. She hears something but it's not distinguishable to my ears. Her tail is protectively covering her butt. There's definitely no woofs coming from that puppy. She's gone to ground.

Two minutes later and everything is quiet. I shout to Val to join me. Reluctant, she finally figures out that she's standing there all alone and exposed. She wrangles Bailey before joining me on the trail.

"Well, that was a bit close for comfort," I wheeze.

"Let's go back, it's too scary."

"Probably was just a moose or an elk. Let's head up trail a bit."

"I don't want to become bear bait," she admonishes me.

Cccrrraaaaccccckkkkkk.

We both jump as another branch breaks 80 feet away.

"I'm going back," Valerie declares.

"No, let's go a bit further; we've hardly begun to hike. It was nothing more than a moose or elk. We've got pepper spray. Come on."

Again the fear factor is overridden by rationale. There *is* safety in numbers. We hike up-trail huddled together with our guard dog squeezed between us. Her normal trail bravado has disappeared. Bailey knows danger is out there.

Our hike continues. It's the only hike I've ever taken where almost every step I walked with pepper spray in hand. We're continually alert, sensing each and every fine little nuance in the woods this morning.

And when we finally reach a point where Pilgrim Creek's trees close in on us and our line of sight diminishes to nothing, better judgment tells us enough is enough. It's time to turn around or possibly get our butts kicked.

The way back goes uneventfully; that is until we reach our last point of noisy confrontation. Fifty yards down the trail from where Valerie stopped to turn around is a steaming fresh pile of bear scat. It's not a huge pile, but it is exceedingly warm and fresh, perhaps only minutes old. This scat definitely wasn't there when we passed.

So that's what Bailey was hearing. Despite our sensitivity and alert searching we didn't *see* a bear(s). Now we have stinky proof positive. Further, we have good reason from all of the tracks to believe it was at least a mother and a cub. Bailey the trail dog heard them sneak behind us after it/they left the copse of trees. How we never caught sight of the bear or bears is perplexing; inexplicable.

I chortle a little bit on seeing the fresh scat. Message conveyed. This bear was sending a memo – "I knew you were here, yet you didn't know I was here. This is my territory, now get the hell out."

Val is more than happy to leave this all behind. Bailey – she just strolls along; testing every now and then for scent, tail up, back to happy dog looking for a squirrel or two to punish.

Me? I'm replaying those nanoseconds over in my mind. I was 100 percent certain that I was about to be charged.

Adrenaline rush? You bet.

Worth the effort and expense to get here? No doubt.

Ready to turn around and do it all over again? Not today.

Nonetheless, I'm already thinking about the next time I'll walk this trail and what excitement might be encountered along this lonesome little stream flowing out of deep wilderness that 99 percent of all visitors to the Grand Tetons routinely pass without so much as an afterthought.

* * *

Many hours later I'm on fast cruise heading home along Interstate 86 out of Pocatello. Suddenly it all comes together. How could I have been so stupid?

Our trips to the Tetons in May and September are decidedly linked; joined in unison by one indisputable fact.

The sow grizzly with three cubs that we nearly encountered in May is still living around Colter Bay. It was their tracks that we saw at Pilgrim Creek; their commotion that tore the bushes apart; their scat that was left as a calling card.

I can't prove this unequivocally, yet I know deep within my heart that May and September are one. I've come full circle.

Late that evening when we reach home I run in to turn on the computer. I enter "grizzly cubs Colter Bay" onto Google. The search engine displays a great reference site with a photo of bear # 399; a 350 pound sow that has been frequenting Colter Bay with her three cubs. These are undoubtedly the same bears that the woman saw at the Colter Bay gas station in late May.

Each year the Interagency Grizzly Bear Study Team, comprised of field researchers from the U.S. Geological Survey; Wyoming Game and Fish Department; National Park Service; U.S. Fish and Wildlife Service; Montana Fish, Wildlife and Parks; U.S. Forest Service; Idaho Department of Fish and Game; and Montana State University; publishes a report entitled *Yellowstone Grizzly Bear Investigations*. From 2001 through 2006 a female sow, Bear # 399, has graced the pages of these reports. Following are the specifics from her monitoring.

DATE	LOCATION	OFFSPRING
8/29/01	Arizona Creek, GTNP	None
9/23/02	Snake River, GTNP	None
10/07/02	Pilgrim Creek, GTNP	None
5/20/03	Snake River, GTNP	None
6/28/03	Cygnet Cr, GTNP	None
7/15/04	Pilgrim Cr, GTNP	1 COY, lost
10/02/04	Colter Bay, GTNP	1 COY, lost
9/09/05	Bailey Cr, GTNP	None
2006	No specific site reported	3 COY

No specific references were made to Bear #399 in the 2008 or 2007 reports. Bear #399 is just beginning to mature as suggested by the detail listed above about her offspring. It is also obvious that she likes to hang out at Pilgrim Creek, Colter Bay and the Snake River.

Scott Armstrong, staff writer for the *Christian Science Monitor* (November 16, 2005), followed Shannon Podruzny of the Interagency Grizzly Bear Study Team in the summer of 2005 as Podruzny and her team tracked Bear #399. Podruzny claims that "'399' is one of 11 bears the team is shadowing this week…She likes cozy daybeds. '399' is considered big (7 feet tall, 350 pounds) and scrappy for a female. She's neither shy around people nor, apparently other bears: Her collar was ripped off in a fight."

Eventually the IGST led by Podruzny comes upon an elk carcass that Bear #399 had been feasting on. The team collects hair and scat samples for later analysis. As they head off to collect additional data, Armstrong writes that "Podruzny bypasses one [promising collection point] near the willows so we can 'go back with our scalps intact.'"

It is informative that Bear #399 was last captured in 2005 at **_Bailey Creek_** which flows out of Bailey Meadows – one drainage west of Pilgrim Creek. Did she have a prescient moment about a future West Highland Terrier guest?

On June 13, 2007 Bear #399 made front page news of the *NPS Digest* (National *Park Service Digest*, Jackie Skaggs). She, or one of her cubs, mauled Dennis VanDenbos, a 54 year-old Lander man near Jackson Lake Lodge. VanDenbos was apparently on nearby Wagon Road below the corrals between 5:50-6:00 a.m. He stopped to watch an elk and suddenly the sow and her cubs approached from his left. VanDenbos yelled and then dropped on his stomach in a submissive posture. He received puncture wounds and lacerations as the bear(s) tried to protect their food source.

Officials concluded this was a case of VanDenbos being in the wrong place at the wrong time. Biologists did not try to kill or remove the bears.

There's another side to Bear #399 that sticks a bit in my craw and that represents an unsettling epiphany.

What does it say about our world when we can't leave a bear in peace? Through the miracle of the World Wide Web I am able to see a photograph of the very bears that crept through the forest of Pilgrim Creek like ghost grizzlies. In the real world I never actually saw them even though we shared an intimate physical proximity.

There's value in knowing about Bear #399 through all of the facts available on various web pages. I feel a kindred spirit with her and the life she lives. Bear #399 gives a precious gift of a fascinating story – about her wanderings, legacy of cubs, and in good time, her death.

Nonetheless a part of me shouts that it's too much. We've encroached on her life too deeply. Perhaps I am the biggest violator. We know more about her than is right. Bear #399 has lost her wildness and mystery. In our rush to learn – to push our scientific knowledge – we've denigrated Bear #399's very essence and special quality that fascinates. Numbered, observed, cataloged, and documented, we've hounded the wildness out of her. And, that criticism extends first and foremost to me.

In the end Bear #399 has become too comfortable with us; too familiar. She is habituated to humans, but not as a food source. Bear #399 doesn't avoid our company, she pursues it. She knows that we offer a safer haven for her cubs. Consequently Bear #399 teaches them that humans can be trusted.

My Teton revelation, my epiphany, screams that this is not what we want in our grizzlies. We want them to be wild and free; stealth-like ghosts moving in the shadows of our minds and the landscape. Knowing that: *they're in there – somewhere.*

5

Comfort Zone

Slightly below timberline is a strip of territory that's neither continuous forest nor stark alpine terrain. It's a land of twix-and-tween where small dense islands of fir, mountain hemlock and Engelmann spruce stage a last stand before succumbing to winter's onslaught and summer's drought. Go ten feet higher in elevation and trees vanish. They can't take the frigid exposure; desiccating wind chill; soil lacking any semblance of essential nutrients; wild vacillations in moisture; or being pummeled by sun.

Above tree line tundra takes over and with it an ecosystem of miniature ground hugging plants that eons ago learned to compromise with this utterly ruthless environment. Many adapted to Venus-like temperature extremes. Some developed an ability to create quasi antifreeze that sees them through sub-freezing periods prevalent in these micro climes. Others have evolved leaf structures that fold into themselves, hugging precious warmth until dawn's feeble light. They refuse to give up even with deeply hard freezes during summer's short nights.

Sub-alpine country, usually a narrow band between woodland and tundra, is fascinating because it typically sparkles with glorious views, luxurious flower gardens in late summer, and crisp air packing a walloping oxygen punch. Wander this parkland with confidence; it's gentler than walking a fine line on stratospheric summits whose conditions are so cruel that life is merely a visitor. Sub-alpine's buffering cushion between thick woods and desolate tundra functions as a transition from robust vegetated jungle to unprotected exposure among rocks, ice and snow.

Sub-alpine country offers a last-chance before extreme conditions. It's the best of both worlds – a pleasing mixture of trees and flower gardens bordered by a mountain's exposed character. Descending a barren peak I always feel a small sense of relief come over me when hitting this special demarcation; if trees can survive here, so can I. Above there are no guarantees; period.

Peak-baggers are usually somewhat ambivalent about the sub-alpine transition. It's just one more hurdle to jump before serious climbing necessary in scaling most summits. For them, a mountain's highest pinnacle offers the best unobstructed views and imparts a sense of mastery over all that reposes below. I also enjoy unparalleled vistas; what a joyous lift they give. But for me a gnawing discomfort, a palpable sense of the temporary, is also associated with sky-high mountain-tops. This gut-feel dissipates when I drop back below timberline.

Peaks reluctantly allow me to visit. Sub-alpine country embraces like a long lost friend.

That's why I see the epitome of backcountry travel as being *in the zone.*

Lunch simply tastes better down there when I'm freed from exposure out on the bleak tundra or off a twisted shaft of granite.

Gentleness replaces harshness. Flourishing patches of healthy blossoms substitute for meager miniature flowers struggling to survive. Gurgling springs and tiny creeks sing joyous melodies. Swirling winds are tamed, buffered by mountainside and convenient windbreaks formed from firs and pines. Heady bouquets of rich soil warmed to perfection waft past.

Being back in the zone is like coming completely, totally, alive – never cognizant of a niggling little thought about errant weather. Over the years I've shifted my paradigm of thinking about wilderness I love most. All those years spent idolizing high mileage treks and arduous peak bagging have gone by the wayside. Now my heart is set on something offering more intimacy – sub-alpine country has become the ultimate destination for me.

When some of my best friends have difficulty understanding why this perceptual shift occurred, I try to explain that I still love to bag peaks as much as the next person. By glorifying the act of conquering a mountain I also denigrate what mountains are all about. Now the comfort zone embodies a more robust, much richer, way of relating to mountains. That's a pretty powerful epiphany.

No other region of the country delivers sub-alpine country quite like the West. The Sierras, Cascades and Rockies with their majestic forested robes set a perfect counterpoint to the zone. It seems like it takes forever to climb to the edge of these endless forests where a ribbon of parkland waits that is polka-dotted with splotches of trees and fringed by krummholz. Beyond this sanctuary, alpine spires are usually smothered in snow.

Krummholz is a German term for stunted sub-alpine forest or twisted wood. This diminutive forest occurs at the very edge of tree-line, on the fringes of sub-alpine territory. Krummholz trees and shrubs are mini-sized with trunks twisted and gnarly. These deformities occur due to great environmental stress caused by constant high wind. In extreme cases trees will not grow branches on a side facing these incoming gales. On the leeward side branches tail out – elongated since almost all growth is funneled away as means of protection.

It would be easy to conclude that krummholz vegetation represents entirely different species of trees and shrubs, but don't let appearances be deceiving. A cluster of oaks just over the lip of a breezy mountain pass will have intriguing shapes and peculiar branches. But, they also may live next to quite ordinary trees that escape because they are somewhat lower in elevation, slightly below the immediate reach of gale force winds. Cut a cross-section of each and growth rings should confirm the similarity of age. Nonetheless, a sheltered oak could easily be twice the size of a krummholz oak that's blasted by wind.

In the mountainous West most krummholz is populated by sub-alpine fir (Abies lasiocarpa), lodgepole pine (pinus contorta), limber pine (Pinus flexilis) and Engelmann spruce (Picea engelmannii). These trees grow closely together, seeking shelter from each other and tailing off into densely matted bushes – trees that have been so severely pruned that they've lost their ability to grow upward so they spread out horizontally.

Patches of krummholz facilitate the growth of new clumps. Studies of sub-alpine fir expansion in Glacier National Park suggest that krummholz in this park is increasing in density and area. Researchers attribute this to soil enhancement and micro climate improvement surrounding krummholz patches. The implications for wildlife are remarkable since many critters not only find shelter in krummholz stands, but also sources of nutrition not otherwise available in these near alpine conditions.

On the eastern edge of the craggy Rocky Mountains, peaks shoot skyward wearing their signature boulder capped crowns.

Drier than the Cascades, the Rockies' sub-alpine zone is often less decipherable and also usually more expansive. Here barren boulder capped summits play counterpoint to softness of the transition zone. There's no Rocky Mountain high quite like a jewel of a tarn tucked in a mountain's crease, liberally sprinkled with islands of trees that offer shelter for a camp, and carpets of wildflowers spread across surrounding meadows.

Being in the zone is the personification of having wildness and loving it too. Exit to alpine country and wilderness carries a perpetual edge, a constantly challenging pressure to remember. Drop in elevation to vast woodland forests and wildness tones down to an almost imperceptible sub-conscious level.

Get a taste of sub-alpine country and you're hooked forever. A walk up Granite Mountain exemplifies what the zone is all about.

* * *

Spring is a fickle and chaotic companion in the Cascades. A day in the mountains may span the continuum from tentative pale sun, to spotty rain showers, then consuming bruised clouds, to snow falling on spruces, and back to promising yellow rays. Yet, despite these vagaries spring is beloved because it delivers hope for full-on wilderness adventures. Spring is a time to gnaw on the marrow of life and there is no better place to enjoy spring than on the high reaches of Granite Mountain near Washington's Snoqualmie Pass.

Grand outdoor adventure waits above on this giant of a mountain as lengthening sunny days and warming temperatures unveil land reborn. Wildlife is more visible, perfect contrast to an epidemic of fragile buds unfolding to a new season as unchecked growth consumes trees, grasses, and shrubs. Spring connotes new beginnings. It's a time to leave unrealized dreams behind; that raft trip not taken last year due to anemically low water, the planned three-day backpack into distant pristine alpine lakes squeezed out by work, or a peak not bagged because lightning-laced thunderstorms stubbornly refused to yield.

Wilderness calls; imploring me to get on with it; to just do it. And, that's the calling I expect to fulfill today. This is a time for action, to turn imaginative desires into concrete experiences; into adventure. I want to savor warmer temperatures mixed with gentle breezes, longer languid days and a destination made difficult by winter's command. Frighteningly humongous avalanches sweep off Granite Mountain in winter, making it a very risky prospect for snowshoeing or mountaineering. But today a perfect spring moment is unfolding in the Northwest, the entire world seems right. There's no place to experience the ecstasy of spring quite like sub-alpine country.

A deafening haughty swoosh of hyper-compressed air from a dingy grease splattered eighteen wheeler parts thrashing Douglas firs as I emerge from my car along Interstate 90. An ominous vacuum fills with the rata-tat-tat of his Jake brakes. Another truck driver high on some miracle chemical is numbly trying to slow down while negotiating the perilously swift descent from Snoqualmie Pass. Reaching for my daypack, fleeting silence is desecrated as this trucker hell-bent for Seattle barrels down the twisting highway. Cars swish by, emitting only a modest moan, but it seems as though the entire world is using busy Interstate 90 today.

Traffic is chalked up as one minor cost you bear in accessing the Alpine Lakes Wilderness on Seattle's far outskirts. Back before the computer and dot.com booms, a modest urban population in Puget Sound loved this territory. As Seattle and surrounding communities expanded, encroachment on wildness accelerated. Now the problem is finding a several hour hike where less than twenty people crowd the trail. Twenty is considered a good day; a bell-wether day of relative peace and solitude, almost untrammeled.

This is Tuesday so I won't have to fight weekenders, but it is also early May which means that most Cascade trails are still snow-bound. Of course there is a big difference between snowbound and closed to further travel in the Northwest. Closed means deep snow obliterates any forward progress. Snowbound simply implies being a little more innovative in defining a route, more cautious in avoiding cement-heavy spring avalanches, and more discerning in selecting south facing slopes that receive full sunny exposure. All of these considerations clearly point to Granite Peak (aka Granite Mountain) as the trail du jour.

Granite Peak is a perfect prescription for spring malaise since its trail climbs mercilessly straight up from 2,000 feet to 5,629 feet. Soft golden sun is shining, a rarity in Washington, and an intriguing path beckons to leave the depressingly gray freeway bound parking lot.

Water? Check.

Snacks? Check.

Ten essentials? More or less.

With spit-and-polish boots, optimism that only hikers nurture at the start of a long climb, and sun warm on my back, I pierce a shroud of thick recently leafed-out vine maples, alders and assorted brush demarcating wilderness from civilization by declaration of the United States Forest Service.

Trail tread is wet, an expectation in the Cascades, and the air is filled with an aromatic fragrance of humus; raw forest is struggling to reach the energy of penetrating sun. Fragile spring vegetation is still in the process of completely leafing out, which means that the forest floor is quite naked in spots. This makes it easier to discern historic logging scars – hemlock and Douglas fir trunks broken off at chest height.

Uncomplicated axe technology was used back in the early days of Snoqualmie Pass to cut down trees. Loggers notched chest-high holes in tree trunks as receptacles for platforms formed by cramming solid boards into the notches. This gave them a little breathing room above both the forest floor and occasional weirdly-shaped root balls. Despite the intervening decades since the late 1880s, these trees are still fighting to nurture life. Their stubby bases slowly decay offering both valuable nutrients and prize incubation medium for others. Don't look closely and the scars will never be noticed, healing processes have gone that well.

Sun beckons through a fringe-line of trees; it's streaming in, finding ways through various holes in the canopy. It's akin to sun bursting past thunderstorm clouds in a dying storm – light that's almost sacred as golden gauzy shafts blast darkness into smithereens. Squinting in this intense holy light, I step out onto a vast wildly green avalanche slope.

The world opens up beyond the forest's shadowy canopy. Leave the Northwest, but the memory of trees can never be left behind – stately tall, brooding, dark green, and ready to reclaim any vacant spot of land. However, this avalanche slope stops trees in their tracks. Granite Peak sheds wonderful wispy-white billowing avalanche freight trains in winter threatening to gobble up the freeway.

At the avalanche path's edge it's possible to see where several decades-old trees have been taken out this year. A once-in-a-hundred-year avalanche has mowed down these survivors with its voluminous punishing mass, speed and longer run of chaotic white clouds filled with ice chunks, blocks of snow – whispering white mist and death bulldozing everything in its path. Those are days past; here in May lower slopes are already displaying a profusion of confident greenery and flowery blossoms. Steam rises lazily from a black-damp log at trail's edge while a profusion of miniature winged insects go about their business darting here, flitting there.

So begins a long series of switchbacks rising quickly above the din of freeway below. As trucks and cars gradually become smaller, rhythmic noise simultaneously subsides from tires slapping pavement, labored gears grinding away, and powerful engines humming at their loads. Views to the south widen and within minutes Mt. Rainier's ice-cream white dome begins to peek up over a distant saw tooth horizon. It's a dominant anchor for so many people — a benevolent and ever vigilant guardian angel — whose presence is celebrated both as a pronouncement of fine weather and affirmation that all is right with the world.

Catching my ragged breath at a switchback, it's interesting to see just how quickly a trail virtually on the edge of suburbia becomes wilderness. Granite Mountain doesn't care about a concrete and asphalt ribbon winding below swollen with busy commerce. It knows little of, and pays no attention to, scurrying humans bent on this insignificant agenda or that. This mountain only knows how to radiate proud grandness, nurturing wild country with life exploding in synch with a fresh season.

I'm gauging progress by how high trees are in the forest bracketing this avalanche path and, of course, the extent to which the freeway evaporates. Eventually the road and its phalanx of ant-like vehicles drops out of sight leaving trees as a barometer of elevation gained.

One thing is for certain, trees have hardly diminished in size since I began an hour ago. I'm fortunate that this trail doesn't wind through Granite Mountain's massive forest. It would be awfully repetitive switch-backing from one contour to the next over the miles, longing for something other than to see tree trunk after tree trunk. Only so many variations accompany Douglas fir, or hemlock for that matter. Here, out on the avalanche slope, there's plenty to focus on: dozens of wildflowers blooming, sun drilling into my bones, wispy clouds determined to ruin a perfect day, little streams running down Granite Mountain's coulees and ravines, and thick forest hesitant to give ground.

Movement at the trail's edge two yards above draws my attention to a grouse feeding; now shedding its white winter plumage. Hunting and pecking among low-lying shrubs like a Wal-Mart shopper for a super bonus special, a bounty of insects faces a feathered grim reaper. As for me, when I make this next switch-back and reach the grouse snowy remnants from winter begin.

Few birds equal the ptarmigan species of grouse as clever masters of disguise. Ptarmigan are typically 12-15 inches in size, weighing 13-18 ounces. Most common in the U.S. are white-tailed ptarmigan (Lagopus leucurus) in northern Washington, Idaho and Montana, but also habiting northern New Mexico, Colorado and southern Wyoming. Willow ptarmigan (Lagopus lagopus) is the largest ptarmigan in North American followed by rock ptarmigan (Lagopus Mutus). Both reside principally in northern British Columbia, Alaska, the Aleutians and Arctic. The white-tailed ptarmigan is smallest of these three birds.

In concert with their hostile habitats, ptarmigan possess feathered feet and small beaks — adaptations for surviving wintry Arctic conditions. White-tailed and rock ptarmigans frequent boulder-strewn territory usually at or above timberline. Willow ptarmigan dwell in low areas of dense vegetations, especially around swampy areas. Solitary in summer, ptarmigan flock together in winter.

Ptarmigan have adapted their plumage to fit snowy environments. In late summer they molt into all white plumage that they retain from October through April. In spring they molt to a brown mottled pattern characteristic of their breeding season. As summer develops ptarmigan go through a partial molt again arriving at mottled brown and black plumage with traces of white on their wings. These molting phases make them masters of disguise. They blend in perfectly with their environments, a very useful adaptation to avoid becoming prey.

Look for ptarmigan among ground-hugging plants and shrubs where they feed on berries, seeds, insects and blossoms. They also like to consume new buds on willow and heather. But, hikers shouldn't be surprised if they fail to see ptarmigan until almost stepping on them. When they don't move ptarmigan are extremely difficult to detect because the birds blend right into the scenery. If accidentally flushed, they will roar up with little wings frantically beating the air. Watch out if you have a heart condition. Ptarmigans could easily scare you to death.

I'm near the sub-alpine zone; a bit of goal-anxiety kicks in to power me those final yards of snow-free hiking. From here things change in a big way.

Scrambling along a rough boot-beaten path on top of disintegrating icy snow, I'm transported many weeks back to very early spring. It's a winter wonder world. Snow blankets everything. Only a few brave firs poke their puny heads above the icy crust, while at the avalanche path's edge patches of fir congregate like school kids at a busy playground.

This is where a trickle of adrenaline begins seeping through my veins. Views of wild land are expansive. Rationally I know that Interstate 90 is only thousands of feet below hemmed in by power lines and clear cuts. But, here in mid-week with nary a soul around, that connection disappears over the rocky hump of Granite Peak's rib. A taste of wildness fills my palette; the perfume of raw earth recently freed from snowy grip glides by on a sudden gust of wind. The beautiful and rugged snow covered peaks of the Cascades Mountains roll and glisten in the distance like white canvas sail-cloth of yachts plying a vast sea.

I'm in the zone.

Although others have paved the way over the last three weeks, persistent melting has erased many of their boot prints leaving me free to choose my own way and to make potentially foolish mistakes. It will be difficult to lose the correct line toward Granite Peak, but dumber things have happened to me out in the open like this – that's part of sub-alpine country's allure.

There's a nasty edge here – a feeling of bad juju waiting to happen. About to enter highly exposed alpine terrain, from this point forward each step has to be carefully placed. It's time to concentrate rather than just bumbling along. It only takes one false step to get into trouble. My biggest worry is plunging through disintegrating snow over a hollowed-out spot in a snow drift above jagged rocks. Little tarns doting Granite Mountain's upper ramparts also pose an impending hazard if I'm not careful. It would be very easy to break an ankle or leg by busting through a snow bridge.

Ahead a scruffy route climbs steeply, almost vertically, over rotten ice, gray precarious rocks and decomposing snow. I've climbed in these conditions hundreds of times, but this doesn't reduce my excitement or attention to proceeding cautiously. I'd like to peak-out, but there still is another 400 feet to climb above this ridge before reaching a fire lookout.

How lucky do I feel today?

I've passed over the most serious obstacle – Granite Mountain's cavernous avalanche gully – without mishap. Now I'm facing either a rock sea along the southwestern face or jumbled boulder gardens if taking this ridge heading west. Neither route appeals.

While making up my mind, I notice an ice-covered tarn that's waiting for its moment in the sun, crouching down in a slight basin on this vast white wonderland of snow. This forlorn little lakelette is smothered by winter's remnants adding to its lonesome cachet and resonating with my deliberations.

Something about the pond's solitude sparks a startling realization about how alone and distant I am from Granite Peak's trailhead. Yet, it was barely less than two hours earlier that I started climbing.

My pulse quickens. Bad vibes seem to envelope me like a full-body aura. Something tangible is at play, but I can't quite put my finger on it.

I've been to the zone and passed through it. I've gone from the embrace of sub-alpine parkland to full-on alpine roaming. Suddenly, for whatever reason, bagging a peak doesn't seem so important after all.

Unable to see down into the valley where electric power lines, naked clear cuts, and noisy mechanical conveyances dwell; high on a gem of a mountain in blazing radiance of sun; possessing a tremendous view of an alpine world with Mt. Rainier as the focal point; and plowing through a glittering world of freezing snow, I'm blessed with the magnificence of wildness. This is more than adequate compensation for meeting the mountain's challenge. Why press my luck when visceral gut feelings are screaming otherwise?

Think I'll drop back down to the fringe of the sub-alpine zone where I ran into the ptarmigan and take a little snooze in the sun. That's an ambitious enough agenda if I ever saw one on a mellow day like this.

* * *

In my eyes, human desecration of the base of Granite Mountain is so extensive that it makes adjoining forests considerably less than wilderness. And, there is more than a grain of truth to support this perspective. These forests have been defiled by loggers' saws and soundly cleaved by railroad and Interstate. Nonetheless, some-one would have to argue pretty persuasively that I failed to attain a "wilderness experience." That moment in the sun on Granite Mountain's shoulder was filled with wildness. My connection with nature would have been no different if I was one hundred miles away deep within North Cascades National Park.

In *The Future of Life*, Edward O. Wilson (2002) examined this very question: "What is a wilderness today in our largely human-ized world? What it has always been: a space that sustains itself, was here before humanity, and where, in the words of the Wilderness Act of 1964, the Earth and its community of life are untrammeled by man and where man himself is a visitor who does not remain." Granite Peak, cloaked on top in a thick blanket of snow, offers a very tangible sense of being untrammeled that fits precisely with the concept of wilderness.

The vicissitudes of summiting snowy Granite Peak presented a splendid experience and allowed me to savor a bit of old-fash-ioned Northwest wilderness. Clearly, my walk up Granite Peak was nowhere as dangerous as a summit attempt on Mt. Rainier or Mt. Baker. But, in profoundly vibrant ways I left behind the comforts of ordinary urban life, deeply drank my share of wildness, and enjoyed the tangy taste of adrenaline-laced danger. That's what happens whenever you enter into the sub-alpine zone – that myste-rious breech from forest to tundra – and beyond.

How quickly conditions can change above timberline. A lit-tle lesson about the alpine zone's illusion of safety was forcefully driven home in a high rocky basin immediately south of Granite

Mountain. Annette Lake is a mesmerizing sub-alpine lake sitting at the base of Silver and Abiel Peaks. People love this elfin lake to death due to its proximity to Seattle and relatively modest 1,400 feet elevation gain over three miles of trail. After negotiating the clutter of railroad tracks, power lines and freeway service roads the path heads steeply up through full-bodied hemlock and fir aiming for distant granite spires.

My hiking buddy, Jim, and I decided that a late spring afternoon walk would be the perfect prelude to a fun-filled weekend. It had been a bear of a winter and many Cascade trails were smothered in deep drifts; they'd remain that way until the end of June. We expected the same for Annette Lake Trail, but prepared for an inevitable plod across rotten snow banks by bringing ice axes.

First surprise of the day was how much snow had melted leaving half of the trail snow-free. We quickly scaled the switchbacking trail gaining 1,200 feet through mature and well-watered forest. It was simply a matter of charging up a well-manicured trail. Just shy of 3,500 feet a deep snowline showed up out of nowhere. We paused a moment to catch our breath and turned around trying to gauge our elevation against Granite Mountain to the north, deeply covered in snow above the zone.

For the next 1 ½ miles our trail was no more than a bootbeaten route on top of a good two feet of snow and ice. Occasional breaks occurred where trees had fallen letting in more sun on these high western slopes of 5,605-foot Silver Peak. Talus slopes were also surprisingly free of snow even though some still owned vestiges of avalanches sloughing off Silver Peak looming 2,000 feet above.

We reached Annette Lake and enjoyed a second surprise of the day – no one was around. Usually you have to share this jewel with other recreationists. Nonetheless, it was tough finding a snow-free spot to sit down and relax, but any inconvenience was swept away by the sun's deeply penetrating warmth. Jim and I luxuriated in a new season – summer – until it was time to leave.

No more than one-quarter of a mile after departing Annette Lake we ran into the first of what amounted to about 15 Boy Scouts making their way toward the lake for an overnight adventure. Most of them were about 8 years old. They carried a bewilderingly motley amalgamation of gear – many cast-off or cheapo packs and borrowed equipment that didn't fit. Smiling at this rag-tag army as it went by, I thought about what really mattered – they were simply doing it.

We exchanged a few words with the Scout's leaders. These men bravely volunteered to make certain that a dozen plus young boys enjoyed a wilderness experience. As stragglers struggled past I noticed how sweaty they were. Their parents had sent them off in down coats and they had dutifully worn them up the trail. Many looked sopping wet.

These thoughts evaporated 30 minutes later as Jim and I came upon our third surprise of the day. We missed the spot where this ad hoc beaten path rejoined the well-defined trail. One minute we were smugly looking at a bunch of neophytes with a bit of disdain and the next as seasoned veterans we were sliding down a slick fern and moss covered ravine. About the third time I landed on my butt with a thud, I shot Jim an unkind look. I'd nearly impaled myself on my ice axe.

It took us twice as long to come down Annette Lake Trail as it took to get up and by the time we reached our car a film of clouds commandeered the sky. A weather change was underway that hadn't been forecasted.

That night Snoqualmie Pass received 11 inches of snow.

I can only think about how miserable that Scout Troop felt when conditions changed and the alarm of its leaders when those first flakes fell. It must have been a very challenging adventure getting them safely off that mountain. The lesson: hikers have to be super cautious about the false illusion of safety whenever entering the sub-alpine zone or going higher to alpine tundra.

Fortunately people can enjoy sub-alpine terrain without going to the extremes associated with hard-core mountaineering. A perfect answer – an epiphany for many who are in the early stages of experiencing the outdoors – is waiting in many of our national parks and national forests. Early park superintendents and supervisors understood the benefit of locating lodges as close to wilderness splendor as possible. Consequently, many historic rustic structures are built right in, or near to, the sub-alpine zone. Most of these famous lodges come with a surprising list of amenities enabling visitors to live in the lap of luxury with bona fide wilderness right outside their rooms.

Crater Lake Lodge in Crater Lake National Park is an ideal example of a sub-alpine lodge serving the public and designed to stimulate tourism to southeastern Oregon. Construction began in 1905 and the lodge eventually opened to guests ten years later. Part of the problem in finishing the 71 room structure was Crater Lake's hostile sub-alpine climate exacerbated by snowfall averaging 533 inches per year. With over 90% of the park managed as wilderness, visitors could experience the beauty and harshness of the sub-alpine zone by looking out their windows.

In 1991 complete rehabilitation of Crater Lake Lodge was undertaken at a cost of $15 million. Its Great Hall was dismantled and reconstructed following proper standards for structure integrity while other portions of the original facility were destroyed. The primary goal was to recreate the rustic atmosphere of the Great Hall and incorporate original materials to the greatest extent possible.

Crater Lake Lodge was a grand experiment in trying to build and maintain a structure at the edge of sub-alpine country. Happily, the facility introduced thousands of visitors over the decades to the vicissitudes of high country environments and was instrumental in encouraging similar construction approximately 240 miles north at Mt. Hood. There, over 2,000 feet above the nearest town of Government Camp, a lodge was built to encourage tourism rivaling that at Crater Lake.

Mount Hood in the 1.2 million acre Mt. Hood National Forest is a very convenient location for accessing sub-alpine lodging. In fact, Timberline Lodge underscores by its very name a location within that magical sub-alpine zone. Mt. Hood's summit tops out at 11,249 feet, the fourth highest Cascade peak after Mt. Rainier (14,410), Mt. Shasta (14,179 feet), and Mt. Adams (12,277 feet). Timberline Lodge, located on the southern flank of the mountain, was built at 6,000 feet. A prodigious amount of snow falls here which motivated President Franklin D. Roosevelt to add a ski chairlift, the Magic Mile lift, to the facility.

Flash back to 1936 when construction began on Timberline Lodge. At that time this country's depression was at its height and the Works Progress Administration initiated this project for economic relief. The WPA retained 350 local craftspeople to build the structure with 70 guest rooms in 15 months using local stone and massive fir timbers harvested from the nearby forest.

Timberline Lodge's signature feature is its hand-hewn construction. Each room is unique unto itself. All furnishings and hardware are handmade including draperies and rugs, artwork, bedspreads and lamps. Craftspeople continue to lovingly repair and refurbish this grand lodge.

The Magic Mile ski lift was the second, and longest, chairlift built in the United States at that time. Roosevelt envisioned a ski

Mecca where thousands of skiers came to enjoy winter play and also become more familiar with the economic importance of the Northwest's timber and ranching industries. Roosevelt's dream has been fulfilled as more than 250,000 skiers dance their magic on six ski areas with the highest lift topping out at 8,540 feet. The lodge offers the longest ski season in the U.S.

Both Crater Lake Lodge and Timberline Lodge grew out of governmental efforts to spur economic development and tourism. In Western settings the federal government more often relied on the private sector to build grand hotels. Glacier National Park is a case in point. A series of lodges was built by the Great Northern Railway at East Glacier, Two Medicine, Cutbank, Gunsight, Sun Point, Belton and St. Mary's Lake. While these lowland lodges offer access to Glacier National Park's vast wilderness, they are far surpassed by the unrivaled sub-alpine experience waiting at Many Glacier Hotel and alpine lodging available at Sperry and Granite Park Chalets.

From Babb, Montana, a battered paved road twists and turns 12 miles toward a fairyland setting. The road is so rough that it seems certain it will succumb each winter. Wilderness parallels the road, a fitting prelude for what's to come once visitors turn into the little valley holding Swiftcurrent Lake. Not only are the views beyond spectacular, but the alpine-style Many Glacier Hotel adds its own large measure of cachet to this remote land.

Many Glacier Hotel was built from 1910 to 1915 in a series of four-story chalets consistent with President of Great Northern Railway Louis Hill's vision of the park as America's Switzerland. The Swiss chalet style was integral to structures throughout the park and a leading motif of the railroad's advertising campaign. Larger lodges at Many Glacier and East Glacier served as hubs from which visitors could access smaller rustic backcountry sites. What phenomenal backcountry awaited tourists then, and now.

Glacier National Park is big wilderness on a level that most visitors find difficult to comprehend. Statistics on the geological and climatic features alone verify the depth of this landscape: 12 large lakes and 700 smaller lakes; 200 waterfalls; 7 mountains over 10,000 feet elevation; a triple divide (sending waters to the Pacific Ocean, Gulf of Mexico and Hudson Bay); 27 glaciers (formerly 150 before global warming); record temperature change in 24 hours (from 44 degrees Fahrenheit to -56 degrees Fahrenheit); and snowfall at any time of the year.

Many Glacier Hotel is blessed with dozens of public and private balconies conveying a Swiss jigsaw pattern. Verandas are strategically placed to direct visitors' attention to the park's glorious splendors. Swiftcurrent Lake is ever-present from balcony and window views. Great Northern Railway's architects created a setting that makes visitors want to explore what's beyond their room's window; to get a real taste of mountains that are almost too spectacular to be true.

Glacier Park is host to an estimated 800 black bears and 350 grizzly bears. Visit Many Glacier in late August when berries are ripening and be prepared to see bears. From the lodge's main balcony I watched a handful of bears rummage through berry bushes hardly 25 yards from the main roadway.

I definitely walk more cautiously along Glacier's trails compared to other mountain places. Knowing a large omnivore is out there that can kill me in one swat makes a difference in attentiveness. The magnificent sensation of being 100% alert is intoxicating — not scared, necessarily, but living fully in the moment and concentrating on every little clue that comes my way.

Grizzly bears, mountain goats, moose, black bears loons, osprey, eagles, deer, waterfowl, hawks and life's great menagerie swarm around Many Glacier Hotel. These sightings add a very special flavor to this sub-alpine country. *The amazing thing is that virtually anyone can access this quaint rustic and historic lodge squatting in the middle of sub-alpine country.* Even if a visitor never left the lodge or its balconies they still have an excellent opportunity to see wildlife; watch a crimson sunrise on peaks glistening with fresh snowfall; or, experience what it means to be in the zone. That's the beauty of sub-alpine wilderness.

You don't need to go on an arduous hike traipsing up Granite Mountain's steep slopes to become immersed in sub-alpine wilderness. Our National Park Service and Forest Service have taken all of the hard work out of reaching the sub-alpine zone.

But, don't be fooled.

Raw wildness waits slightly beyond the trailhead. The joys and unexpected surprises of being in untamed land begin the moment you step off pavement. Accessibility doesn't make these at-the-fringe experiences any safer compared to a Boy Scout troop sweating its way up to Annette Lake for a night in remote wilderness. Even a walk along a heavily-traveled nature trail carries many of the same risks as my climb 3,000 feet up Granite Mountain's snow-riddled peak.

All of life carries perils that can't be anticipated. People have been killed sitting in their living rooms watching television as a car smashes through their front window or shot in a hail of bullets when a gang-banger high on meth mistakes their house for the crib of a rival gang member. When seen from this perspective, any possible danger associated with sub-alpine and wilderness settings seem fairly irrelevant.

That's the sweetness – and epiphany – of being in the comfort zone.

Overcoming Primal
Challenges

6

Winter Revelation

People are attracted to outdoor recreation for many reasons including, among others, relaxation, rejuvenation, physical challenge, exercise, access to visually stunning locations, chasing wildlife, and adventuring with family or friends. Some folks become so infatuated with the goal aspect of outdoor sport that they pursue the elusive dream of being first — conquering an unclimbed peak, snowboarding a new run on a near-vertical slope in deep wilderness, forging a new-fangled bike track across Mongolia, or surfing a virgin Tasmanian break. In many respects it's all good; there is no one best reason for getting immersed in the outdoors.

During my initial al fresco forays I too fell in love with the notion of seeing how many laborious miles I could rack up on a grueling day hike, how many days in a row I could cover marathon-like long distances, and how many dangerous mountain peaks I could tick off in the course of a summer month. It was quite gratifying to test my day hiking mettle with impressive physical feats. Nonetheless, in time these victories became a little shallow, a bit boring.

That's when an important realization gripped my mind.

My greatest pleasure from outdoor pursuits distills into comfort about knowing my way around wild country. By conquering some of the most serious physical and environmental life-threatening trials that untamed country and critters can throw my way, I progressively learned how to overcome primal challenges. It hasn't always been pretty. There were more than my share of moments when I tucked tail and ran, or when disaster happened. I scrapped by to try again.

As my collage of bellwether day hiking moments accrued, another epiphany slapped me in the face…I needed to become more proficient at a broader range of backcountry activities such as fly-fishing, white-water rafting, and snow-shoeing. It was time to strap on a pair of snowshoes and go meet the mountain.

* * *

A thick coat of fluffy white cotton progressively creeps lower on the Cascade and Olympic Mountains as winter tightens its frigid grip. Trapped in Seattle, I look forlornly at wonderful mountains calling with adventure. Snow doesn't fall on the Cascades like magic while avoiding the city; we're also coping with a daily onslaught of rain or sleet falling in great heaps alternating with persistently steady drizzle. One thing is exceedingly clear when gazing out on vanilla dappled peaks – an enormous amount of the right equipment is needed to explore the backcountry in winter.

The Cascades' legacy of relentless storms is bitter-sweet. Snow lovers can't wait to get out – snowboarders, cross country ski aficionados, downhill ski bums, snowmobilers and snowshoers. In winter many people go to ground in the city, hunkering down and enduring the long wait until spring. Others who feed off outdoor exploits know that these conditions are perfect for winter explorations.

This weekend is my first foray into snowshoeing – a straight-forward extension of walking in the woods, or so I think. To hone technique and sort out my gear, I'm joining an outing with the Seattle-based Mountaineers, a non-profit group of outdoor fanatics. A call from Tom, the trip leader, the night before explains that I'll hitch a ride to the trailhead with him at 6:00 a.m. sharp. A forecast of thick clouds and possible snow means that we are good to go so long as we watch our back. His battered old yellow Volkswagen Beetle pulls up in front of my house; gear is loaded and we're off to wild lands near Snoqualmie Pass.

Two hours later a patchwork group of fifteen people assemble at Snoqualmie Pass Ski Area (also known as The Summit at Snoqualmie) intent on climbing Mt. Catherine, a 5,052 foot peak east of Seattle. There's not a lot of discussion beforehand as almost all of the participants – women and men, young and old – are seasoned snowshoe veterans. I'm the only neophyte. Once everyone is geared up, Tom spins 180 degrees at the crunchy edge of this snow-covered parking lot and begins breaking trail north of the ski area.

I fall in two people behind Tom shuffle-hiking with anodized aluminum Sherpa snowshoes in a sloppy path formed by our leaders. It doesn't take too many clumsy steps to conclude that this is almost twice as hard as normal walking. The trick is to follow in the same precise gigantic steps as those who went before. It's really not all that difficult. With a few steps the remarkable ease of walking over fresh snow and joy of vigorous exercise has me grinning from ear-to-ear.

Think snowshoeing is a relatively recent phenomenon? That would be a very natural conclusion when looking at all of the high tech snowshoes available in the marketplace today and the proliferation of snowshoe manufacturers. Think again.

According to Jim Tucker, Northeast (New York) Regional Representative on the United States Snowshoe Association Board of Directors, snowshoeing can be traced back 6,000 years to central Asia. Snowshoes provided indigenous people a means to travel great distances over snowbound terrain. Frontier explorers followed suit. Today many are familiar with the importance of snowshoes in winter-bound locales. However, it is less well known that snowshoeing experienced a recreational revival beginning in the 1970s.

This rise of snowshoeing as a fashionable sport can be traced to technological improvements. Until the late 1960s, snowshoes were constructed of wooden frames with rawhide laced decking. In the 1970s manufacturers introduced neoprene decking which did not stretch and aided flotation. Solid decking material allowed designers to make snowshoes narrower and shorter, raising flotation and in effect improving their function. However, a significant drawback remained in rawhide bindings holding the decking to the shoe frame. Once new designs and materials for bindings were introduced, even uncoordinated recreationists could enjoy a day conquering snowy slopes.

Citing statistics from the National Sporting Goods Industry, Deb Acord (Gazette.com, http://www.snowrideguide.com/full-story.php?id+5596) estimates that in 2005 1.4 million people went snowshoeing at least twice that year. In January 2002, *Outdoor Retailer* claimed that at least 5 million people went snowshoeing in 2000. These statistics provide insight into a national love affair with what at one time was a clumsy means of negotiating snowy terrain.

Several firms are credited with making significant improvements to snowshoes. Sherpa Design's Bill and Gene Prater of Ellensburg, Washington fabricated aluminum-framed snowshoes with neoprene decking in the early 1970s. They incorporated a steel hinge and crampon-like claw to significantly advance traction and lateral stability. Redfeather Snowshoes founded in 1988 in La Crosse, Wisconsin and Tubbs Snowshoe Company in Stowe, Vermont founded in 1906 also are credited with advancing the state-of-the-art.

As snowshoe design has improved a corresponding rise in consumers followed. Lighter weight, better stability, increased traction and heightened reliability have encouraged many consumers to try snowshoeing. Since snowshoes have slimmed down they are much easier to walk in unlike their predecessors. Technological innovations have helped to convert and retain new participants in this sport. Judging by the growth of sales and snowshoe-related events (e.g., group trips organized by hiking and mountaineering clubs; races sponsored by the United States Snowshoe Association), snowshoeing is here to stay as a vibrant winter sport.

Chic skiers in trendy garments with colorful skis and fashionable accoutrements peer down on us from overhead lifts. I can almost hear them saying, "Who are those Bozos anyway? What a waste of effort when they could be riding these lifts and avoiding all that effort." Baggy wool pants, thick boots, frumpy parkas and clumsy snowshoes do not evoke images of dashing and daring people off on an adventure. We more closely resemble snowboarders. Who cares? Our obsession is breaking trail, plowing through a foot of fresh snow on a three-foot base.

One awkward clown foot in front of the other.

Repeat endlessly.

Waddle like a duck.

This cadence goes on infinitely while gasping for all the oxygen we can possibly pull out of this fragile mountain air.

Huff. Puff. Wipe dripping snot from under my frozen nose with the back of a black leather glove. Keep those legs churning. I don't want to be run over by the fellow riding my ass.

Almost seven hundred feet of well-earned elevation gain later, this workout has all of us blowing hard. Most, like me, are retreating into ourselves, deep in thought and asking, "How did I ever get so pathetically out of shape?"

Tom jukes sharp right at 45 degrees headed toward a cave of snow splattered trees. Quickly ski runs are left behind while massive silence of these snowy woods becomes almost overpowering. One second we're part of the known world and the next it seems as though we've been transported deep into Alaskan backcountry.

Snow muffles everything like a blanket of ash after Mt. St. Helens' eruption. Douglas firs wear a thick shroud of feathery white snow reaching down to their trunks. It's beautiful, but surreal, so quiet, so cold, so detached from a green embracing forest in summer. At the edges, almost like an ominous subtext, there is a distinct hint of danger lurking in these woods. It's most intimidating when icy winds blow down from peaks, swirling gray cloud and mist gobble up trees and meadows, or when a light snowfall begins to rain from clouds only scores of yards above our heads. No one is saying anything about it, but these combinations are just ripe for disaster if a white-out suddenly hits.

A little swirl of wind blows past. Trees start slowly swaying in their upper reaches like groupies grooving to tunes with cell phones held aloft at a rock concert. Suddenly a hard push of air sweeps across the forest blowing moss, flakes of snow, random pieces of bark and fir needles. Guess what's on its way?

A white-out is a snowshoer's nightmare. Anyone who goes long and deep in winter wilderness — snowshoers, snowmobilers, cross country skiers, sledders – justifiably fears running into a white-out. This weather phenomenon characterizes conditions where visibility and contrast have deteriorated to the point that it is nearly impossible to discern which way to go. Terrain may be difficult to judge because dimensionality is lost as light is equally absorbed/reflected by the ground, trees and hillsides.

Most people associate white-outs with blizzard conditions; that is, excessive amounts of snow blowing fiercely. Winter storms are often mistaken for blizzards. If visibility is less than one-quarter of a mile or wind speeds exceed 35 miles per hour, a storm has reached blizzard proportions. However, it can be perfectly calm – no wind whatsoever – and a white-out occurs. Diffuse light causes surface definitions to meld together. White-outs also arise when snowfall is so heavy that it is impossible to see objects except those in very near range.

When snowshoers encounter white-outs they usually have a convenient life-line in the trail they compacted. However, it is surprising how quickly such a life-line can disappear when snow is falling at prodigious rates. Therefore, experts highly recommend that extra precautions be taken when venturing into winter's wilderness.

A good rule of thumb is to carry enough proper gear to survive two unanticipated nights in the wilderness including: shovel for digging a snow cave; sleeping bag and/or thermal blanket; extra layers of clothing with special attention to a hefty parka, gloves, hat, and underwear; extra food; and, candles and matches/butane lighters (for melting water and starting fires). These additional supplies will make any pack seem like an unnecessary burden and a constraint on the free spirit of snowshoeing. However, all of this inconvenience pays off when it's clear that getting home won't be a viable option.

For the moment there's no trail to follow; only our concern to get above the ski lifts before heading south on a small plateau that eventually curves upward with Mt. Catherine's higher ramparts. By now Tom and two others have exhausted themselves breaking trail. My turn, so I ratchet up the pace while wading through drifts at least five feet deep, and higher, in spots.

Plowing my way to the top of a ridge, terrain suddenly flattens and the ski area disappears. We're snowshoeing through dense forest and then breaking out into openings smothered with decidedly deep snow. Small lakes are underfoot – Divide Lake, Surveyors Lake, Rockdale Lake, and Frog Lake – hidden by winter's largesse. They are down there somewhere, but I'd never know it because all I see is this cottony blanket broken sharply by firs like inverted white carrots.

Eventually the easy stuff – consistent steady climbing through snowy meadows and muffled forest islands – runs out. I run smack straight into an ice-encrusted cliff. Good time for a breather. I'll let Tom figure out where we go from here. Besides, I hate to admit it, but I'm getting more than a little tired.

Taking off his snowshoes to climb these vertical white cliffs, Tom uses an ancient ice axe to chop half-foot-long steps and miniature handholds up a particularly steep section. The rest of us remove our snowshoes and plunge them into surrounding snowdrifts. I can't help but chuckle to myself because they look like a bunch of headstones in a lost and forgotten cemetery.

Waiting for Tom to finish chopping the ladder, I look around as our group slowly coalesces into a puddle of people. We've been strung out over a half-mile due to varying physical abilities. Several look worn out and ready to stop, others rummage through packs seeking a piece of gear, clothing, or some snack; but, no one – not a single soul – complains about being cold or tired.

Leaving snowshoes sticking up like a menacing prophecy, we post-hole our way to Mt. Catherine's upper reaches, literally clawing our way toward the summit. Those with heavy duty plastic and leather mountaineering boots are leading the way kicking steps into the initial holes Tom hacked out of snow and ice. Thirty minutes later on a windy, frigid northern slope huddling in a copse of small conifers, we stop.

It's hard to see each other because everyone is blowing out big misty clouds of nearly frozen fog – sucking as much air as we can grapple for after the tough climb. Most are bent almost in half at the waist, seeking to recover from our strenuous exertion.

Mt. Catherine is wreathed in a cloud of fog adding further to the eerie feeling of being right at the edge. People fade in and out of focus as cloud swirls around us.

Wwwwoooosssshhhhhhhhhh.

Wwwwoosshh.

Mini-gales dart past followed by pressing wind from the west. Weather has continued to deteriorate and with it prospects for ground blizzards are rising. Another half-hour and we might not be able to make it off this summit.

Not one word is said about the dangerous exposure we've reached, but one false step and anyone can lose a life.

Wwwwhhhuuupppp!!!!!!

Wwwwhhhuuupppp; wwwwhhhuuuppppp!!!!!

These spindly sub-alpine firs are shedding great piles of snow. It's like being surrounded with mortar fire in a hostile engagement. We're dodging to keep spindrift off our backs; our necks free from a noogie of ice cubes.

Another bout of chilling wind buffets past flash-freezing our sweaty bodies. Nervous anxiety reeks from my fellow explorers; most of all me. It's the scent of humans near their mental and physical limit.

There's a choice — either have lunch or finish the climb. About half of our group decides to stay put while the rest continue the remaining two hundred yards to the peak. Following a route carved by Tom, it isn't until the last one hundred feet that I discover why so many in our party have stayed behind. Until this point everything was calm and reasonably safe. Now danger accompanies every movement.

Adrenaline kicks in like an unexpected explosion.

Visibility is no more than fifteen feet. Unfortunately I can see that the near vertical slope along which we are dancing falls into nothingness. There's a gray void that is thousands of feet deep. I can't see it, but I can definitely feel its sinister pull inviting me over for a little look-see.

Thoughts race back to lessons we received on avalanche danger as slope gradient increases. It's tremendously uncomfortable picking my way across three treeless couloirs that funnel snow — and possibly bodies — to rocky talus piles hundreds of feet below and from there 2,300 feet into aptly named Cold Creek at the base of Mt. Catherine. Too late to turn back, I just keep going and soon I am standing on a summit staring out on absolutely nothing except gray cloud. It's like staring at a perfect canvas of the lightest gray — unblemished, dimensions indecipherable.

Bunched together like meerkats with a predator hovering in the bushes no one is saying very much; we're too nervous. Surrounded in dense cloud with absolutely no view, I wheel around and quickly head back to safety in the trees. There's a fifty-foot section of extreme exposure that I virtually run across to safety.

This winter summit of Mt. Catherine is definitely more out there on the edge of danger than I expected for my first snowshoe trip. Judging by pinched and creased faces of my compatriots, we all are wondering what we've gotten ourselves into on this Saturday.

Despite the great exposure we pull it off safely and retreat for a quick lunch or to change our pants.

There's almost no conversation on the way off Mt. Catherine's steep face. We're just focusing on the task at hand, trying to find slippery handholds and randomly placed footsteps backing off the mountain. Lost in an endlessly dense cloud of gray, it's apparent that going up a steep wall is easier than coming down. But, no one peels off or suffers the indignity of a crash. This mountaineering section without snowshoes is not complicated except when you plunge up to your hips in a snow bank.

Returning to the cars should be easier because it's all downhill from this point on. At least that's what we're not so silently telling ourselves. Furthermore, we have left such enormous tracks that it will be almost impossible to lose our way going back.

At the base of Mt. Catherine's steep slopes, we finally reach our snowshoes and begin the arduous process of putting them on. By now the miles have added up. People are sore and tired, cold and ready to be home. Several haggard faces look dejectedly down our packed powder path carving up through the forest. We walked in here, now we will have to walk out. There's no choice under the circumstances and unspoken code of the Mountaineers.

To make the task all that much more difficult it begins to snow great big globs of flakes. They're enormous, almost like millions of white potato chips fluttering down from above. It's approaching white-out conditions. Tom pushes us down the trail with urgent encouragement. We're walking the thin edge of safety.

Danger continues to float down gently from the sky across the plateau with its hidden lakes and forest maze. As day eases toward night, as gray absorbs the sun's reflection on contours, our trail is becoming very difficult to read and negotiate. Fat flakes are filling what once was easily discernible trail, and they add greatly to our labors. The temperature drops a bit causing ice to form on bindings and the bottoms of our snowshoes.

We lumber along focusing on putting one foot in front of another. As packed pure white snow falls from the comical extensions of our feet with our rag-tag group still high on Mt. Catherine, the bitter taste of peril lingers in my mouth. I thought I was going on a casual stroll not a winter ascent of a Cascade peak.

It seems like forever but eventually the cursed ski lifts break through the snowy din. Never have I been happier to welcome a return to civilization. By the time we reach The Summit's parking lot its flood of skiers have disappeared – long ago chased off by this monstrous storm.

I clamber into Tom's snug-as-a-bug VW exhausted. With a jaunty step he reaches the driver's side, crams his snowshoes and pack in back. Flopping into his seat he says, "Well, that was a bit intense."

The old air-cooled four-banger engine kicks over grudgingly. Tom lets worn wiper blades scrape across the windshield while using a mittened hand to swipe at huge icy drops of condensation. He clears his throat and then suggests…

"Want to check out what conditions are like up Commonwealth Creek across the highway?"

My earlier suspicion is confirmed – I didn't think old Tom was trying hard enough as point person on our hike up Mt. Catherine. Now I know for certain that he was holding back. Still, it took everything I had just to keep up with him when he wasn't trying hard. Snowshoe enough and you too can build this sort of endurance.

"Snow is probably real good along the creek by now."

His question hangs suspended in the car; a massively pregnant pause that I'm not responding to. Unanswered, we merge onto

Interstate 90 heading west to Seattle and join a flow of vehicles racing to beat an incoming blizzard.

* * *

Snowshoeing opened my eyes — in epiphany fashion — to an entirely new side of winter. Instead of lounging around like a couch potato for half the year, snowshoes symbolized freedom from the indoors. Downhill and cross-country skiers as well as snowboarders might find this revelation a bit Pollyannaish, especially those addicted to cross-country skiing. They have long known about wilderness coyly waiting less than 50 yards from snow-packed roads. The problem is convincing others that this is paradise and not the first steps toward an insane asylum.

It is truly astounding to discover how quickly wilderness engulfs those who venture away from a roadside or parking lot in winter. Take a few steps or glide a couple of strokes on skis and wild country slams home. At first it's a bit intimidating to understand the consequences if you are new to skis or snowshoes. And, fitness is paramount to survival. A descending blizzard can erase any visual tracks or landmarks in no time at all leaving a body out there and all alone with only their wits to come to the rescue.

For many people these realities are chock full of risk and downside potential. Consequently they would rather stay in the comfort and safety of home, the mall or other urban hangouts. Coming from Southern California, I'd have to say that I was more than skeptical about winter sports. Added to this doubt was recognition that travels to prime snow play areas — ski and snowboard slopes, cross-country and snowshoe tracks or even trails for post-holing — meant serious winter driving conditions.

My penchant for hiking translated elegantly to snowshoeing. As a result I could not find a reasonable excuse for avoiding winter backcountry explorations. This was a monumental conceptual shift and despite the arduous first Blitzkrieg trek up Mt. Catherine, I was willing to give snowshoes another chance.

One month later….

Wwwhuup.

Wwwhhhuuup.

Wwwhuup

Wwwhuuppppppp.

Wwwhup.

Tom Lobb's muffled steps reverberate behind him as he breaks through five inches of the freshest powder imaginable. The back neoprene platforms of his custard-tan snowshoes are already caked with chunks of ice like shelves in a freezer months overdue for a good defrosting.

Wwwhuup.

Wwwhhhuuppp.

Wwwhhhuupp.

Tom hasn't broken stride in the last half-mile. Not once. Never missing a beat. Head bowed to a face-full-of-wind from the south-west; harbinger of the next storm that will add a good 6-12 inches of white stuff. Bet this time it will be more like cement rather than powder since a Pineapple Express is building – the Northwest's euphemism for a relatively warm front riding up from warm Pacific waters.

Doesn't matter to Tom.

He's not going to be bothered.

Tom's on a mission.

He's headed to Reflection Lakes and, if time allows, Louise Lake on the south side of Mt. Rainier.

Friends kid about winding Tom up and then letting him go like a child's mechanical toy. Tom keeps going until he reaches his pre-determined destination or he runs completely out of gas. Trouble is we have never seen him run out of gas. He basically walks, snow-shoes, skis, hikes, runs or jogs until reaching the stopping point. No fuss; no muss.

No whining.

No superfluous conversation.

Breathing in and out.

In and out.

Never stopping. Never faltering.

The Machine.

At moments like this a bit of resentment builds up. How was he blessed with all of the right physique and stamina? I could use a few inches added to my legs to improve my chances of matching him step-for-step. Without such a miracle, in the next few minutes he'll pull farther and farther away.

Wwhhuupp.

Wwwwhhhuuuppp.

Wwhhuupp.

I'm qualified to comment because I'm trying desperately to keep up with Tom's long stride. He has a couple inches on me. I've got a bit better conditioning on him. Still, he seems to be gain-ing ground even though that isn't his intention. Tom merely has a destination to reach and he'll be damned if anyone or anything will prevent him from reaching those lakes lying cold and lonely up over this intervening ridge smothered in winter's magic.

We began this day in the road maze below Paradise Inn, some-where near 5,000 feet. The idea is to stretch out after weeks of heavy weather. Snow reaches down to Longmire at 2,761 feet and lower. Up here the mountain, which has a tendency to make its own weather, looks like a super thick coat of white insulating foam was hosed over everything.

Five thousand feet doesn't sound very high; does it? Believe me; it's lofty enough to face the most treacherous storms the Arctic and Pacific spin off. This elevation is sub-alpine and exposed to monstrous snow dumps – more so than above 10,000 feet where hyper cold flash freezes everything. Blankets of snow – that's what has brought Tom and me to Paradise Inn and a little backcountry exploration winter-style.

Paradise Inn is an aptly named sub-alpine lodge located at 5,400 feet elevation on the southern side of Mt. Rainier. This site is spectacular from several perspectives. In winter the lodge receives an average of 630 inches of snow – that's over 12 feet of precipitation. When all of that snow finally melts surrounding meadows go ballistic with wildflowers. With Mt. Rainier's upper ramparts looming overhead, the scenery is almost too good to believe.

Trails wander throughout Paradise Meadows offering many people their first taste of what sub-alpine country is like. It's a land of sharp contrasts – carpets of blooming foliage juxtaposed against mottled gray glaciers and deflating snow banks nearby. One second the temperature can be boiling and the next a rapid chill blows off surrounding snow fields sending the unprepared running for Paradise Inn's comfort with its crackling fires.

The two-and-a-half story lodge was built in 1916 over 90 years ago. Accumulation of heavy snows over the decades has essentially tweaked the wooden log frame structure in all of the wrong places. The National Park Service closed Paradise Inn for a two-year reconstruction and renovation project. It reopened on May 16, 2008. Work focused on repairing the lodge's two signature stone fireplaces, improving the overall structural integrity, and modernizing the facility for handicap accessibility.

Natural materials were incorporated into the construction of the lodge. Ancient weathered Alaskan cedars were harvested from a former forest fire. Their sliver patina added character to this historic structure. Stones were quarried locally for the foundation. Cedar shingles covered the roof and sides of the lodge. All of these elements helped to meld Paradise Inn with its pristine sub-alpine setting.

Intent on climbing 14,410 foot Mt. Rainier? Paradise Inn is launch point for a 4,680 foot climb up to Camp Muir resting at 10,080 feet. In 2005 a little over half (4,604) of all climbers who set out for the peak (8,972) actually made it to the top. In that same year there were four fatalities and 20 major rescues. Sudden weather shifts are primarily to blame for injuries on Mt. Rainier including, hurricane force winds, impenetrable fog, blizzards, and plummeting temperatures. Climbers also have to dodge rock falls, avalanches and crevasses.

Tom falters for a moment as he stops to kick off some of the crud piling up on his snowshoes. He faces a tough and aggravating dilemma – he wants to kick the shoes together to shake off the ice wads, but he doesn't want to damage his precious snowshoes. On the other hand he doesn't want to go to all the effort needed to remove each shoe, swipe them clean and then tighten up the bindings. So, he's using the head of his ice axe to swat at the offending build-up.

It's my chance to catch up and wisely engage him in a bit of conversation to keep this brief rest stop lasting longer than three nanoseconds.

"Tom, you must be getting old, stopping so early like this. Have you run out of gas already?"

"Very funny. These ice balls are beginning to pile up under my right boot. Can you knock them off for me?"

"Pleasure is all mine. It gives me at least one salient reason to justify carrying this ice axe. I'm beginning to think that a ski pole would be far more useful."

"You're right about that until we hit a steep slope – then you'd be sorry."

I look up the ridge we're climbing and note that most of what passes for terrain is probably steep roadbed in summer. But, it's hard to tell given the billowing piles of snow everywhere falling toward Longmire.

Swinging around to take a gander at Mt. Rainier I notice a new development to keep track of. When we started this hike there was only a thin veil of the most fragile clouds overhead. Now, high above the summit a lenticular cloud cap has formed. *That's bad news.*

Those who go exploring in the backcountry are wise to freshen up on reading cloud formations. Over tall summits, such as Mt. Rainier, or high altitudes lenticular clouds signal approaching storms. Large volumes of moist air flowing from the Pacific bump into mountains and are pushed up. Moisture progressively accumulates forming a succession of waves, visually apparent as clouds.

"Tom. There's trouble in River City."

"What's that?"

"Look behind you."

"Uh…oh. Well…what me worry? We'll be all through before any storm hits. Besides, I think I remember hearing the weather anchor say it will rain in Seattle tomorrow. This is probably just the leading edge."

"And, by the way, we better get going if we want to reach Lake Louise."

End of break. But, I'm satisfied. I managed to stall Tom just long enough to catch my breath, snatch a swig of water and put myself back together. In fact, we've stalled around too long. I'm beginning to freeze.

Tom launches back into his Paul Bunyan stride.

Wwwwhhuuupp.

Wwwhuupp.

Wwwwwhhuuuppppp.

Wwwhhuuppp.

Seemingly in seconds I'm grabbing air like a Kmart shopper fighting for a Blue Light Special. Tom doesn't care; he's already thirty feet out front and on a mission. Nothing's going to stop him, or so he thinks.

I retreat into myself and ponder all sorts of crazy little notions. It's captivating to see how flat the light has become, almost like being inside a gigantic marshmallow; this has reduced all contrast and the ability to discern dimensions. We have to watch carefully for sinister little depressions and gullies that can easily trip us up. More often than not I anticipate a continuing rise in this climb and then step into an unforeseen hole falling heavily on one snowshoe. A basketball court length of little moguls has us looking like staggeringly drunk winos that are too clumsy to find the way home.

I'm also turning over in my mind the contrast between the dead of summer and the dead of winter. This place is bursting at the seams with color in summer – lupine and paintbrush relatively late in the season; glacier lilies where snow banks lingered; Reflection Lakes' cobalt blue-black against an indigo sky; and, the looming presence of glacier clad Mt. Rainier drowning out everything by mirror-like reflections of Washington's ever-present sun. Seems funny to be thinking of summer as I lift these Bozo the Clown extensions on my feet.

Eventually Tom crests a ridge and begins dropping toward Reflection Lake hunkering down the other side at 4,861 feet. Once

I catch up, I pause a moment to turn left and take in the grand vis-age of sub-alpine lake nestled in the lee of this ridge before sweep-ing south toward the Tatoosh Range.

There's trouble ahead.

My gaze goes from the rapidly descending cloud cap on this stratospheric peak to a line of purple-black clouds welling from the southwest. We have incoming weather and it is moving at an incred-ible speed. Something has changed in the atmosphere – a slight shift in the Jet Stream, a sudden variation in barometric pressure, or a powerful storm that's overcome drag associated with the Cascade Mountains. Whatever has shifted it is undeniable that prior fore-casts are about to be tossed out.

Tom's got his head down, nose to the ground and headed to the shore of Reflection Lake. I don't think he's aware of how much the weather has shifted. I've got to catch up with him before he keeps trucking toward Louise Lake. We need to turn around now if we want to avoid slogging back in a whiteout.

How easy is it to run into serious trouble on high mountain peaks in the Cascade Range and northern Rocky Mountains? Just ask three well-experienced and equipped climbers who apparently lost their lives on 11,239 foot Mount Hood in December 2006. The tragedy captivated virtually all media for almost two weeks and the public became intimately informed about the lives of these three climbers during this time. Of the three who set off on a two-day expedition to climb the legendary north slope of Mt. Hood, only the body of Kelly James, age 48, has been recovered. Brian Hall, age 37, a personal trainer from Dallas, and Jerry Cooke, age 36, a lawyer from New York City, are still missing in action and presumed dead.

Of the trio, Kelly James had the greatest expertise having climbed Alaska's 20,320-foot Mount Mc Kinley (Denali) and various peaks in Europe and the Andes. All three had climbed together on Mt. Rainier. Searchers understood that these mountaineers had sufficient knowledge and experience to cope with trouble in the event that their planned alpine style ascent ran into trouble.

The one factor that they didn't count on apparently was a very lengthy spate of horrendous weather accompanied by massive snowfall, brutally cold temperatures and ferocious winds.

James, Hall and Cooke had purposefully set out to climb the highly difficult north side of Mt. Hood and then descend on the south to Timberline Lodge. They prepared well in advance taking great pains to carefully determine equipment, route and contingencies. Underlying this preparation was lengthy experience – 8 years – Hall and James had climbing together at State University of New York, Stony Brook during the late 1980s. Cooke had attended mountain climbing courses and was an accomplished ice climber.

When seen in this light it is perplexing how things went awry, but that's the conundrum that world-class mountains present for even the best-of-the-best. There are literally no guarantees and disaster is merely seconds away from one benign mistake.

Searchers were pinned down by weather after Kelly James' family received a four-minute cell phone call from him, a Dallas landscape architect, on December 10; two days after the trio had begun climbing. He indicated that his party was in trouble and that Cooke and Hall had gone for help. James was later found dead in a snow cave. An autopsy revealed he died of hypothermia.

The discovery of his body is where the mystery begins.

Weather cleared crisp but cloudless on Sunday, December 17. If rescuers didn't find the trio that day it was easy to understand that they had probably perished during the huge storms. Searchers were clued into Kelly James' location near the peak of Mt. Hood by a large "Y" made out of climbing rope and anchored in the snow. The bottom of the "Y" pointed to the snow cave where James' body was found. I was returning from Portland to Boise on December 17 and as our jet passed over Mt. Hood we could clearly see the rope and search commotion below.`

A second empty snow cave or ledge was found 3-400 feet below the summit along with two ice tools, climbing rope and half of a sleeping pad. Rescuers found footprints into an icy chute that ends 2,500 feet later at the Newton Clark Glacier. It is hypothesized that Cooke and Hall were blown off the summit by wind or an avalanche, or fell down the ice chute. This trio joins more than 130 people who have died in climbing related activities on Mt. Hood since records have been kept.

Whupp.

Whup.

Whup.

Wwhup.

My snowshoes sound like slow motion shots from a semi-automatic pistol as I struggle to catch Tom. He's plowing ahead entranced by a grand view over the deeply buried Reflection Lakes. Mazama Ridge rises steeply overhead to our west, a barrier to Paradise Valley and safety.

It's easy to appreciate Tom's enthrallment. There are perfect scenes of Mt. Rainier in winter and then there are moments like this where its beauty is indescribable. Tom has stopped at the edge of the largest lake with his back to me. He's off somewhere in meditation, surrounded by celestial music of the spheres.

I slow down to a trot, uneasy about pulling Tom out of his litany to this anchor that's central in so many people's lives. Tom's reverential moments are about to fade away, but before they do I capture their sublime heavenly bliss. His body is merely thirty feet away, a slumped and hollow shell; his spirit has melded with the mountain. Tom has gone home.

Pausing for a couple of minutes, I puff awhile and supercharge depleted muscles with a fresh batch of oxygenated blood. They'll need it if we're going to make it out of here safely. I'm antsy to get going, but adamant about not destroying what is clearly a sacred moment for Tom.

Something changes in Tom's posture; his deflated body straightens – shoulders flex back up. He slowly pivots to greet me.

"Pretty spectacular," he says softly.

"I know what you mean, Tom. It's like Heaven on Earth."

"Well worth the price of admission."

Yeah…thank you for this gift."

Tom glances up to a swirling curtain of spindrift blowing over Mazama Ridge and settling gently over the Reflection Lakes basin. "I think it's high time we got out of here. Have you noticed the storm building? I've never seen clouds lower that quickly over Mt. Rainier."

His assessment is summed up in a few brief sentences before he pulls out a water bottle and snacks. Having seen this posture and routine many times before, that's a signal Tom is preparing for the battle ahead. In turn, I'm already peeling back a Snickers Bar trying to stoke my internal fires for the slog ahead of us.

Fat flakes rain down and with them a wave of frozen air that's a good twenty degrees colder. Tom's not ready to move yet so I pull out the Fat Man – a monstrous bulbous down parka with hood that inflates like a pop-up doll surrounding me in blessed warmth. Granted, I'll just have to stuff it back in its sack in a few minutes. But, the effort is worth it for a Hawaiian moment here on Mt. Rainier. We'll be racing to the car with maximum exertion and I don't want this safety net to become soaked with sweat.

For this brief blink in eternity I'm swaddled in its care and the whole world seems right. Yes, we're on the razor edge of danger here. But, there's something comfortingly secure in these huge friends – parka and hiking buddy – that let me know this won't be my last snowshoe trip.

In a flash Tom crams everything back in his pack as snowflakes triple in volume. We're leaving now – right this second. I bobble the lid on my bottle, but eventually get everything packed away and protected.

I look up and Tom is 20 yards ahead.

The Machine cranks up his turbocharger determined not to be defeated by this pittance of a storm.

Wwhhuuppp.

Wwhup.

Whup.

Whup.

Already our tracks made coming in are filling with snow, while half-light of early dusk starts to fade to night.

Mt. Rainier releases her embrace and we retreat into a methodical cadence of a long bone-weary slog home.

7

Dancing Down the Deschutes

Harpham Flat is a riot of rainbow colors as boisterous parties inflate bulbous blue and red rafts or unload fluorescent pink and banana-yellow kayaks for a scintillating day on Central Oregon's Deschutes River – the river of falls. Campground and launch point have little to distinguish themselves from other high desert river access points. Scraggly junipers mixed in with an occasional pine say it all. It's a land of sparse rain; bone-dry except for this slithering snake of a river. Shade trees are at a minimum, almost more valuable than bulky plastic coolers laden with precious brew.

Paths crisscross our launch point like a drugged-out spider's web running from parking lot to river's edge and back to the outhouses. There's a lot to unload at the outhouses – excess adrenaline for first-timers, processed libations for the veterans, and platefuls from cocky bull-slingers. People are darting everywhere in a confused dance that makes Grand Central Terminal's hordes seem orchestrated by comparison.

Chaotic splashes of color rivet attention as 12- to 16-foot rafts gradually rise from collapsed heaps of high tech fabric. From afar the shoreline looks like a late spring flower garden gone hyper. It's as though a gardener overdosed the place with Miracle-Gro® and then went back with a second helping. Interspersed are slivers of incandescent neon; injection molded plastics whose vivid sheen assaults the eye. High-priced sunglasses are needed for more than the sun's harsh glare.

Kayakers tend to be a little more serious than rafters while simultaneously over-confident. On big rivers such as the Deschutes safety is at a premium. Kayaks are much more maneuverable and in experienced hands probably safer on this river than slow-to-respond rafts. Today's paddlers unload their vessels from roof-tops and place them oh-so gently on gritty gravel. Soon these paint pots will push off for Sandy Beach waiting 9 miles downstream – take-out situated several hundred yards above a death trap at Sherars Falls.

Depending on the time of year and flow, the Deschutes offers Class II to IV whitewater and Class VI for those foolish enough to miss take-out. In mellow summer when high water has eased and sun bores down on rock-strewn shores, boaters often seek relief from mid-day heat by floating rapids in life jackets. Given the relatively short length of this float, level of difficulty, and convenient access, the Deschutes attracts rafters like a party tavern that's giving away free samples on Saturday afternoon.

Placid sections enable floaters to work on their tans, have water fights and lay back to enjoy a cradling ride on the swiftly flowing river. However, don't be too fooled by the easy stuff; these rapids have an insidiously evil character.

There's enough danger amid swirling whirlpools to keep adrenaline intensity at a max.

Unless floating the Deschutes in mid-week, expect lots of company onshore, in the campgrounds, and throughout the twisting gorge. Extremely heavy public use and commercially guided trips create an attractive side-benefit for the friendly town of Maupin – economic development. Throw in the side road paralleling the river which serves as a shuttle loop and it's easy to see why this doesn't represent a wilderness experience.

Today's goal isn't a pristine backcountry adventure but rather honing rafting abilities without a seasoned guide holding our hands. Going on a crowded weekend offers some safety in numbers. If we crash and burn there are many eyes to catch the embarrassing ineptitude, but there are also lots of hands to pull our soaked and battered bodies out of the Deschutes' maelstrom. If by chance we safely navigate this run and graduate with honors then we can go after tougher rivers.

Too many rafters tends to increase the Bozo-factor and raises probabilities that some nincompoop will spear innocent and well-skippered rafts broadside. That's the price to pay for accessing overly loved rivers. There will always be those callous self-centered few who don't care about others or don't know how to navigate the difficult sections. It's not a big deal; just something to be aware of. But, we're not about to let them chase us off. We'll focus on show-ing others how the Deschutes should be run with style, grace and a bit of panache.

* * *

Maupin is a two-hour plus drive from Portland on Interstate 84 that runs along the Columbia Gorge until The Dalles. From there, 40 miles of painfully slow State Highway 197 twists and turns progressively climbing up and down between massive roll-ing hills. This is monotonous rain-shadow country that's seldom forested except on northern slopes of ravines or down in shaded canyons. The Cascades' green east slopes are perfect counterpoint to these barren hills and dusty gulches.

On reaching a precipice jutting out like a swollen jaw over the Deschutes' canyon, things change dramatically. This pathetic road spirals down toward a ribbon flowing inexorably north that's determined to join the Columbia. The humongous Warm Springs Indian Reservation is just south of Maupin bordering the Deschutes' eastern bank. Maupin sits at the nexus of the state highway and river. It's here where permits are purchased from the Forest Service and last minute supplies are garnered before heading off for a little adventure.

For some whitewater rafters this Maupin section of the Deschutes is too overwhelmingly crowded for enjoyment. Those who abhor running cheek by ruddy jowl with other thrill seekers do have an option – White Horse Adventures (www.whitehorseadv. com).

Recreation and tourism by the Confederated Warm Tribes is personified in the Kah-Nee-Ta High Desert Resort and Casino a ubiquitous center for commercial tourism. But, for adrenaline junkies who are more interested in gulping down heaping doses of outdoor adventure, the Tribe has developed affiliated guiding services for horseback riding, rafting and kayaking, among other sports. White Horse Adventures is the rafting arm devoted to half- and full-day explorations of the *lower* Deschutes.

Highway 26 at Deschutes Crossing is launch point for a full day trip with exclusive access to the river from Tribal land. For 10 miles the river carves through barren canyon wilderness surrounding the Mutton Mountains ending, for lunch, at a confluence with the Warm Springs River. Both the full and half day trips cover 10 miles of float down the Deschutes' scenic canyon from this confluence with the Warm Springs River. Downriver waits infamous

White Horse Rapids, a half-mile of seething Class II, III and III+ whitewater complete with standing waves and enough turbulence to scare even the most intrepid rafter.

The advantage of rafting with White Horse Adventures is the ability to see territory with limited access. Independent souls may find this option too restricting, but it is an easy way to avoid the throngs and sit back while someone else does all of the work.

We're using Chad's blue 12-foot Northwest River Supplies paddle raft today. After shuttling one car to take-out at Sandy Beach we backtrack up to Harpam Flat where we off-load equipment and proceed to put on our game faces. Chad and I lug the bulky raft over to a quiet edge of put-in and begin manually pumping this monster up. There's no rushing this job because the pump only produces so much output – it blows out great breaths of air filling the raft's empty caverns.

Chad and I switch places frequently, spelling each other in rotation and giving us a chance to laugh at the circus taking place around launch site. It's literally a mad-house of unbridled chaos as groups gear-up for the coming float. People are running around like chickens with their heads cut off, scrambling to assemble rafts or kayaks and making final preparations for launching into the Deschutes. The river is patient. It was here before they arrived and it will continue rolling on to the Columbia long after everyone has departed.

I'm focusing on what to wear. It's one of those deceptive days in the high sixties headed toward mid-seventies with plenty of sun. Seems perfect on the beach working up a sweat while filling the raft, but we know that it will be much cooler on the water even though almost no breeze is blowing today. It only takes a few good splashes in the first mile to set the tone for the rest of the trip. If you're under 25 odds favor that you'll be wearing t-shirts and bathing suits while more cautious old fossils wear partial wetsuits. We're aiming for something in the middle with dry-suit tops.

Rachel, Chad's friend is determined to soak up sun after Portland's dreary weather. She's ridden this bucking bronco several times before and is confident that conditions will be extra toasty over the next few hours. Valerie and Rachel are piling paddles, life-jackets and assorted gear next to the raft while a few final pumps make the rubber skin as tight as a drum. The chambers are trimmed to balance the bulbous craft and we're good to go. It's only then that this little journey begins to shift from a virtual image planned over the last few weeks to a full-on reality – a descent of the river of falls.

Two sixteen-foot paddle rafts and a fourteen-foot paddle raft filled with rambunctious teens launch minutes before we're ready to shove off. We'll give them breathing room since no other party appears ready for another fifteen minutes or so. Chad and Rachel have their bright yellow paddles ready for action in the rear. Val and I will be up front providing forward thrust according to Chad's instructions.

There's nothing complicated regarding what our responsibilities are and where orders will come from. Everything is snug on the raft and a safety throw-line is within easy reach of any paddler. The time has come to face up to a series of challenging rapids – some gentle, others not so gentle – that could extinguish a life or two if a serious error is made by us or another raft.

Danger waits downstream.

Sitting on the raft's edge, ready to stand up and push us off into the current I'm watching across the 75 yard wide Deschutes to the other shore. It all seems so straightforward. The river's current is definitely swift; it is pushing relentlessly toward Sherars Falls. Spring run-off is well past so this is mid-high water, but it's a big, powerful Oregon river several feet deep and more in spots.

A booming thump accompanies each precious heartbeat as blood squirts at high pressure throughout my body. These are moments to remember as anticipation is climaxing and seconds remain until furious action is underway. Time seems to stand still waiting for a shift from virtual visualization to realized adventure. Glancing back at the others, I'm ramped up and ready for the doing of it but I don't know what Val, Chad and Rachel are thinking during this prelude to our dance. There's good reason for them to be a bit introspective because it's the deceptively easy-looking floats that often cause the greatest trouble.

On June 2, 2006, Daniel (his last name has not been disclosed by his employer due to pending litigation), a rafting guide for the Grand Teton Lodge Company began his fourth season on the Snake River in Grand Teton National Park. Launching from Deadmans Bar, he was guiding a 10 mile trip to takeout at Moose Junction.

Normally the Snake River is a placid float through the park. However, winter 2006 delivered a bumper crop of snow that continued to accumulate well into May. Then, as the seasons shifted, melt-off quickly rose to enormous proportions. Huge cottonwoods and sections of riverbank were consumed as the Snake swelled to flood level.

Reed Finlay, a guide for Baker-Ewing Float Trips, made 4 runs down the Snake the day of June 1. On his final 10 mile run, Finlay came round a bend only to discover that a gigantic dead cottonwood blocked the main channel. Reacting quickly, Finlay was able to barely skirt the downed tree snagged on a gravel bar. Its limbs bobbed like tentacles sweeping the river of debris. At the end of his run, Finlay posted a note on the company's bulletin board to warn fellow rafters about the danger downstream.

Daniel never received word about the obstacle. He was totally unprepared for the cottonwood blocking his raft's path.

The 20 foot raft carrying 13 passengers could not squeeze through the logjam. The raft was sideways as Daniel struggled to get off the main channel. He almost made it through, but his raft slammed into the cottonwood and lodged. The powerful current drove the raft's back third down into the river while the upper two-thirds climbed crab-wise vertically up the root ball.

Shortly after 10:40 a.m. John and Betty Ann Rizas as well as Linda Clark, three of Daniel's clients, were swept under the logjam. They never made it out alive.

Daniel was guiding the second float of the day for the Lodge Company. The Company's first raft made it safely through by swinging hard to the west and negotiating an unblocked channel. Shortly after Daniel's wreck, the third and fourth Lodge Company rafts of the day came upon the disaster and began to help in the rescue.

This story is compelling because it underscores how quickly things can turn deadly on what normally is an uncomplicated and quite innocent outing. Despite the Lodge Company's efforts to keep facts about the disaster quiet, there is a plethora of public documents available about the trip and its consequences.

A rafting wreck on the benignly inviting Snake River reinforces the deadly serious repercussions of guiding and guides' relationships with their clients. We literally place our very lives in the hands of these unknown strangers – people who intend to do no wrong but who are not infallible in keeping us out of harm's way.

Shifting my right leg to gain better purchase and to prevent our raft from being sucked out of this eddy, my skins rubs against red hot rubber. What a contrast – scalding hot above waterline; ice cold below. Once we launch, staying in the raft becomes more difficult with everything slippery wet as the raft bounces and twists in concert with the river's command.

A slight puff of wind blows erratically cross-stream. The raft's bow is already bobbing, impatient to get on with it. Sunlight glistens off the Deschutes in silver glittering bullets as small waves and wind-blown chop dimple its liquid surface. Dark brown algae cover most of the river rocks close to shore, vanishing in the river's depth. A faint rippling rumble fills the air as the river slides by.

What a perfect day for a float.

Totally in the moment, I'm also chewing over what great happiness there is just sitting in the intensifying sun as the Deschutes slips toward the Columbia. There's blatant wildness in those depths that can't be masked by rowdy throngs of folk preparing for life on the edge. The river of falls is, after all, a Wild and Scenic River, but on this little stretch our human imprint is pretty heavy.

Wildness becomes a background mosaic; it is always there ready to resurface whenever SUVs, rafting culture, kayaks, party boats and whitewater junkies depart. How utterly quiet and absolutely wild this same spot will be in twelve hours when a quarter moon wanes on the horizon and the Deschutes continues to live out its destiny.

Starring at diamonds sparkling on tiny waves washing over the sandy shore I think about what it takes to get past the detritus of our lives in order to make a connection. Our raft's gentle rocking in cadence with the river's flow and ebb becomes a metaphor for larger rhythms.

I'm drawn to these rhythms until Chad shouts "push off." Then the brief connection evaporates as the thrill of adventure rises in our adrenaline-parched throats.

Val and I paddle for all we're worth clawing toward mid-river. I can't tell what Rachel and Chad are doing back there but our raft runs cockeyed with the current. My exuberant thrusts are overpowering Valerie's efforts, yet Chad isn't compensating by steering. The

Deschutes' forceful current catches our raft and spins it around, drifting every closer to Wapinitia Rapids half a mile downstream.

Not to worry.

For all our effort we end up beaching on a huge Half-Dome shaped boulder only one-quarter mile from launch.

This is the most impressive screw-up I've seen all day, despite the river swarming with neophytes and half lucid rafters. Worse, we're only yards downstream from Harpham Flat and totally visible to the huge crowd congregating at launch point. The left front of Chad's raft is sticking a couple feet in the air and on the verge of riding further up the boulder. That's disaster waiting to happen. Bouncing up and down to shake loose doesn't do the trick. Eventually Chad has to get out on the rock and shove for all he's worth to pry us free.

Caught by the current we once again drift toward mid-river and set up for Wapinitia's undulating wave train. Fortunately there isn't a narrow tongue of water to aim for – only a broad set of 2-3 foot waves delivering a rollercoaster ride. Despite our incredible ineptitude these rapids are wide enough to compensate. We'll survive this first challenge in good order, but we're going to be forced to improve our style if we hope to make it off the Deschutes alive.

Val and I are paddling furiously trying to keep the raft headed straight downstream. Desperate flailing keeps our raft parallel to the shore and we drop into Wapinitia's jostling wave train. It happens so fast that there's no time for mid-course corrections. We're entirely at the mercy of the Deschutes' current and lay-out of the boulder garden.

Seconds zip by and we spin around in an uncontrolled drift toward oblivion. This crew isn't getting things sorted out very well. Our lives could depend on how we coordinate our efforts because one-mile downstream is Boxcar Rapids — a fairly serious challenge for the Deschutes.

"Ahhhhhhhh, Chad; are you back there?"

"Yeah what do you want? A brewski?"

"Noooooooooooooooooo. How do I say this politely? Is there any chance that you might actually help steer this wash bucket?"

"Chill out. Everything's going fine."

Valerie adds a little zinger, "Chad, start steering back there."

This exercise in futility is repeated at Boxcar Rapids. Val and I are thrashing away trying to steer a straight course and line toward the oncoming rapids. We see frothing waves just ahead. Water is thundering down a washboard rock garden in huge rolling waves. Mist roils up in gossamer clouds before settling over the Deschutes like cotton candy on steroids.

This thunderous booming is getting closer and closer. It's enough to snap everyone to attention....everyone, that is, except for Rachel and Chad.

What are they doing back there?

As far as I can tell I'm the only one paddling on the starboard side — Rachel's paddle lies limp trailing in the water. Is she asleep at the wheel or terrified out of her designer bathing suit? Maybe she's too scared to move? Whatever the reason I'm expecting Chad to take up the slack or compensate in oar strokes and rudder adjustments on his side. Fond wish — it's simply not happening.

Val looks over at me in exasperation and turns to give Chad a sharp retort. He's not listening, or doesn't care to. Our baby blue raft is reduced to a bobbing toy about to be swept down a major league rapid. All I can envision are sticks I used to throw into rushing streams as a kid. They always took a beating and were righteously doused before resurfacing at the end of small rapids. We're in for the same.

Class III Boxcar Rapids loom directly ahead. Unless something is done now – immediately, not a second later – we'll go into them broadside instead of at an angle that could prevent capsizing. In a last ditch effort, Val and I dig deep to send our raft through at a 45° angle. It's not pretty, but it's enough to hit Boxcar's wave train with some semblance of control.

We wash through the pounding rapids and twirl again.

Before I can even begin to articulate my feelings, Valerie sends an uncomplicated message filled with expletives to the two rafting superstars in the rear. It goes something like, "What the heck are you two doing back there? Paddle in unison with us; use you paddle to steer in a proper line; or, get the #*&% up front!"

Several minutes of silence go by without so much as a peep from the Olympic Whitewater Crew in the stern. Boxcar Rapids' rock garden, a product of a massive landslide in the early 1950's, rolls past. It's so quiet you could hear a salmon breach the Deschutes' surface. Unfortunately for Rachel and Chad silence is bad news because Valerie isn't going to let their transgression slip by so easily.

"Chad, get your &*#%@!! paddle in the water and use it to steer a straight line."

More silence ensues as we drift in a brawny current hurling us toward Maupin.

Finally after a black hole has seemingly swallowed up all sound, Chad issues his thesis, "Just let the raft drift where the current runs strongest. That's the best line."

Good try Chad, but Valerie isn't buying this lame excuse. She regales him for not trimming the raft's line and for failing to set up properly before Boxcar Rapids.

Then Chad blows it big time.

"Who cares if we crash and burn? A little swim will feel good on such a hot day."

I glance over at Val. If looks could kill, Chad is toast. So, that's the plan. We're not going to get serious about this trip. It's only a party float where capsizing and silly antics are the modus operandi. Val is seething as our raft spins and bobs the next two miles toward Maupin.

After Chad's confession it's as though a thunderstorm has blown past and the air sparkles with freshness. His intentions are out there now for all to see. Not a good move on Chad's part. Lacking any sort of orchestrated sanity from the stern, Val and I will have to try to control our line. It won't be easy, but now we know the game. There's no counting on help from the rear.

A little thought crosses my mind: it may be Chad's raft, but it's our lives.

Maupin dominates mid-run. Several rafts in front of us pull over toward shore to stock up on beverages, change passengers or to use the facilities. We mimic their line until right before reaching shore. Then we see it — a large sign shouting warnings about a landing fee. It'll cost some precious Dinero to pull over for even a brief respite Free enterprise at work.

Our paddles bite water as we back out toward the current. No way are we going to pay toll to the Man. Sweeping downstream we get a good look at Maupin which radiates a carnival atmosphere. Kids and dogs are playing in the city park. Like dimples on a golf ball, dome tents liberally sprinkle the Deschutes' eastern shore. Cars and trucks are racing along the access road. In a matter of minutes we go from semi-wilderness to semi-metro. The gentle quiet of the Deschutes morphs back into civilization writ large.

Now that Val's histrionics are over and Chad's agenda has come out of the closet, we relax a bit. We've been so focused on perfecting technique, safety and style that we've forgotten to have some fun. Grey Eagle Picnic Ground is an eighth mile away so we aim for the shore. Only God knows whether we'll make it or not given the two Bozos in the stern.

Time to break out soft drinks and lunch; celebratory brews will wait until later per government regulations. Chad guides the raft into a reed-filled eddy. Gliding to a halt, I leap off to pull us firmly on shore. Unfortunately a bed of softball-sized rocks lines the river bottom. It's as slick as an oily concrete street in Los Angeles after a heavy rain; covered with mud, muck and brown algae goop.

In full view of three raft groups and legions of picnickers I make a most fabulous butt-flop – a new standard for lack of coordination.

While my pride recovers and others seek Grey Eagle's facilities, I reflect on untamed moments in the course of our float. Perhaps it's the Deschutes' Native name or the view down river toward a watercourse that will transfigure into a snarling set of rollercoaster waves at Class II Surf City Rapids. My mind is racing. What must it have been like to live day-to-day along this beautiful river some 300 years earlier? The Warm Springs Tribes frequented this spot throughout the year. In those days did someone spot an unusual grey-colored eagle fishing for salmon in this desert valley? Or, was this a preferred fishing-hole named after a tribal member?

The Deschutes offered a bounty of salmon to early indigenous people now known as the Confederated Tribes of Warm Springs. Their descendents continue to fish along the river's length, especially at Sherars Falls where time-honored dip-net fishing continues to this day. Steelhead (Oncorhynchus Mykiss) and Chinook (Oncorhynchus tshawytscha) headline a vital fishery since time immemorial.

In 1855 formation of the Warm Springs Reservation was underway through leadership provided by Oregon Territory Superintendent Joel Palmer. The reservation initially was established for Wasco bands of Indians living along the Columbia River and Warm Springs bands that migrated seasonally along the Deschutes and other rivers in this territory. By treaty these bands gave up rights to almost 10 million acres of land in exchange for the reservation. They were joined by 38 Paiutes of southeastern Oregon who also migrated seasonally.

Although the Wasco and the Warm Springs bands share a common dialect, the Paiutes do not. The Paiutes did not settle on the reservation until 1879. The three tribes finally organized as the Confederated Tribes of the Warm Springs Reservation of Oregon in 1937 and proceeded from that point with self-governance. A major differentiating characteristic for the Paiutes was food. Both the Wasco and the Warm Springs bands incorporated fish, especially salmon, in their diets. The Paiutes hunted game as well as subsisting on roots and berries found throughout the high plains and forests.

Seventy years after organizing the results are impressive on many dimensions, but particularly in economic development terms. Nearly 4,000 tribal members now live on or in the vicinity of the Warm Springs Reservation. They have numerous employment opportunities available with the Warm Springs Economic Development Corporation including hydroelectric power, forest products (timber, sawmill and plywood plants), ranching, and vacation resorts, museum and outdoor recreation.

These enterprises focus on building long-run sources of employment and revenue to benefit tribal members.

After the turn of the 1800s, white trappers "discovered" the Deschutes. But it wasn't until 1825 that trappers gave the river of falls its name as Rivie're Des Chutes. Undoubtedly they encountered many tribal members fishing along the Deschutes' banks, deriving sustenance as they had for centuries. After the Willamette

Valley was settled white homesteaders commandeered the ancestral fisheries and began commercial exploitation of forests and rivers throughout the Deschutes basin.

Evidence of tribal habitation is readily observed along the Deschutes including ancient pictographs. "She Who Watches" is famous rock art located near Sherars Falls. The Deschutes drew indigenous people to it as a source of sustenance. Tribal rituals embraced the cycle of life surrounding salmon, in turn shaping how tribal members viewed the world.

Sitting on this 12-foot balloon of rubberized fabric has given me a brief moment to contemplate the larger scheme of things. Such moments won't last very long as Chad, Rachel and Val come jogging down from the sandy bench chiding each other for our previous wreck and anxious to float.

Time for adventure.

* * *

We're a little less than two miles from Surf City Rapids a sometimes Class III but in this water Class II+ set of rolling waves. We want to get this right because half a mile further is the monster of them all – Oak Springs Rapids, Class IV. Our apprenticeship is about to be tested to the limit.

Chad and I push and bounce our awkward craft for all we're worth, but it's not budging. Valerie jumps out and shoves forward as we flex the raft sideways, up-and-down, and backward-and-forward until the muddy bottom's cohesion gives. In a split second we catch current and it's a rocketed sleigh ride out into fast flowing hydraulics determined to speed us toward the river's ultimate test.

This canyon is narrowing and losing elevation causing the Deschutes to pick up speed and gain depth due to the constricted walls. We're not quite ready for this slingshot experience as everyone is getting situated with their life preserves secured and clothing stowed. To make matters worse, a quarter mile downstream a little nubbin of rock snags the bow and whips us 180 degrees.

We're hung up *again*.

This is exasperating. We clearly do not have our act together at a critical moment when we most need to be working seamlessly in unison. Chad steps out to push us off but he can't do it. Valerie decides to help but miscalculates the river's depth. There's a good 5 foot hole below the rock and she steps right into it just as Chad gives a mighty heave freeing the raft.

Val goes under and then floats to the surface. I have one chance to pull her aboard before our raft leaves her behind bobbing like a soon-to-be-bruised Macintosh apple in the rippling current. Educated instincts take over. Prior training from rafting guides bubbles to the surface – grab the person and roll backwards into your raft letting momentum and gravity lever the unwitting rescuee into safety.

There's just one little problem – Valerie doesn't have her faded orange life vest zipped up. As I begin to pull her up using the vest which I've frantically clawed, her arms come out. She dunks down for a face-full of liquid pleasure; coming up spitting and choking but still partially wearing the vest. Some guides exhort rafters to grab floaters under their arm pits instead of their life preservers for precisely this reason. What sounds simple enough on shore is entirely a different matter in the heat of action. I was lucky to glom onto her life vest.

The second try I get it right, grabbing Val under her armpits and rolling backwards. It's not perfect or graceful, but it is just enough. Val's half-in, half-out. Flailing away for a handhold, she's desperately grasping for something solid to hold onto. A quick tug on her shorts and she sprawls perpendicularly across the middle of the raft like a beached Chinook. I'm on my butt, feet poking up skyward and somewhat dazed but relieved that the bobbing princess has come home.

Our little drama happens so quickly that I've forgotten all about Chad and Rachel. Only now at the end of these few seconds has Chad finally negotiated five feet of rafting gear to come alongside. It's not as though he isn't making the effort; rafting calamities like ours unfold in a matter of split seconds – that's part of the intrigue and allure of whitewater adventure.

Seasoned river rats like to call an unanticipated departure from a raft "going for a swim." By definition, those who fall overboard are entitled "swimmers." How should people prepare for an unexpected swim so that they survive and live to raft other beautiful rivers in the course of their lifetimes?

More than any other preparation, mental attitude is an essential prerequisite. Bold and courageous know-it-alls are precisely those most likely to spend an excessively long time sucking water in a big hole's washing machine agitation. Bravado overrides common sense and makes them susceptible to those avoidable little errors or to dangerous conditions screaming that backing off is really the better part of valor. In short, show respect for a river and the chances of surviving a swim are increased.

Even people who are highly proficient in swimming can run into significant trouble when they get pitched out of a raft. Fortunately all is not lost. A properly worn high quality life preserver with all snaps, zippers and belts cinched up completely is the single most important piece of survival gear. Wear a U.S. Coast Guard personal flotation device rated Class I or V because they are designed to keep an unconscious person afloat face up and on their back. These bulky vests may not necessarily be fashionable, but they're better than the alternative – wearing your Sunday best in a coffin after you drown because you were too damn stubborn and proud to wear a life jacket.

Avoid Class II and III vests. Although they are svelte and lightweight, they may not turn an unconscious person face up in the water. They definitely are not designed for rough water.

Intelligent rafters wear protective headwear, ostensibly a helmet. Swimmers are at the mercy of the river once they've been dumped out of a raft. Whitewater rapids occur where a riverbed drops in gradient exposing rocks that create pounding waves and turbulence. In these conditions a person's entire body is susceptible to being slammed against an immovable object; something as solid as a rock. Add to this equation jagged edges associated with lava and granite boulders to better understand the wisdom of wearing a helmet.

Clothing is another important factor to consider before rafting. Even though a river may flow through a baking hot canyon, its temperature can approximate ice cubes. In these situations it doesn't take very long to become frozen to the core while all of the fun slips away.

Drysuits are made of water-repellent fabric. They are effective in keeping people dry. However, don't expect that even the most expensive equipment will repel every drop of water. A drysuit's defenses can be breached in too many places such as the wrists, neck and waist. Sitting or leaning against the raft can force water through fabric. Synthetic underwear that whisks moisture away from skin can help relieve the cold.

Wetsuits are highly recommended when water temperature is life threatening. If someone is going to take a swim in these conditions their best prospect of surviving is a wetsuit which helps insulate against cold water. However, for those who have never worn a wetsuit before be forewarned. It's possible to become quite chilled sitting on a raft with wind drilling though the suit while ice water periodically splashes over from errant waves. In these circumstances add a drysuit.

Finally, remember your extremities. Do not – repeat DO NOT – cheap out when buying gloves and boots for whitewater rafting. Your body protects its core first by redirecting heat from hands and feet. High quality boots and gloves will keep toes and fingers toasty. If bucking through a set of vicious waves rafters will want all of the manual dexterity possible in their fingers to hold on to that raft for dear life.

And speaking of swimmers and their rescue I gawk at Rachel wondering how she reacted to our little crisis. As might be predicted, Rachel is still sitting on her princess booty with mouth wide open.

I shoot her a quick look that could kill; she gets the message and begins to stand up.

Unfortunately for Rachel I'm already getting my slippery Teva Proton II's under me and as I rise to catch my equilibrium I step on an errant paddle. It's lying on a dry bag chock full of stuff with the plastic handle end up and the yellow paddle down. The blue middle rests squarely on a dry bag. When my foot clomps down on the handle a predictable turn of events unfolds.

The paddle is catapulted upward at the speed of light and smacks Rachel dead center on her lip and nose. Blood begins to fall.

Chad doesn't know who to attend to first – the wallowing Chinook; the fair but bloodied damsel in distress; or the irate big guy. He chooses the damsel. Not a good choice since his mother, Valerie, is now on her knees and looking around for a hand up.

A few more seconds and we all scramble back to our positions; putting gear in order and fumbling around to see where we are on the river.

I take stock of the situation. It's surprising how fast the raft has picked up speed as it approaches Surf City Rapids.

A hollow feeling hits my gut. I don't think I can stand anymore fun and games, or a lackadaisical attitude toward our float.

Rachel's lip has doubled in size. I can't tell if her nose is broken, but there's no doubt it is tender. Tears are in her eyes as she gently dabs at wounded flesh blooming like purple-red irises on her sweet face.

A pang of guilt washes over me and I apologize to her for my clumsiness. She's not buying it.

"Hey, it really was an accident."

Rachel ignores me, turning her head to the side.

Valerie is sputtering and shouting orders about trimming the raft.

And then we're in the middle of Surf City.

Chad has come out of the ozone to steer like he should. Welcome back Chad. We shoot straight and true down the middle rocking-and-rolling our way on this super roller coaster with spray splashing over the bow. When it all comes together like this there's nothing more exhilarating than a challenging, but not deadly, rapid.

We eddy-out and whoop with glee over the run. Excitement replaces frowns. Even Rachel with the Rudolph-the-Reindeer nose has a smile on her mug. Val shouts, "Let's do that again."

For the first time on this trip I begin to relax a micro-smidgen. When Chad focuses, he can paddle and navigate with the best-of-the-best. The problem is getting him motivated. If he decides that he will get serious we'll be able to survive Oak Springs Rapids waiting four-tenths of a mile downstream.

Chad suddenly rises to the occasion.

"Stow that dry bag against the side."

"Flip that water bottle out of the way and get your foot under the tube so you won't fall out."

"Tighten your vests."

Chad stands up to read the river.

I search to see the safest path. To my eye it's a run left of a skinny lava rock island splitting the river. There's a gaggle of standing waves ending in a large and frightening hole. Right is disaster — an enormous hole waits at the end of the drop with a mishmash of frothing current.

"We'll go right," Chad orders.

"Are you sure?" I reply.

"We'll go right," is all that Chad says.

There's perhaps 30 seconds before the current will catch and slingshot us toward the massive hole. It's like looking into a tunnel. I'm not at all distracted by the riverbanks, steep sage and grass infested hills, or dozens of onlookers in vivid colors watching for, fondly hoping for, a train wreck by some neophytes who don't know their paddle from a hole in the ground.

For a second I catch the sensation of sun drilling onto my legs and arms, but it's only a fleeting sensory gift. Spray from the looming falls and wind-chill from our accelerating sled drowns out the warm-and-fuzzy feeling.

Then, we're into Oak Springs Rapids.

More than anything else I'm conscious of the noise. Water is falling in powerful volumes over the hard volcanic rock, literally roaring like a freight train. Valerie is shouting with excitement; even Rachel lets out a peep of a shriek.

Chad? He says nothing. I quickly glance back and see him in full concentration. He's got his game face on now and deftly adjusting his paddle to cope with the Deschutes' forces that conspire to flip us over like a clumsy turtle on its back.

Chad's not taking anything from Oak Springs Rapids.

We hang on and reach the fall's lip; staring death in the face.

For a fraction of a second we hang and then swoop with a rush down to the monstrous hole with our bow flying upward, bending our raft partially in the middle. Like a spring we pop straight flat and eddy-out.

Chad lets out a whoop and starts talking trash about the run. He's finally earned the right to speak his mind. That was masterful. In fact, as we slowly pull away from the falls I hear cheers from the onlookers and one fellow shout, "Great run."

Yes. I couldn't agree more; Chad rose to the occasion when he needed to.

We have another mile and a half of rapids left so the party isn't over. But, if you can live through Oak Springs Rapids, you can easily handle the rest of the way. Or, so it goes in theory.

White River Rapids loom next – a Class II+ ride. We're still celebrating the phenomenal skill deployed at Oak Springs when these next rapids suddenly materialize. It's an easy roller coaster of waves, but a bit more challenging than I thought it would be.

As we eddy out Chad is searching for his paddle. It's disappeared!

All eyes scan the swirling water. It's simply vanished. How can you lose a canary-yellow paddle?

Chad peels off the spare paddle strapped to the side of the raft. That's why you carry a spare.

When we return from our voyage, a stop in Maupin sheds light on the missing paddle. Photographers line the Deschutes at critical rapids. Using digital technology they transmit prints to a central shop in Maupin. Preliminary photos are then posted for rafters to look through. Several large boards are plastered with often entertaining photos – a person flipping out on a rapid; a raft climbing a rock; or, swimmers clawing back on a raft. If you see a shot that you like it can be purchased several days later from a website using a downloadable format.

After hunting through dozens of sequences we finally find three sets of photos targeting our raft. Our run through White River Rapids was caught on film. With the raft shooting toward the bottom of a wave and three of us digging in with our paddles, only Chad is left paddle-less. His paddle is standing vertically straight-up in the wave with a good two feet of handle sticking out of the water, floating along several feet away from him. For whatever reason, Chad let go of his paddle on the crux of the wave. Thank heavens it didn't happen on Oak Springs Rapid.

For the last mile we have Upper Elevator rapids and Lower Elevator rapids, both are Class II+. Compared to Oak Springs these seem like gentle riffles. They're like a comfortable old set of slippers after the travail of Oak Springs.

After these runs we float a bit less than a half mile and take out at Sandy Beach. Go further and we'll die in Class VI Sherars Falls.

* * *

We're spent from a day in the sun and being riddled with adrenaline. Right now all we want to do is sit here and think about dancing down the Deschutes. Unfortunately all the gear needs to be stowed away and packed for the long trip back home.

Somewhere along the way the brilliant blue sky has clouded over with a gray veil. We're shivering in our soaked clothes struggling to break things down and get out of the slight breeze blowing downstream.

Slamming the trunk lid closed, I look back up river. It looks so innocuous out there. Lower Elevator Rapids do not appear to be any big deal. How could you get in trouble on this gentle river?

They don't call it Wild and Scenic for nothing. Look at Rachel's red nose and purple lip – that's testimony enough to the thrills of rafting one of Oregon's premier water courses.

By the time we enter Interstate 84 along the Columbia much of the day's excitement has been stored away deep in my brain. Noodling the fascinating mosaic of events I'm continually weighing the merits of what I consider to be the high point. No doubt the threats that confronted Valerie's little swim will always rank up there as the most adrenaline producing moment. However, a Class IV rapid is nothing to sneeze at as far as the excitement meter is concerned.

On further reflection I don't think that it was an action-packed moment that took the prize on this trip. As we tool down the freeway a revelation pushes to the surface of my mind. No two ways about it, I'm drawn back to that quintessential moment right before push-off when time seemed to stand still and I *became* the precious river.

Funny how it works like this on so many backcountry trips – where the goal isn't really what the trip is about, after all is said and done. I went searching for adventure and found it. Make absolutely no mistake about that. But, this trip will always be remembered for those introspectively quiet reflections before pushing into the Deschutes. I half think that if an enormous thunderstorm had suddenly materialized and drowned out our launch I still would have taken a full measure of joy with me…reward for melding with a river rather than conquering it.

8

Praying to the Weather Gods

Great curling waves fan out from beneath his mustard-yellow Toyota as Jim screeches to a halt in front of my house. Pulling back a curtain to have another look at our dismal weather the sight isn't pretty. Buckets of rain continue to cascade like a car wash stuck on heavy rinse.

When will it let up?

Our rules of wilderness engagement are sacrosanct after years of backcountry trekking: if it's snowing, go; if it's raining, go; if it's sunny, go; any combination of the preceding, simply go. Not hard to make a decision since we live in the Pacific Northwest. Don't give weather a second thought. Just do it, or we never will. This explains why we're driving toward Mt. Rainier through an unbelievable flood in another drenching spring storm. Jim and I aren't weather wimps – at least that's what we're silently telling ourselves while his car plows through twin channels, tire-track depressions on the asphalt. Spray squirts everywhere in massive sheets.

Bravado begins to trickle away when we reach Enumclaw some ninety miles from the trailhead. An unplanned stop for dinner seems like a divine inspiration– a veggie burrito supreme at Taco Time will fortify our hardy souls.

Damn, it sure is raining and has been all day, as well as yesterday, and the day before. Jim and I share nary a word until he breaks the silence.

"This deluge will stop at some point; won't it?"

Unlike many all-day drizzles that add up to a measly quarter-of-an-inch, this is honest-to-God Washington state rain. Pelting rain drops from depressingly gray-leaden skies. It's like being in a perpetual rainforest.

"The forecast calls for rain tapering to showers tomorrow. It could let up any minute. Then again; maybe not."

That's not what Jim wanted to hear.

Leaving the diner on a flat-out run for his rent-a-wreck, a single solitary thought roots in the back of my mind – all hope is lost; *there appears to be no end in sight.*

Our unwritten rule is that we never raise a question about horrendous conditions even when it's obvious that disaster looms. I'm holding my tongue while dark thoughts slide by in quick progression and Jim steers his Corolla toward mountain heaven. Fantasies flash through my mind about a warm dry bed, good wine, and a pleasant evening at home. We've already violated the holy sanctity of this trip by stopping for dinner. Meanwhile an expensive freeze-dried meal remains deeply ensconced at the bottom of my filthy pack. It will stay there – useless – until another trip at another time when good weather prevails.

Taco Time was brilliant under the circumstances.

Many miles later at the junction to Crystal Mountain the weather hasn't gotten any better. Glimpses of the White River to our right are downright scary. It's a violently frothing, hurling mess rampaging toward Puget Sound. This could be trouble.

Ahead are gloomy grayness and a solid curtain of rain. Is there any hope of making it over 4,694-foot Cayuse Pass before dropping to Ohanapecosh and the final drive to our destination? Or, will rain turn to snow?

Shy of the summit, rain tapers off a bit changing to sleet — dicey conditions but passable. Jim has that kind of luck. If I was driving they would have closed Mt. Rainier to any backcountry travel. We drop down the other side of Cayuse Pass.

Nothing has been said over the last ten minutes because it's so tense. Then he violates our honor code by observing the obvious.

"This doesn't look very good."

I'm not biting on that one. If you want to turn back Jim; turn back. But, this would be the very first time we tucked tail and ran.

Silence fills the Toyota to bursting until we reach Ohanapecosh and turn west toward Nickel Creek.

Like a massive blackout curtain, night is descending on the parking lot as we pull up to a trailhead across from Box Canyon. Nickel Creek is raging toward the Cowlitz River splashing in unchecked torrents beneath a picturesque stone bridge.

This is plain butt-ugly.

Jim shuts off the motor and we sit there listening to rain hammering the roof. No; I'm not going to be the one to give up. He doesn't either — looks like we're not turning back after all.

Time to dress for battle. Rain pants secure, I wrap on a much ballyhooed storm proof parka and exit to an unbelievable and inevitable fusillade. Let's get this over with. Jim jumps out, unlocks the trunk, races around to lock the doors, and returns to find me holding his pack up high so that he can back into it. We're off.

Rain gear has rapidly advanced with high technology fabrics incorporated in outdoor equipment. An astonishing array of innovative material has spun off from research and development.

Nonetheless, despite several decades of progress a question remains regarding what is the most reliable gear to survive extremely adverse conditions.

Forty years ago outdoor aficionados could choose from three basic types of rainwear. Leading the way in terms of rugged, bullet-proof raingear were rubberized parkas and rain pants. Typically found in fishing, logging, agriculture and construction where weather can be horrific and rough use even worse, heavy rubber coated garments are impervious to moisture – they are indisputably impenetrable. Unfortunately their heft makes them essentially impractical for most mountaineering, hiking and backpacking situations. Furthermore, those wearing this gear become soaked with perspiration when involved in any mild form of active exertion.

In non-commercial settings cotton-based anoraks and parkas with extraordinarily tight weaving set the standard for tough mountaineering conditions. These garments followed a grand European tradition and were precursors to Carhartt brand coats and their clones. Weighty armor, they kept most of a deluge off, but they required wool clothing underneath since water eventually penetrated even the best woven models. Cotton-based parkas usually grew supple with wear adding to their charisma. However, their fit-like-a-glove patina came at a high cost: water resistance progressively deteriorated.

A third alternative arrived on the scene some forty years ago in nylon parkas and assorted nylon spin-offs. For total weather-proofing and astonishing light weight, a coated nylon parka set the standard in the field and eventually became the base from which today's high tech parkas evolved. A thin film of impervious petrochemical coating over a nylon shell essentially functioned like rubberized coatings. The primary differences were weight and ruggedness. Coated nylon parkas kept the rain off and like their rubber counterparts delivered a sound soaking from perspiration in humid conditions or under any mild form of exertion. With extensive use the thin coatings would either rub off or peel away thereby compromising waterproofing.

To counteract problems of breathability manufacturers began innovating with combinations of cotton and nylon. For a period the ubiquitous 60/40 parka – 60% nylon and 40% cotton – was a favorite because it shed all but a steady rain and it could take significant abuse while providing comfort unattainable in coated nylon models. This line of gear crossed over from outdoor recreation to urban wear thereby opening a huge mass market. It also provided an incentive for manufacturers to incorporate high tech fabrics being developed at that time.

The light weight, highly breathable and wear resistant parkas today evolved from this heritage. Manufacturers continue to make startling improvements that enhance performance. This has stimulated a massive proliferation of specialty applications. Parkas are designed for just about any outdoor activity. Virtually all of these optional fabrics eventually fail when pitted against pathetically wet conditions for a long period of time.

In the final analysis heavy rubber-coated raingear is the only reliable barrier capable of withstanding wet weather day-after-day. That's what they use up in Alaska.

Jim and I have only a bit over a mile to Nickel Creek and not much of a climb, if any. Can we make it there before it's too dark to see? The answer is before my eyes. Clouds and rain have already obscured everything regardless of the hour. We've run out of sunlight, and there's no other option except to keep sloshing along. This is the ultimate waterproofing test for our gear, especially for my boots that earlier today were freshly coated with weatherproofing in anticipation of the worst.

Hiking through the mud and the muck and the rain not a single word passes between us until we broach a slight rise signaling the descent into Nickel Creek.

From behind comes a muffled expletive. I believe the polite way to put what Jim uttered is "this stinks." I'm not responding because I'm fully focused on avoiding a possible slip in the mud. Seconds later there's the soaking backcountry campground.

Thank goodness.

Nickel Creek is roaring like a jet engine. No time to worry about it overflowing, we're focusing on setting up tents as quickly as possible to keep them from blowing out in this storm. This is one of those times when it pays to be intimately familiar with our tents. Success hinges on erecting them in less than three minutes. Take longer than that and they'll be soundly soaked. The trick is to roll out the tent and almost simultaneously cover it with the rain-fly; then worry about the poles. I beat the three-minute test by a narrow margin and concentrate on tightening staked-out corners and lines. No use trying to dig a trench because the ground is already saturated, this is one instance where the tent floor's waterproofing will be tested to the max.

Tossing my pack under the vestibule to keep it sheltered, I run over to help Jim tighten his lines. Another 30 seconds and we're done. That's the last I see or hear from Jim for twelve hours.

Rain continues to drum like a tympani off the taut shelter.

Backing under the rain-fly I shed rain pants and coat with as much grace as possible under the circumstances. Extricating soaked-feet from what should have been waterproof boots I'm finally able to close the tent door. Rain has not missed a beat the entire time from when I exited the car until this very moment. It's pounding like a crazed drummer on the tent fly. Frankly, this is more than a bit scary.

In extremely wet conditions the value of a reliable tent goes up exponentially. With so many models out there in the market, which type of tent is best for withstanding inclement weather primarily consisting of rain and occasionally a light snowfall?

Focus on backcountry tents for 2-3 people that the majority of people actually use. This excludes expedition tents which only a small percentage of adventurers need. Expedition tents are notably capable of withstanding extraordinary wind, rain and snowfall, but they are dreadfully heavy due to their design and materials, and they are very pricey.

The correct answer to the question of the best tent for surviving ceaseless rain essentially distills to one consideration – the rainfly. However, there are many different factors to consider about a rain-fly and how it will function. Is the tent single-wall or double-wall? What fabric and coating are incorporated into the fly and how is it constructed? Does the tent's design allow sufficient air movement to assist the fly in shedding moisture?

For many years I labored under the erroneous assumption that I simply had to have a double-wall tent whenever venturing forth into country under extremely rainy conditions. As I discovered, a solid tent body is primarily useful for retaining heat in very cold conditions or where wind might invade beneath a fly essentially whisking precious heat away. I've found that even mosquito/bug netting has the ability to retain heat. And, a rain-fly covering a tent body made entirely of mosquito/bug netting is very effective in creating a womb of life-saving warmth – so long as there isn't heavy wind blowing up under the fly.

It's all about the fly.

In the interests of go-light fanaticism manufacturers are innovating with extremely thin fabrics coated by silicon or some variant. It's amazing where technology has led us. For a sporadic shower or even a significant thunderstorm these light-weight high-tech rain-flies excel in conditions the average backcountry explorer experiences. But, above tree-line or day-after-day of rain, the fallibility of light weight materials and construction is all too evident. Usually when these high tech fabrics are saturated with no prospect of drying out, they begin to breakdown.

When heading to country for which almost ceaseless rain has a good probability of occurring, go prepared. You don't need an expedition tent, but you do need something with a high quality fly that is highly water resistant and supported in such a manner that air can easily move underneath.

Back at Nickel Creek it's hard to see anything in my tent due to near total darkness. There's no moon tonight and pitch blackness is intensified by incessant rain and clouds. To make matters worse, we're hunkered down beneath trees under a double coating of nylon – tent body and rain-fly. No wonder it's like a black-hole in here.

Using a flashlight I scan the tent floor – no leaks. Then I unroll a sleeping pad   followed by my down sleeping bag. Given the overwhelming humidity there's not going to be much loft tonight. I make a mental note to see if my budget can handle another shopping trip for something, anything, other than down. Synthetic bags suddenly look like winners despite their weight.

I had been wearing a wool sweater over long underwear beneath a parka. Now I find that water has found its way past the sweater; a disconcerting amount of liquid. The parka fabric didn't fail; there are simply too many ways – zippers, hood, and cuffs – for it to be compromised. It's no big deal because we're only a mile-plus from the trailhead. But, how would this feel if I was scores of miles into extreme country after several days on the trail? Such a potential disaster tends to make me a gear freak.

Jumping into the sleeping bag, I'm home for the night. Switching off the flashlight, I wait for things to stabilize. Down slowly lofts and I begin to grow accustomed to the cadence of raindrops pounding nylon. Eyes grow heavy, and I'm about to take that blessed next step when something scurries across my face.

What was that?

Frantically grabbing my flashlight, I strobe light the entire tent. A narrow column of brilliance darts crazily around the tent like opening night for a Hollywood movie. Movement past the foot of my bag gives the culprit away — a drenched gray mouse runs for cover under a stuff sack. Can't blame the little rodent for wanting to find someplace warm and dry; but, not in my tent tonight. I unzip the blue door and swish it out. Hunker down under the tent floor little fella. The rainfly is doing its work. You'll be dry if you play it smart.

Then, it's lights out.

Fast forward almost twelve hours. I've been awake for more than two hours. When I first gained consciousness I fully expected to hear huge rhythmic drops from overhead — big splats as the sheltering canopy of alder shed last night's gift. Unfortunately that's not quite what greeted me this morning. It is *still* raining with the same unforgiving intensity of last night. Nothing has changed, except that this hollow is a bit less dark. Gray daylight tells me that this storm is nowhere near through with us. There appears to be no end in sight.

Nickel Creek is gushing over its banks like the Columbia River on steroids. Thrashing into the campground it begins carving a new channel toward our tents.

Time to get out of here!

I hear a bit of rustling over at Jim's tent so I unzip my door and call out, "How's it going over there?"

Jim sums it up quite well, "I don't know about you, but Nickel Creek is about to flood me out."

"I'll meet you at the car Jim." Now it's a race to see who can break camp first. He wins, but not by much. Then we retrace last night's imaginary puddle-filled steps. Hours ago rain obliterated our distinctive boot tread depressions.

Throwing my pack into the trunk, I scoot around to the passenger side, flop in the car and close the door. Water slides down to the floor in great sheets. We're soaked, but content. Jim sits there for several minutes before twisting the key. We've both seen big storms before. We've experienced rain falling at a faster pace, but never as long and as consistently as this.

With a lusty hearty laugh Jim puts it in gear we swing out on the road headed home. We'll never forget this storm and nature's powerful message – only the dedicated should be presumptuous enough to explore Mt Rainier's backcountry in a multi-day spring storm.

* * *

An up-close-and-personal confrontation with nature's power is one of the most memorable experiences possible when wilderness adventuring. It is one thing to lounge in a cushy threadbare recliner with libations in hand watching "Storm Stories" on the Weather Channel® and quite another to be out there in the melee. From inside a building, life-threatening hail the size of golf balls – and larger – carpeting the ground several inches deep is traumatically frightening; that is, until you survive such a storm camping out in the wilds. Hail takes on an entirely different meaning under those conditions. A winter blizzard is incredibly awe-inspiring as wind whips crystalline snow into beautiful deathly drifts, but you're comfortable standing at the window with a steaming cup of hot chocolate for nourishment. The same blizzard has different panic-raising signifi-cance if you're cross-country skiing, miles from the car.

Crazy weather is a special gift associated with wilderness for-ays. It represents a force that we can't control, testing our mettle and commitment to get outdoors. The revelation I discovered about horrific weather is that it makes me search deeply within myself to build character — patience to wait out peppering hail under a spruce; endurance to battle persistent rain day-after-day; wisdom in selecting a camp protected from lightning bolts; prudence in carrying more essentials than I expect to need — more water, more clothing, more food; courage to laugh at ugly conditions; and spirit to keep from being a pain-in-the-ass by complaining.

Some will argue that the very best outdoor memories are those coupled to big storms. They philosophize that rising to the chal-lenges of bad weather adds to our moral fiber. All things considered, those unexpected twists in weather — whether a laughably persistent downpour at Mt. Rainier or a freak thunderstorm smothering the Quinault drainage at Olympic National Park — offer highpoints that keep me coming back for more. They endow me with fascinat-ing respect for nature's power and a thirst for more adventure.

Enduring miserable weather has also reversed my thinking about what I expect when making it to the backcountry. I used to pine for superb weather; but now I've come full circle. Just as abysmal weather becomes burdensome, superlative weather can lead to monotony. As a result, instead of planning trips around weather patterns, I'm finding more reward in simply setting an itinerary and sticking with it. Many times what looks like a horrendous catas-trophe waiting to happen ultimately distills into a pleasant col-lage. Failure to understand this phenomenon can lead to a startling epiphany — a lot of trips will be missed if you are too conservative in tackling less than calm conditions.

I think Jim and I had the right equation to begin with. Just go... set a date and stick with it. Carry proper gear and don't turn back. Those images of White River frothing at its banks were inspiring; few others had the privilege of seeing that monster unleashed. The knowledge that I had survived a night of arguably one of Mt. Rainier's most despicable rainstorms made all other storms seem pretty wimpy. It's all a matter of perspective — and epiphany — when remaining committed to doing what you love most instead of settling for the easy way out.

Willis Wall and Mystic Lake at Mt. Rainier

Grand Tetons and the Snake River

Paw Prints from Grizzly Bear #399 and her 3 Cubs

Granite Peak

Forest Camp

Wilderness Columbines

Glacier Peak

Alpine Gardens

View from Mt. San Jacinto in Winter

Deer Lake

Shaping -Identity

9

Unconventional Wisdom

Backcountry adventuring has played an enormous role in defining who I am and in influencing how I think. I've discovered that over time my identity — my very sense of self and character — has been molded by the accretion of enriching sorties into vastly wild lands. Along the way, for better or worse, these experiences have shaped me through subtle changes and vigorous insights. Even the mundane process of acquiring requisite gear to negotiate wild backcountry has touched me deeply, opening the doors to epiphany.

In the beginning I didn't know anything about camping, hiking, climbing, or backpacking, much less the requisite equipment needed to survive in bona fide wilderness. It didn't matter that I was blissfully ignorant; I simply sensed that something rather tremendous and extraordinary waited for me up in those hallowed California hills above Los Angeles where I lived. Little did I know that once I took my first hike I would be hooked forever — an addiction necessitating an entire repertoire of new gear centered on trusty boots, tents and packs essential to surviving the wilds. I was about to take a journey that would define who I am.

John Robinson's *Trails of the Angeles: 100 Hikes in the San Gabriels* (1971) opened my eyes to infinite possibilities. It was a revelation. Life in oppressive Los Angeles provided the incentive – I was desperate for some peace and quiet as well as exercise. Virtually right outside my front door were the southern Sierra Nevada Mountains laced with scores of trails to all sorts of enticing glens and challenging mountain tops. From my Santa Monica flat it looked like these mountains waited solely for me.

Robinson's book taught me where to go and what to look for; I was ecstatic. In the city occasionally an outline of towering mountains would appear through the brown-gray, grimy smog. I thought, "It's just a backdrop; a repository for the infamous 'Hollywood' sign. Does anyone really go there?"

Much to my surprise a few hardy souls regularly use the mountains as a tonic. One sparkling Saturday I took a little drive up the Angeles Crest Highway following directions to a trailhead that unveiled a great mystery. Here was relatively untrammeled wilderness at the fringe of a sprawling metropolis.

My first mid-week hike in Arroyo Seco Canyon proved to be electrifying. The decomposed granite trail followed a stream down from Switzer Camp. It was difficult to imagine a rollicking little brook in those Mediterranean hills – water in the desert! I had no idea that miracle creeks were waiting up tortured canyon bends. In truth I didn't know what I was doing, where I was going, or what to expect. I prepared for the walk by purchasing a tan teardrop pack, a plastic quart bottle and some snacks. After throwing in a long-sleeve shirt, matches, nut bar and toilet paper per Robinson's recommendations, I was ready. I didn't set any mileage record, but I did bite deeply enough to get the full flavor of mountain magic.

Similar to anyone hooked on a new habit, I had to have more gear appropriate to the task. Plenty of equipment purveyors were around to meet my growing insatiable demand. The most expensive item that had to be purchased for day hiking was a pair of boots. Rough terrain called for something substantial and I knew just the place to seek wise advice.

Machinists with whom I worked – men who stood on their feet all day without complaint – waxed eloquently about Red Wing boots. According to them, Red Wing's Irish Setter set the gold standard for rugged footwear. In no time at all I was at the local Red Wing Shoe Store buying a pair of my first boots. Hooked lure, line and sinker, my new obsession was tamed…for the moment.

The Irish Setters were beautiful – red-orange leather high-tops with a patented oil-resistant injection molded comfort sole and boxed moccasin toe. In fact, you can still buy an up-dated equivalent today. I hurried home with a can of their secret sauce – proprietary oil to keep them supple and resistant to rain, sleet, and snow.

It was love at first fit.

As a starter pair, my Irish Setters were probably a good choice because they weren't too heavy; they shed water after stream crossings; they provided support without weighing a ton; and, best of all, they looked the part – rugged. In those days boots were worn for heroic jobs – driving monstrous earth-moving equipment, digging the Panama Canal, building ocean-going liners, mining for gold, cutting down old-growth trees, farming vast tracts of land, and fearlessly hiking the Angeles and San Gabriel National Forests.

The Irish Setters worked perfectly for several hikes until the inevitable happened – it rained. Their molded wavy bottom sole offered virtually no traction. Machinists walking on a concrete floor need minimal traction, that's why they relish these pillow-soft boots. For me, sloppy clay-ridden muddy trails with slick polished granite boulders only spelled disaster.

I graduated to sophisticated hiking boots when relocating to the Northwest with its legendary precipitation. Many weekend warriors from temperate climates cringe at the thought of cramming their precious tootsies into the constricting confines of massive leather hiking boots. Why go there when technology has created so many lightweight and durable options?

If the only challenge hikers face in the backcountry is a day or two of rain along with root and rock infested trails, then it's unlikely that they need a leather boot. But, throw snowfields, scree or ice into the equation and an altogether different recommendation emerges.

Undoubtedly legions of backcountry fanatics tackle these conditions with trail running shoes or ankle-high fabric composition boots. Such footwear will often enable them to reach that lonesome alpine lake. However, they are also tempting fate. Without the requisite ankle support offered by high leather boots, it's very easy to twist a knee or ankle on those slippery and instable scree piles. Boots properly treated with wax, mink oil or silicon compounds have a better probability of shedding moisture over the course of a long and dismally wet hike. Leather boots tend to have rigid soles which help when kicking steps in snow and ice. Throw in a heavy load such as a backpack or climbing gear and the merits of leather boots become obvious.

Fancy fabrics and high tech materials have revolutionized outdoor footwear. But, when a glacier appears around a bend, a cloud burst douses a sub-alpine forest or there are miles of naked rock shrapnel to cross, seasoned trekkers can look down at their leather boots and smile with a beatific grin knowing their footwear can take whatever a mountain throws their way.

When searching for the perfect boot. I didn't wade through the morass of options available in the market because I had been sniffing out a lead on what were reputed to be the finest boots in the world – Limmer boots custom-made in New Hampshire. I contacted the Limmer firm about making a pair for me. Although very pricey, they were tailor-made. Limmer sent detailed instructions for measuring my foot and laying out a template. A year after sending in my dimensions the boots would be ready.

The Limmers eventually reached my door and I tore through the packaging, spilling them out on a table. What followed was an extraordinarily profound moment of worship. These boots were aesthetically beautiful and their fit was like sitting in a finely-crafted automobile – a car that literally embraces; envelops with grace. Such accolades precisely capture the Limmer experience. Craftsmanship was marvelous: triple-stitching at seams, the finest leather, thick soles and spare design. In all, a perfect blend of form and function.

Limmers have a cult following and justifiably so. These boots represent a splendid blend of art, design and materials. But, it is their function that trumps form. An apparent anachronism in a day when light is right; Limmer boots prove that there still is a place for old country leather boots.

I will never forget the Limmers' golden moment in the sun. I was meeting friends on the slopes of Mt. Hope, 12,800 feet high on the Continental Divide, to launch a several day backpack. With a moderately heavy pack, I needed good foot protection. From the moment I took that first step on the stone-infested trail I felt as though I could take any condition the Rockies might throw my way. The Limmers unequivocally took all the shock and abrasion. Fabulous boots, albeit at 4.5 pounds a tad bit heavy. I strode along with great confidence, stepping on rocks without care; almost leaping summits in a single bound.

Boots have progressively transformed from all-leather construction to leather-fabric combinations. It simply isn't de rigueur to be hiking around in heavy, hot, leather stompers. In response to this market change and the realization that few buyers were actually backpacking, manufacturers redesigned backcountry footwear to focus on day hiking. Gens X, Y, Millennia and younger hikers don't need, or want, heavy boots. Low-cut boots became the rage, a trend that was accentuated by the fastpacking craze.

Manufacturers have improved their products and designs to render full-leather boots almost unthinkable except for the most rugged backcountry or extreme conditions. And, I say good riddance to extraneous weight that I might otherwise have to carry. This is especially true given an old hiking admonition that cautions a pound on the foot is worth five on the back.

Conventional wisdom is being trashed as a new paradigm comes rushing in. Ten-plus years ago backpackers began paring down their excessively heavy loads by substituting modern light weight gear for the latest generation of *feather weight* equipment. Backpacking loads have dwindled to day hiking loads. A corresponding shift has occurred in footwear. Where hikers once thought a proper pair of leather boots was absolutely essential to survive the rigors of the trail, fabric and composition boots soon dominated the market.

From all appearances light appears to be right. Hikers can be confident in dreaming about a world where gear weighs nothing but ounces and performance is not the least bit compromised compared to heavy equipment of the past.

Those who buy into this wistful fantasy may be in for a big surprise down the road. It's not about the high tech fabrics and materials; *it's about genes*. If you have the wrong genes – and you probably won't know this until it's too late – then all of those years pounding trails with the skimpiest footwear imaginable will make themselves known in flattened arches, bone deformities, venous collapse and a multitude of other maladies demanding payment for those oh-so-carefree miles of youth.

Light always seems right – until your aching dogs turn you into a couch potato. That's an iron-clad guarantee. Outdoor recreationists need to think more unconventionally.

Plan ahead. Don't scrimp on protection. However, don't weigh yourself down with unnecessary pounds. You can always survive in a second class parka, but in the end you'll pay for having worn second class footwear.

Over the years I find that I have slipped from being an owner, of boots, to being owned by my boots. I am highly dependent on them to fulfill my passion – to feed the gnawing obsession to get outdoors and experience raw weather and rough terrain. In view of this dependence I have inadvertently made myself a pawn of the industrial complex. And, in a concomitant paradigm shift, large manufacturers and retailers have slickly changed into service organizations that corral the largest number of buyers for their current line of fashion-oriented products. In order to secure the highest sales, manufacturers and retailers must, by necessity, continually introduce new models.

Certain small specialty niche manufacturers, such as the Limmers, can count on a limited market for their handcrafted products at exorbitant prices. But, they cannot possibly compete in a global marketplace in any sort of large-scale fashion. That's not a problem because usually they don't have to, their small operations are financially sufficient for their self-sustained aspirations.

Where will all of this lead? Simply looking at the trends, expect to have more choice and heightened innovation in the future. Errors in design, fabrication or fashion will be made along the way. Such boot models will die a quick death as will their manufacturers. Consumers have become accustomed to appreciating a one-year life span for boots (and other outdoors equipment) while accepting their dependency on manufacturers.

It is also clear that things will lighten-up ounce-wise. Footwear is destined to become lighter and more durable because face it; no one wants to schlep around heavy boots unless conditions absolutely warrant it. I envy generations to come because they will benefit from all of this technology and in the end extend their hiking and backcountry lifespan. Why not enjoy the best that Nature has to offer by capitalizing on the best that humans can devise in their laboratories. Light is right.

Although I initially fought this revolution being forced down my throat, eventually I saw the light. Talk about a great epiphany! Heavy wasn't necessarily more macho or gallant. Dropping pounds and ounces on my feet meant a richer experience. And, a possibility loomed that I might add years to my ability to explore the outdoors. This represented a reversal in how I looked at hiking boots. Little did I realize that a similar trend would affect my thinking about tents.

Whenever I head to stratospheric country I take along a serious high altitude tent. It's difficult to enjoy the power of a thunderstorm if I'm cowering beneath flimsy nylon praying that my tent will withstand the onslaught. The operative word here is "enjoy." With the right bombproof tent I actually take immense pleasure in thumping hail bouncing off my rain-fly. Let the torrent fall, it won't get past the high-tech fabric over my head or up past that well-engineered bathtub floor. Lie down and relax – let the soothing sounds of water cascading off my little home lull me to sleep.

Undoubtedly a high percentage of those visiting remote backcountry all over the globe survive frighteningly powerful thunderstorms in the most pathetic kinds of tents. Luck is on their side.

Many are lured into a false sense of security by sophisticated light-weight fabrics. Blinded by obsession to "go light," they place unwarranted faith in claims of tent manufacturers about three-season capabilities and silicon impregnation. These aren't proper tents if they aren't able to withstand rigors of big time, high altitude country. A friend can testify to this. I lent him a popular three pound ultra lightweight solo tent. The morning following a humongous storm the tent was sopping with nary a spot of dry fabric. Another day or night of precipitation would have been the final — fatal — straw. Fortunately for him the temperature was uncharacteristically balmy; his synthetic fill sleeping bag kept him warm despite being semi-soaked.

Endure one of these storms and realization hits that what experts say is indeed true — whenever near or above sub-alpine country, take an appropriate high altitude tent. However, like so many others I had to learn this lesson the hard way. First it was a failed tarp tent in Washington State's Glacier Peak Wilderness. Luckily I was able to hunker down in a decrepit, leaking log shelter and weather an unanticipated storm that moved in. Next it was a generation-one Gore-Tex® single-wall tent getting hammered somewhere at 12,000 feet on the Continental Divide. A hailstorm threatened to cave-in the tent's crown; when that failed, zippers began leaking profusely.

Once during a week-long hike on Mount Rainier's Wonderland Trail I had the extremely bad fortune of experiencing day-after-day of incredibly lousy weather. When it wasn't pelting rain it was misting. If I wasn't becoming soaked walking through a descending ethereal cloud of ultra-fine vapor, I was tightening up my raingear to stop a deluge from soaking everything I was wearing and carrying. After forty-eight hours of an almost non-stop battle I began to laugh at my predicament thinking that at any minute the fusillade would stop. It didn't. Humor turned to depression and I sought solace through a growing stubbornness and determination to outlast the ugly beast.

The biggest lesson I learned on that trip was how heavy wet nylon becomes once it is saturated. My tent's fly was thoroughly soaked after the first night of fending off a sweet pitter-patter of raindrops. Each morning the rain-fly seemingly took on more mass and within no time at all it weighed a ton. I man-handled the fly into an equally saturated stuff sack, lashing it on top of my pack in hope that some water would escape by sheer force of gravity. No such luck; it sat there soaking up more moisture throughout the day.

In conditions of almost continuous precipitation campers have to be extraordinarily meticulous about keeping gear dry. Sleeping bags and clothing should be protected in plastic bags before being stuffed in sacks or a pack. Enter and exit tents with great care to leave as much water as possible outside in a vestibule or under the fly. The rule of thumb is to remember that once something becomes wet, it is unlikely to dry out given high humidity.

Having learned from my experiences with hiking boots, a similar epiphany about tents was inevitable. Match equipment with the conditions rather than bravely defending a misguided philosophy.

After I was hammered by hail on the Continental Divide and barely lived to tell about it, I immediately went out and bought a stout North Face Westwind tent. Its hoop design offered lots of head room with an aerodynamic profile. The rain-fly of this model didn't incorporate a vestibule and as a result, the tent only weighed 5.5 pounds. This was a fabulous tent with first-rate length (96 inches), width (60 inches) and height (44 inches) – plenty of room for two people.

Like most things, selecting the proper tent for any specific backcountry trip hinges on many variables such as anticipated temperature, precipitation, number of people that must be accommodated, and weight. However, a tent's weight inevitably surfaces as a (if not *the*) prime factor affecting the selection decision. Most often a tent is the heaviest item of gear that mountaineers and backpackers carry, although packs and sleeping bags can also contend for this hallowed honor. Therefore lots of attention has historically focused on downsizing tent weight.

A convenient rule of thumb is to plan on three pounds of tent per person. A solo tent should not weigh more than three pounds and a solid two-person tent should not exceed six pounds. From there conventional wisdom begins to break down.

With respect to one-person or solo tents, manufacturers have achieved the three pound threshold and begun to reach for the elusive two pound goal. Incorporating ultra-light and high tech (e.g., silicon impregnated) fabrics has been an effective strategy for reducing weight and winning the battle of the ounces. An equally effective approach has been ingenious design – such as replacing solid tent-body fabric with mosquito/bug netting, or reducing proportions (length and width). At the end of the less-is-better continuum, ultra-light aficionados argue that only a light tarp is needed to repel rain or that a bivy sack can function as the main shelter.

Anyone who thinks that a tarp or ultra-light tent can handle high country weather hasn't had the benefit of experiencing storms that I have ridden out beneath less than substantial shelter. At some point, typically below three pounds, a tent or rain-fly/tarp isn't tough enough to handle extreme weather.

The ultra-light folk argue that when an ugly storm strikes, with less weight they can simply retreat to the relatively safe forest scampering quickly under a light load. With fewer pounds they are more mobile and agile. This sounds logical, but too often in forest settings I've seen plenty of thundering hail threatening to rip my ultra-light rain-fly to shreds. Perhaps a camper can dodge this bullet once, even several times, but eventually odds will catch up. And then the consequences are painful.

There were no conditions that my Westwind tent couldn't handle with ease. Hot weather in the Gila Wilderness reaching the high 90's was no problem because of its well-orchestrated venting. Spring backcountry treks to frigid snow-filled wilderness? Send it my way. Hurricane winds at Olympic National Park? Let it blow. Summer rain storms at Mt. Rainier? I laughed in the face of cloudbursts. It didn't take too many extreme situations for me to realize that this tent simply worked. My confidence in it grew to unwavering. I literally had no fear.

All good things seem to come to an end and such was the case for my beloved Westwind tent. Heavy use wore out the floor and compromised its waterproofing. Things started to get wet – sleeping bag and pad – which pushed me to consider the unconscionable. I would have to get a new tent.

One sad summer day I slipped the Westwind in its light tan carry bag and after a respectful ceremony and outpouring of grief took it to the Goodwill. Somewhere a lucky person may still be deriving shelter from the tent that could. Thus began a several year search for a suitable replacement.

It pains me to think of the money I spent on my many tent experiments. Express mail purveyors came to know my address by heart. I turned to North Face and its Bull Frog model. I bought less room than the Westwind while adding more weight. An intricate three-pole dome design produced a freestanding tent but at the cost of space and pounds. A Mountain Hardwear Trinity model was bombproof and lightweight, but lacked headroom and space for two people. Various Sierra Designs models came and went, victims of excessively light fabric, poor design (such as rain-fly zippers running along the tent poles) or short length/width.

Disruptive advances, or innovations, that are an order of magnitude better create short-run competitive advantage for the inventive firm until larger manufacturers have time to incorporate mimicking innovations within their product lines. A case in point is Go-Lite's line of super-lightweight gear. Over time established manufacturers adopt and refine advances that eventually erode the competitive vigor of smaller firms like Go-Lite.

Product innovation begins to slow down when small, medium and even large size manufacturers go out of business or change ownership. This is precisely what happened when REI bought Mountain Safety Research, Moss Tents and Walrus Tents among other acquisitions in the 1990s. Product innovation in these small manufacturers was progressively re-oriented toward the existing REI brand and line of goods. This may have had a serious dampening effect on new product development.

Vanity Fair, a large corporate conglomerate, purchased The North Face. Such an acquisition tends to reduce innovation because successful research and development costs money. The corporate parent seeks healthy returns on investment through larger production runs of existing goods. New product introduction is treated more conservatively due to its expense.

On a lark I turned to eBay and put in "North Face Westwind tents." Nothing came up. Out of desperation I went to a search engine and entered "North Face Westwind tent." Bingo. Up scrolled all sorts of links to European web sites. I searched further only to discover that various United Kingdom retailers were selling the North Face Westwind tent. I couldn't believe it.

Eight years after I tossed out my beloved friend, the new Westwind tent has improved ventilation (courtesy of a larger rear window), strengthened floor and tent sleeves, and a light-weight silicon-impregnated rain-fly. A smile spread over my face. What a beautiful sight to behold.

Ah, the marvel of an almost perfect market – the magnificence of the Internet. I placed my order to the Adventure Centre in the United Kingdom and, with a bit of delay in shipping, the Westwind tent came home to roost. I am thinking about buying a second just to have a backup. My sleep is much sweeter. I welcome those ferocious storms and everything they can throw my way. Let it hail, snow, rain or blow. I'll be safe and snug as a bug in a rug. After 8 long years I have finally come full circle.

Or, have I?

Consider the third leg of backcountry adventuring's holy equipment trinity (after boots and tents) – the dreaded stone on your back, also known as the backpack.

For decades I used a Kelty external frame pack. I carried that pack thousands of miles across alpine trails, down desert hollows, up to sub-alpine lakes, around enormous mountains, and on almost every trip into the backcountry. Friends had long chided me about getting with the program by purchasing an internal frame pack. I had resisted steadfastly despite their petty allusions to my torture rack. The Kelty worked best when light; worst when heavy. I endeavored to keep it light.

In a weird twist of fate some bastard lifted my Kelty out of my pickup's bed. What kind of punishment does such a despicable deed deserve? This is akin to shooting a person's dog. I fumed, but the pack was gone, long gone. I decided it was time to follow the crowd. There must be some rationale for everyone buying what Edward Abbey called "infernal" frame packs. My friends were all too willing to help me chose what they thought was a pack from heaven.

At the local REI outlet a Trigon brand (now defunct) pack fit like a glove. I couldn't believe how comfortable it was in the store — just perfect. The belt was so cushy and soft, unlike the hard back of the Kelty external frame and constricting waist strap. I walked away a very happy camper. Not many weeks later the first field testing was underway.

I would like to say that the first trial went perfectly. But, it didn't. With the external; frame I walked erect. With the internal frame I hunched forward. Everyone had suggestions for reloading it to shift the weight. But, no matter how many different combinations I tried, inevitably this pack pulled me backwards. And, I was now paying a weight penalty of several additional pounds over the light aluminum Kelty. I fiddled with the pack throughout summer and by fall had purchased a Gregory, also internal frame, since it came highly recommended by the Godfather of long distance walking — Colin Fletcher.

I should have known better.

Epiphany eye-opener #3 regarding gear was about to unfold.

I gave up entirely on internal frame packs and went to an REI external frame pack. What a hunk of junk. Not only did it ride uncomfortably, but it squeaked and groaned with every step, every shift of weight. Its first, and last, backcountry outing was to New Mexico's Gila Wilderness. After only one trip the pack soon found its way to the Goodwill store. I dropped it off in the dead of night so that a future owner couldn't trace it back to me.

When fall rolled around and snow was beginning to cover the high country I caved in and bought a Super Tioga from Kelty. This puppy hauled everything I owned and more, but it tended to pull me backward. Instructions warned about overloading the pack or incorrectly loading heavier items since this aggravated a tendency for the pack to pull backwards. I adjusted the pack to perfection. It rode absolutely flawlessly with nothing inside.

There are many problems with the quality of modern Kelty packs and it's probably a good thing that Dick Kelty passed away. He would be embarrassed by the current designs. Old Kelty frames were made from high quality aluminum with impeccable welds and attendant craftsmanship. Traditional Kelty pack bags were made to last forever. They didn't incorporate tightening straps (thus adding weight). Zippers were of rugged metal fabrication (thus lasting forever). Numerous side pockets offered easy access to small items and easy-to-access rear pockets ensured you could reach a rain parka in nothing flat.

Is it truly possible to go lightweight and have a reasonable level of comfort? Frankly, the statistics are against a satisfactory combination of light weight and reasonable comfort. Consider the figures for extremely lightweight gear: 2-3 pound pack; 2-3 pound tent; 1-2 pound sleeping bag; and, ¾ to 1 pound sleeping pad. At the low end, without any clothing, food or water, minimalists are looking at a base that weighs at least 6-9 pounds. This sounds light until adding a quart of water (2 pounds), a water filter/purifier (1 pound), insulating and protective clothing (5-7 pounds), food (7-8 pounds) and miscellaneous safety/camping equipment (4-5 pounds). The combined weight of ounces translates into a heavy pack that takes much of the fun out of backpacking.

Legions of backpackers and mountaineers focus on building the lightest platform possible. In their minds it is possible to go minimal and still have a light pack. But, there's the rub, and what turned out for me to be a highly significant epiphany about why I treasure outdoor adventures.

Many, if not most, people define comfort as *hiking* with the lightest pack possible. To them comfort relates to the journey; not the end – a comfortable campsite. In contrast others believe that comfort relates to the *camping* experience – sleeping comfort; quality of food/meals; warmth around camp on a frigid morning or ability to remain safe in a monster storm. For the latter they would rather schlep a few extra pounds and be comfortable in camp than comfortable on the trail.

The ability to go lightweight also varies according to the intended backcountry trip. In the Cascade Mountains of Oregon and Washington night temperatures (during summer) rarely fall below freezing. This means that thick insulation isn't needed. Sleeping bags and clothing can be lighter. But, it is often wet in the Cascades implying heavier tents to cope with persistent moisture. The deserts of the Southwest offer a sharp contrast. Temperature-swings between night and day are startling – perhaps 40-60+ degrees. This enables campers to carry goose down products for sleeping and flimsy tents if not just a tarp.

In the end it may be inevitable that hikers will substitute weight for comfort. The question is where will the replacement occur – on the trail or in camp? Personally, I don't relish freezing my rear-end off in camp or on the trail. Therefore I tend to take more equipment and heavier items than minimalists find acceptable. However, when the temperature drops 20-30 degrees as a thunderstorm slides through camp, my muscles may be sorer from carrying additional weight, but I know unequivocally that I will make it back to the car.

It's all a matter of trade-offs.

Again I searched the web for an alternative. Up sprung Deuter's series of lightweight packs. I couldn't resist the price or the minimalist design. Could I finally have found a lightweight internal frame pack that rides comfortably?

After field testing I concluded that it's the perfect summer pack for warm conditions and lowland backcountry forays. But, it doesn't carry much volume. As this pack came out of its shipping carton and I strapped it on, I realized that like my tent and hiking boots, I had *come full circle — it was a surprising revelation.*

There's a much deeper message here than merely ranting on about my preferences for footwear, packs and tents. I began to see that my contrarian way of thinking applied equally to equipment as it did trail adventures. Backcountry travels reinforced that the most deeply satisfying experiences were often in rather mundane spots without compelling vistas, majestic scenery, or mind-boggling challenges. Similarly, when it came to gear, the anticipated seldom became the realized. Thinking that only tough leather boots would suffice overlooked the advantage of lightness. On the other hand, pursuing lightness in tents compromised the ability to handle horrific weather. With respect to external frame packs, stubborn dedication to external frames prevented me from lightening my load *and* from attaining comfort.

Truth be told, I've found that most fashion trends in backcountry gear are just that: a fabrication designed to sell more product. Wilderness junkies should be careful not to be swept up with these trends fueling a maniacal drive to buy more.

I believe that the outdoor equipment industry operates like many other industries where style is concerned. Outdoor equipment manufacturers have actually used fashion to instill planned obsolescence in their products. This enables them to annually introduce new models that are "bigger," "better," "more rugged," "safer," and "more desirable." They have sold out function for form thus ensuring that their avowed bombproof gear isn't really bombproof. Another "better" version lurks around the corner when new spring (or fall) catalogs hit the street or web site.

What attracted me to the North Face Westwind tent model in the first place was value. Here was a tent that could handle any weather and that provided sufficient room for two people. The addition of a vestibule was preferred by the vast majority of consumers. They wanted somewhere to store their gear during inclement weather. A few tweaks here and there – siliconized fabric and sleeves for poles – improved the tent without adversely affecting either its form or function. Eight years after my original tent gave out; the Westwind still shines in its original design.

The same story characterizes a classic Kelty pack. Despite almost two decades domination by internal frame packs, classic external frame packs can still compete with the best internals for backpacking. The operative word here is *backpacking*. When you consider rock climbing, high altitude mountaineering or global traveling, internal frame packs still trump the old Kelty external frame packs. But, for comfort on the trail in carrying 30+ pounds, there is no substitute like a Kelty. The load rides well. This pack is capable of taking considerable abuse. Your back is ventilated and cool in hot ambient temperatures. There is easy access to important pieces of gear. It simply works. It may not look beautiful – all sexy and glamorous like slim internal frame packs – but it functions perfectly.

I can only speculate about improvements that might be made in the Westwind tent if North Face went aggressively after reducing the tent's weight. By incorporating the best materials in poles, rain-fly and tent body, while leaving the design and dimensions alone, my new Westwind is 5.75 pounds. That's just .25 pounds heavier than my First Generation Westwind whose rain-fly didn't include a vestibule.

And, how about the classic Kelty pack? What market leader might surface if Kelty went back to original high quality materials and design rather than bastardizing what worked so well? If both Kelty and North Face went full circle they might discover huge markets for their products both from those who knew the old models and younger folk who are attracted to something that works beautifully.

I'm not advocating a retro phase in backpacking, camping and mountaineering products. But, when manufacturers and their design teams go off in the wrong direction and introduce gimmicks as innovation, then it's time to speak up. Despite superlative advances made in materials (i.e., fabrics, lightweight metals, plastics), there hasn't been sufficient corresponding improvements in design. It will take more than sophisticated software and tinkering around with computer-aided design to get the job done. It's time to learn from the past and integrate the new.

At the same time it's difficult not to fall under the alluring romantic spell of ultra-lightweight gear. GoLite, Ray Jardine and many others introduced a radical shift in how we think about traveling in the backcountry. However, product design and functionality remain vulnerable in extreme conditions that most campers can unwittingly stumble into. Furthermore, *comfort on the trail is not equivalent with comfort in camp*. Manufacturers have yet to reconcile these seemingly diametrically opposed objectives. We can remain hopeful that in the years ahead a pleasing balance will evolve blending trail comfort with camp comfort.

Looking back over many years and thousands of dollars spent on the holy trinity of backcountry equipment, it is interesting that the same sorts of epiphanies I experience in the wild also surface when purchasing gear. I've learned that the obvious isn't necessarily what's best. Consequently I now spend more time in reversing how I look at things. I'm more willing to question prevailing conventional wisdom about products and trends. This may not fuel the gross domestic product, but it certainly leads to better balance both on and off the trail.

Think differently the next time you consider purchasing a piece of equipment for the outdoors. Challenge the assumptions you hold regarding form and function. In the final analysis unconventional thinking may add inestimable spice to your backcountry getaways, and fat to your wallet.

10

A Spirit of Adventurousness

*M**osquito Valley.*
Wickedly nasty name; absolutely perfect forewarning. It ensures that the faint hearted won't be crowding precious wilderness this weekend. Snowmelt is running at full throttle and a smothering snow pack blankets the high country. This is another reason why sprawling forest and lake country around White Pass east of Washington's Mt. Rainier will be lonely. These are ideal preconditions for a little weekend adventure until really primo country slowly resurfaces from hibernation.

Gorgeous sub-alpine and alpine country for which the Northwest holds a legendary reputation comes at a cost. Access to knock-dead beautiful country is obstructed by lingering snowdrifts until very late in June or even mid-July in some high mountain basins. Outdoor aficionados face the prospect of waiting interminable weeks during which lovely summer days fall away like leaves from a tree. It's maddening to watch the best days of the year slip away while the epitome remains snowbound, tantalizingly out of reach.

There's never any guarantee that the high country can be reached once trails are free enough of snow to permit travel. Balmy sunny days without the slightest hint of June rain can easily morph into depressing summer storms – drizzle dampens the wonder of reaching prime mountain territory. Such is often the case for the Cascades where snow melt stalls when cloudy periods block the sun or when summer storms add their own dismal gray.

The secret to enjoying alpine country in the Cascades is to just do it – scramble over the snow while slipping-and-sliding along. Fair weather hikers wait until all conditions are absolutely perfect, unknowingly missing some of the best wild possibilities.

At the Cascade Crest Trailhead near Leech Lake a flawlessly sunny morning is beginning to morph into a blazingly hot day. Sun is so bright I have to squint to read the trail sign even though wearing high-end Bolle´ sunglasses. Clear skies are definitely something to be treasured having paid my dues with six gray months of perpetual mist, drizzle and rain. Good weather means that I can go long and deep into new territory; fully take the measure of the land rather than merely picking at the margins. We'll see how much my boring winter exercise regimen has paid off after mounting miles have passed under scuffed and tread-worn boots.

Hoisting threadbare pack on back; a brief shiver of exhilaration floods over me. It's like this at the start of new forays into the unknown. I don't know what to expect, what complicating obstacles must be overcome, how razor-close I will come to harm's way, or whether this might be that final, terminal exploration. It's not a looming obsession in my mind, just the tiniest seed of doubt about how things are going to unfold. That's why I'm standing here in the first place – to experience adventure.

After walking a hundred feet up the squishy trail masked as streambed a depressing reality is evident. Here at 4,412 feet snow banks are everywhere, up to two-plus feet deep off the trail. Some people might simply turn around and head back to town. For me vast snowfields heighten the challenge and raise hopes for a more memorable experience. Later on I'll be able to share an awesome tale at my local watering hole or around the next flickering campfire.

Within one-quarter mile any semblance of trail has completely vanished and I slip and slide along a vague path rutted on top of the snow. In sunny spots gray snow festooned with a cover of dark green needles, black-brown bark, gray wispy moss and other forest detritus evaporates. Then I wallow along a black muddy path only to tediously climb back up on an icy carpet. Navigation will require reading vague blazes hatchet-hacked onto trees, scouting for where trail tread inadvertently resurfaces, and consulting map and compass.

One-half mile later shake-down is out of the way and my muscles are limber. Now all I have to do is keep track of where I'm going. Forest litter strewn on top of the snow begins to obscure this virtual trail. My concern meter kicks up several notches. It's going to be impossible to cover all of those fantasized miles that not too many minutes ago were a given. Still, there's no panic because I seem to be following a trail. Faultlessly sunny weather adds confidence and I keep plodding along.

Minutes later I meet a couple of fellow backpackers surfing through slush as slick as Teflon. After exchanging greetings I try to gather valuable reconnaissance – they're headed to Deer Lake. Good, I'll avoid it. Sharing a campsite would be sacrilegious this weekend. Sometimes adventure is best when you go solo. It adds an extra helping of perspiration-inducing uncertainty that flavors things when you can't rely on someone else to save your sorry rear-end.

Sand Lake Trail continues to slowly climb 800 feet through sporadic forest toward Deer Lake. Eventually a gaping hole swallowing this forest of spindly firs signals the lake laying mirror flat without so much as a wave. A number of bare spots hug the shoreline offering campsites, but the thought of stopping only two-and-one-half miles from the trailhead is absurd. This doesn't meet the litmus test of an adventurous weekend. I'll keep hiking and save Deer Lake for the fellows I passed a half-hour ago.

As the path skirts north of Deer Lake a few nuisance mosquitoes show up in loose buzzing clouds around my legs and head. Snow cover and an ever-so-slight breeze help to keep them at bay, but I'm suddenly mobbed as I briefly hesitate to find the route. A whining swarm seemingly materializes out of nowhere. Brushing them away with a few swats of my hand, their attempts to irritate on this gorgeous day will go for naught.

Leaving Deer Lake, a metronome thrums inside my brain: time to be attentive since I'm entering lonesome wilderness. From all appearances, it doesn't look like anyone else has been this way today, and perhaps not for a week or more. No fresh steps have been kicked in the snow; all puddles have clear water standing in them. If others did travel here they were extremely light walkers; either that or they followed a completely different route in.

Unthinkingly, I've become more alert to my surroundings. What lurks behind that copse of trees huddled so close together that it resembles thick hair on a shaggy German shepherd? Why did that branch break behind me three minutes ago? This late in the year bears must be out roaming and looking for something nourishing to eat such as me — good honest protein with a whopping dose of trans-fat from too many burgers.

By the time I slip down the sloppy trail into Sand Lake, another half-mile distant, it's almost impossible to read where this indecipherable route is headed. Blazes on trees and rusty metal Crest Trail markers have become quite vague. I'm spending too much time looking for the next marker and at this pace I'll never reach Beusch Lake six miles from my car.

Adding to this confusion about which way to go, I've become tentative and edgy. My pulse is rising and I'm walking way too slow. I've got to get my wits together. Time for a break to settle down. A little snack and some water gives me a moment to look around and to erase any thought of hobgoblins or errant bears skulking around tracking a doofus lugging a monstrous pack.

A quick snack both for the mosquitoes and me and I'm ready to plow ahead. I want to reach Beusch Lake if possible. Three miles doesn't qualify as a wilderness adventure by most standards. I've got to keep going if I have any intention of later bragging about this hike.

But, what direction should I head? An exposed section of trail following the vector I've been heading is almost two-feet beneath glass-clear water. I skirt around on a grainy snow bank and pick up a blatantly distinct trail that angles left just past a copse of fir.

It's extremely frustrating hiking on relatively flat terrain that barely undulates – down into little snow filled vales and then up along level stretches of forest among impenetrable trees – due to few physical landmarks for orienting travel. I can't get a reference point on any peak. There are too many trees and not enough variation in the terrain. The easiest thing would be to take a compass reading. However, it seems like a wasted effort to drop my pack and search for my clear plastic Silva compass somewhere inside. After all, the trail is readily visible in spots.

Travel frequently in the backcountry and eventually even the finest woods person will become disoriented. Conditions at Mosquito Valley are ripe for such a misstep. It's essential that I don't panic because there is a big difference between being disoriented and being lost. The best recipe for becoming disoriented is to not pay attention to where I am walking. Sounds unbelievably simple, doesn't it? THINK about where I am walking. Notice unique trees and rock formations. Keep assessing the tread my feet are covering. These are the primary rules for not becoming lost.

How easy is it to become disoriented? All I have to do is head off trail a few feet into a heavily treed forest and the way back can be confusing. A classic case occurs when running off to the bathroom. Numerous times I've dropped my pack along a well used trail and scrambled 100 feet-or-so into the boonies looking for privacy and spot to do my duty when nature calls. Out of common courtesy I try to ensure that lots of bushes and shrubs are screening me and my privates from the trail.

After finishing my business I often dawdle for a moment listening to beautiful silence. While taking in the view and quietness inevitably from somewhere deep in the recesses of my brain pops a perplexingly discomforting question: "Can I find my way back?" A couple times I discovered that I couldn't even find traces of my boot prints. It's as though I had never walked through the area. There's no doubt in my mind that the trail and my pack are only 30 yards or so away, but, *exactly where?*

Occasionally when making my way back I detour around a big fir or dense shrub to avoid being scratched. Sometimes the trail doesn't materialize quite like I think it will. My palms become a bit damp with perspiration and my breathing ratchets up as I move in a herky-jerky way darting around to find the trail. A few times I have come crashing out onto the main path, thankful the trail suddenly materialized. How fortunate to never run into anyone with a look of desperation on my face.

I've honed a proven recipe for staying found whenever going off trail. First I stand in the middle of the trail facing the opposite direction from which I will initially be headed. This gives me the exact same perspective I will have when trying to come back (in the opposite direction of that which I initially took). Next I note how the trail travels to my left and right. Is it running straight? Does it bend? What is the gradient and are there any distinctive features such as a gully or ravine? How was the trail contouring before I stopped? These observations add further perspective for the return trip.

When I turn around and head into the bush I casually count off the number of strides I make so that I know how far I have wandered off trail.

Finally, I take as direct a vector as possible both going and coming.

Sometimes I become momentarily disoriented. But, I have never been lost.

Fortunately trail markers – blazes gouged into the trees and an occasional Pacific Crest Trail emblem – continue to turn up at the last minute when it seems as though all is lost. These little discoveries convince me over-and-over-again that I'm following the designated trail toward Beusch Lake and camp for tonight. Adding to my confidence is the fact that mosquitoes are slowly receding.

Perhaps I should have stopped at Sand Lake?

Nope; it's too early in the afternoon.

I plow ahead, but again a niggling little feeling that something isn't quite right comes sneaking back into my mind.

Thuunnkkkk!!!!!

Without warning I suddenly crash through the snow to solid earth. I've got my right leg mired to my thigh in freezing ice pellets. This isn't smart, but it is an excellent way to break an ankle. Shaken, I heave a couple times and clamber back up on two quivering legs.

Time to blow out a bit, steady my thoughts, and reconnoiter again.

It doesn't look like anyone has been this way in a long, long time – that's good news because solitude will be guaranteed tonight. And, with every step I take, mosquitoes seem to be dropping off – Mosquito Valley indeed.

Full speed ahead.

So it goes for another half hour, but somehow it just doesn't feel right.

A nagging sense that something is awry grows when a rocky mound 120+ feet high appears to my right. It's a bit more prominent than what my topographical map indicates the terrain should be...*if my reading is correct.*

Going slowly now. Sighting carefully on the trail markers. Gradually apprehension invades my questioning mind and a sickly trickle of adrenaline courses through my veins.

The trail begins to progressively lose elevation and my senses amplify. This is no longer just a weekend stroll in the woods. I'm attuned to everything – hot yellow glowing sun, fickle caressing breezes mixing warm air with frigid layers lying several feet off the snow, and a junco flitting about among the branches. There's a sudden absence of whining mosquitoes due to a gathering breath of wind. Sloppy, slushy purchase of boots on snow makes me skate in place while thinking about whatever lies unexpected around a screen of almost black evergreens.

Uuunnnooohhh!!!

The increasingly skimpy forest abruptly opens to glorious sun and a dramatic view of dazzling Mt. Rainier. That shouldn't be there; nor should the hillside falling 2,000 feet and more down to a valley.

No matter how many times I have seen Mt. Rainier, the majestic mountain always takes my breath away. Eastern slopes above Summerland and Indian Bar – Ohanapecosh, Emmons, Ingraham and Cowlitz glaciers — remain covered in a dense mantle of blinding white snow. From here it looks like a healthy dollop of vanilla ice cream impervious to harsh sun.

This moment's dreamy contemplation doesn't last very long because the trail's direction is plainly visible heading two thousand feet straight down to a valley. It's as though I've reached the edge of the continent. What happened?

Checking map against panorama it's clear that I've blown it. Somehow I've angled southwest to Cortright Point instead of traveling directly northeast. The mistake was relying on infrequent trail markers rather than also reading the map *and* compass to verify my bearing.

Veterans of search and rescue teams often marvel at how little it takes for people to become confused and inexplicably lost under the best conditions. It's rather alarming to think how easily it is to become disoriented in the middle of rough terrain that you have never visited. Much of the problem can be traced to the psychology of being lost. And, virtually every outdoor recreationist can vouch for how queasy that feeling is — they also have been there sometime, someplace.

Recently I was returning back down one of my hometown's most popular and freeway-like hiking, walking, running and biking trails. The path is normally 10+ feet wide. One minute I'm walking along thinking about a nice clump of big sage proliferating along this trail; the next I'm wondering where the hell I am.

All sorts of little shortcuts and side trails peel off from the main trail. As it switch-backed 180 degrees around a steep hillside, an alternative trail hardly two feet wide dropped to my left. I was so busy looking at the sage down this route that I didn't recognize the shift from a 10- foot wide trail to a 2-foot wide path.

Shunted onto a completely different trail, I had walked perhaps a quarter-mile before realizing it.

I'm still flummoxed about the lapse, but it certainly confirms how easy it is to lose my way.

Most important was the immediate psychological bewilderment I felt – even, I will admit, a bit of panic. This cognitive confusion is a common phenomenon. Failure to immediately stop and calm my mind usually leads to further errors and eventually losing my way.

When I sensed that I was lost, I stopped immediately.

That's exactly what I did at White Pass as well.

I took a few deep breaths. I didn't go stumbling blindly around. I fixed my current position with my pack; it can also be done with a bright piece of clothing. I thought about what I last saw on the actual trail. I began to take methodical forays from my current position looking for this detail – trees, logs, rocks or other distinctive features that captured my attention.

Keeping visual track of my pack builds confidence as I began to search away from it. The ability to repeatedly return to this spot informs my brain that I'm not lost – only momentarily disoriented. Conquering the psychology of being lost is usually the first and essential step to survival.

Gradually there's less fear as I twist and sway checking out Cortright Point and Mt. Rainier. Big deal, I'll just turn around and go back the way I came following boot prints and trail markers. But, by the time I reach the next marker adrenaline rises like Old Faithful Geyser.

Searing hot sun is erasing my boot prints.

Compounding my dilemma is the extreme difficulty I'm having in finding trail markers. They were much more visible going the other way – not necessarily easy to find, but enough that I was able to keep going. Now, it's hard to tell where the next one will be.

For a brief moment terrifying panic begins to override reason, but I catch myself and calm down, albeit with pounding heart. I wanted adventure and a story to share with my friends back home?

I sure found it.

Some will read this little tale and conclude that an early summer's journey on the edge of Mosquito Valley wasn't much of an adventure. Certainly I was disoriented and close to being lost, but I carried all I needed to survive several nights and days. I could simply have followed the trail down into the valley and ultimately have reached busy Highway 12.

I didn't break a limb or slip and crunch my noggin on a protruding rock leaving a messy red swath tainting the snowy blanket of white.

The most dangerous form of wildlife encountered on this little expedition was swarming mosquitoes. I had plenty of food; and water was definitely not an issue. The trip wasn't to a distant foreign country where I don't speak the local language and political or civil unrest allowed travel only in daylight surrounded by bearded and heavily armed guards with scratched and dented AK 47s.

No, this little jaunt on frozen hills above White Pass wasn't to the Himalayas, African plains or Arctic National Wildlife Refuge. But, it was the sort of trip that the vast majority of us contemplate taking. This was a jaunt that many pursue while building toward more ultimate moments of adventure on the edge.

Are these little adventures somehow any less – any less at all – compared to a trek through Burma, a bicycle ride across Siberia, or traversing the Outback of Australia? I can end up just as dead in the wilderness above White Pass as I can on any adventure in more exotic locales.

Dan Flores eloquently captured the essence of this point in *Big Sky Journal*. Flores had just returned jubilant from a four-day trek across Glacier National Park from its western boundary to Blackfeet land on the east, across some of the finest grizzly habitat in the Lower Forty-eight.

Flores notes that "Back when high summer burned its brief, bright flame in Montana's Glacier National Park, a friend and I – seized with an inability to resist the call of the wild – loaded up our backpacks and headed off for the Northern Rockies backcountry. No one drowned in the river, got pounced by a grizzly, toppled off a glacier or got struck by lightning amongst the peaks. But, nonetheless, this little trip was a kind of adventure, a mild modern form of the *adventurousness* that the Northern Rockies have been about for a very long time now."

I didn't drown in Deer Lake or Sand Lake. I didn't crash through a snow bank's icy crust and in the process shatter my leg to smithereens. I didn't end up wandering aimlessly with ravenous hunger through hostile wilderness for days. But, like Flores, I did have an adventure, and I can certainly say my adrenaline rose above its normal placid level.

As Flores implies, the last best adventures may be those that are part of our daily outdoors regimen – those special spots on the trail we normally ply; moments when we've gone off-trail to discover a little fern-infested glen with dripping spring; a coastal cliff that's marble-slick and has to be carefully negotiated to reach a small crescent of bone-gray beach serving as magnet for the most amazing drift; or single track with startling solitude and silence waiting patiently to be used simply because it offers no rowdy downhill run.

Carefully making my way back toward Sand Lake adrenaline eventually evaporates and equilibrium returns. Now I'm thinking rather than reacting; buoyed by the realization that if all else fails I can simply turn around and follow the trail down to Highway 12. From there I can hitch a ride back up to the trailhead and my car. I don't want to be forced into this strategy, but I can if I must.

Calmed down, I make a game of finding the next blaze, and then the one after that. It only takes a few in a row to build confidence and eventually spot a few of my tracks lingering in shade. Once again I'm a fearless explorer weaving through White Pass' forest still decked out in winter finery beneath a blistering July sun. Little jogs and detours are refreshed in my mind as I shuffle from one blaze to another. Two tenths of a mile away I sense the forest falling away to Sand Lake.

When I finally reach lakeshore the error of my ways is readily apparent. In negotiating around a low spot in the trail which has been smothered by two feet of standing water, I inadvertently kept going southwest instead of hooking around to the northeast and my path to Buesch Lake.

I now have two choices: either I can keep walking toward Buesch Lake and hope that the route finding and snow drifts aren't any worse, or I can call a halt to it right now. In many respects I would dearly love to go much farther. However, not only have I used up most of the day, but I also am a little gun-shy from my unintentional detour to Cortright Point. Tomorrow I've have to backtrack and I don't want to spend all day searching for the Holy Grail of trail markers.

Time to set up camp.

A sliver of bench beside Sand Lake has caught the sun offering a possible perch for tonight. With calculated maneuvering, my tent can be placed half on dry ground and the other half on damp ground – that's pretty good considering that most of this forest is either under a couple feet of snow or melt water. So begins the pleasant tasks of emptying my pack and erecting a modest home for this evening.

I'm looking forward to a little relaxation now that my exercise is over. After walking on all of those rotten snowdrifts I've discovered that my calves possess muscles I never dreamed existed.

With camp situated it's nearly dinner time. I break out my trusty Svea stove. It may be archaic, but it always works and weighs less than other high tech alternatives. I've set it up on muddy ground bordering the lake, 15 feet away from my tent.

Tonight is like so many other camp nights. It will be macaroni and cheese plus a few freeze dried vegetables – peas, green beans and carrots – to increase nutritional value. The freeze-dried stuff has been soaking in water the past hour. If this technique isn't followed once these ingredients land in my stomach they immediately begin sucking all of the moisture right out of me.

Macaroni and veggies are dumped in the requisite water and left to boil while I retreat for a little snooze in my tent. I figure another ten minutes or so before the pot begins to boil and then 15-20 minutes for everything to cook.

Laying with my head to the rear of the tent, I'm drowsy but not ready to fall off to sleep. Besides, it's massively hot in the little bugger; sweltering in fact. How hot has it gotten – 80 or even 85 degrees? One thing is for certain, the snow will evaporate at this rate. Thank heavens I didn't try to make more mileage on that rotten snow. I'd be plunging to my thighs if I had kept going. That would have been a lost cause.

A watched pot never boils, but that admonition isn't worth much to a hungry man. I go over and peer into the pot after gradually lifting the lid. Still no rolling boil, only a few tiny bubbles launching off the aluminum pot's bottom. Peas, beans and carrots float agitatedly while making little circular swirls around the universe of this pot.

I ratchet up the Svea's output and reach to lift the lid to avoid a nasty boil-over.

Ouch! That handle is scalding hot.

A few more minutes pass by as I stand in my diminutive kitchen gazing out on a nearly placid Sand Lake. It's when I'm almost breaking my arm patting myself on the back for honing my orienteering skills in finding my way back to Sand Lake that disaster happens.

Fire in the hole!!

Without warning a three-foot flame similar to one etched on the front of a tarted-up candy-apple red 1940 Ford comes squirting out of the Svea like a geyser out of control. First thought entering my mind is fear that this little metal bomb is going to blow.

Sand Lake is two feet away.

The flame gains a one-foot extension

Two seconds have already been lost

I'm not about to touch the turn-off key – been there; done that. My thumb and fingers still ache from being singed. Ugly blisters have already welled-up.

With one swift kick the whole kitten-caboodle goes flying four feet into Sand Lake with a resounding *pphhhssssffffttt*.

Crisis over.

Little concentric ripples spill away from the now extinguished Svea.

Lime green peas, fluorescent orange carrots, black green beans and pale yellow macaroni bob contentedly toward shore.

There's no dinner, nor any breakfast for tomorrow. Hunger claws at my stomach. Only a Snickers Bar waits in the pack – that wouldn't be enough to see anyone through the night. Standing there watching the Svea's tiny ripples finally dissipate; one elegant thought comes to my befuddled mind.

There's still enough time to make it out of here tonight.

On reaching the trailhead I clamber into my run-down car and think about this extremely long day. When all was said and done I discovered a lot about myself on this trek to Mosquito Valley — lessons that accumulate and in the course of time will enable me to better pass through wilderness areas.

I honed orienteering skills that lay dormant especially those of negotiating dense forest without certain clues about where a trail ran because it was resting 2-3 feet below snow. I learned about how important positive psychological attitude is for someone traveling solo in remote wilderness. My self-reliance proved durable when conditions suddenly deteriorated and I crashed through a vulnerable spot in the snow almost breaking a bone.

I also learned about how quickly little errors add up to spell trouble. Unanticipated slippery tread on the snow pack meant that I wouldn't cover impressive miles to Beusch Lake as intended. If a disaster occurred it might take a very long time to reach the trailhead. Pushing a stove for more heat when the ambient temperature was too hot trashed food I was counting on to get me through till morning. This blazing afternoon was rapidly melting snow, raising Sand Lake, and drowning exposed trail tread. The sum of these little variances pointed to an early exit.

In all Mosquito Valley clarified why I love wildness as well as helping me understand how it was molding my character. A person is a whole lot more likely to persevere in civilized contexts after they have overcome near calamity in the wilderness. When only I am around to look out for myself, confidence naturally percolates into my character.

All of the preceding insights are well and good, but they substantially miss the mark compared to an unequivocal milestone moment in this humble trip to Mosquito Valley. The defining high point of my voyage of discovery, the epiphany, was realizing that no wild area is bereft of adventure if I only open myself to the possibilities.

No doubt those who walked the same trail I did three weeks later would laugh a bit about my histrionics. They hiked trails that were virtually snow-free and the way to Buesch Lake was never in doubt. From their experience Mosquito Valley is nothing more than a trivial walk in the woods.

Our society could use more folks who are in touch with wilderness, people who see the inherent greatness of wildness and wild areas. We won't get there if the standard has to be the *first* to scale some peak, to float a twisting dragon of whitewater, or to snowboard backward down a deadly couloir. However, a spirit of adventurousness can thrive if it is viewed as a natural attitude within the context of all natural areas – a pristine Southern swamp, dense northern forests, a sandy beach hidden along a Texas lake, or a vacant lot in downtown New York. Connecting with the vibrant wildness of commonplaces is truly the last best adventure.

11

Under a River's Spell

Frosted rime coats gray-green leaves of grass that flop over one another like papilla on a swollen tongue. An undulating bed of alien vinca is hunkered down waiting for afternoon's dose of full-on sunny rays. It's nippy indeed this morning, somewhere in the high 20's, but not bad at all for late fall.

ssqquuAAACCCWWWKKKK!!

ssqquuAAACCCWWWKKKK!

squawwwk!

sssqquuaawwkkkk!

squawwk!

SQUAWK!

A fuming mallard hen lets a meddling Canada goose know she's not at all pleased with vacating the inches deep shallows she and her mate have been standing in all night.

Geese and ducks love to nestle down along the Boise River's broad cobblestone beaches. As the river's flow slows to a comparative trickle, narrow shallows form like spokes of a wheel etched into otherwise high-and-dry banks. Avian guests in the side waters are

204

able to enjoy a bit of food and a clear view for hundreds of yards making them somewhat secure from predators. A goose hardly ever knows when a coyote or fox may decide to call. Spread out on the cobblestone beaches like candy sprinkles on vanilla frosting, there's safety in numbers; game, set and match to hundreds of eyes.

As sunlight begins to ignite trees and bushes into a wild kaleidoscope of vivid colors, I'm out for a very early morning walk along the Boise River that dissects this charming city. A greenbelt with extensive trails and pathways runs 26 miles through the heart of Boise. Many such as me believe the river *is* the city's heart.

Ooooooooooooooooonnnnkkk!

Oooooonnnnnnnnnkk!

Onnkk!

 Onnkk.

Onnkk.

Five Canada geese lift off from the shallows leaving three dozen comrades gawking to see what caused them to leave in such a hurry. Four seconds pass and then 12 join the flight. The remaining 24 spin and twirl trying to read what's going on; determining whether they've been left as sitting geese.

Three kingfishers in classic "vee" formation dart upstream while flying two feet above rippling waters. The two-dozen laggard Canada geese hardly pay them any mind. It's not that they're unwary; the simple truth is that the geese have something larger on their minds – two eagles have recently taken up residence in ancient black cottonwoods several miles upstream by Boise's Shakespeare Theater.

All of this little drama unfolds after a couple minutes' stroll over an icy-slick footbridge a few yards from my office. The bridge leads to a main pedestrian trail and bike path paralleling the river. I'm treading extra carefully because the thin layer of ice could unceremoniously dump me on my butt and over the bridge's edge. A thirty-foot fall to the Boise is fun, even if illegal, in the middle of summer when water levels are four times higher. Right now, I'd break a leg if I went off the side.

There's delectable comfort in abruptly shifting from urban life to wildness in a split second. Dressy work clothes hanging back in the office seem like a lifetime away. I've entered the no-zone: no email, no busy-bodies, no complainers, no tasks waiting to be procrastinated on, no cell phone or copier, NO MEETINGS; nothing!

Although squarely in the middle of downtown, I've mentally migrated to the wild. Thick weighty air riddled with humidity carries a punky scent of decay from leaves fallen over the past 5 weeks. Riparian forest is a wild mosaic of stark deciduous skeletons balanced by vivid colors from flaming leaves that are seconds, minutes or sometimes days away from their fall to grace. Dark green fir and a few pines shroud the riverbank. Background white noise – rumbling tires, accelerating engines, a random honk, jetliner overhead – soften to a non-existential state.

That's when the quiet is broken.

Boise River is cascading over thousands of rocks. Small riffles everywhere sing a distinct, but hushed melody for those listening closely. It's a forceful dominating burble that rises to a sharper crescendo when the river's broad cascades narrow into mini-rapids schussing into a massive pool waiting patiently below. This pattern repeats itself over and over again as the Boise River makes its way to the Snake River.

A quixotic song hums persistently from the river channel. It's ever-present – gurgling, burbling, splashing, tinkling, swishing, and, yes, even roaring every couple miles when larger falls take center attention.

It's more than background noise; more than pleasant sound.

River music is what makes this greenbelt a slice of wildness in the midst of imposing, but seldom oppressive, human habitation. River song bores into my soul. It cradles me in comfort and wipes away trivial cares of uncivilized life paralleling its banks. A good stiff walk with dancing river at my side, singing harmoniously, inevitably places all things into perspective.

It's a river of life.

When I'm done walking it's as though I am glowing with a sort of innocence and purity. I feel a palpable joy that radiates with good cheer. As corny as this may sound, the river recalibrates me, blending body and spirit with the river's undeniable soul. A part of the river – its very essence -- departs with me when I leave; the river and I become one.

It takes a pretty callous person to walk along the Boise River and not be soothed by its melody. And, the tonic leaves me wondering how many others feel a deep sense of gratitude for the nurturing power of Boise's river music. Perhaps this explains why life is so civilized in The City of Trees – Le Bois as early explorers exclaimed.

A favorite section of trail takes me past a copse of young sequoias. I get a bit goofy when I see these trees just beginning to stretch toward heaven. They seem like they don't really belong in Boise; but, there's no denying their presence. Here in the most unlikely places of all – high desert – moisture and cool temperature loving sequoias are doing just fine, thank you. Several have stretched to 60 feet tall with lush full growth girdling their trunks, testimony that Idaho is truly a northern latitude kind-of-place.

Mallards spread over the surrounding lawn like ants on a hillside beneath these soon-to-be-gigantic coniferous trees and neighboring monstrous maples and oaks. As long as no dogs are around, mallards are content to remain grounded; ever alert to flight. They slowly waddle around in pairs, quacking about whatever it is that ducks talk about.

Boise River is partially hidden from the greenbelt path by a screen of trees that has gone to the extreme with color. Black cottonwoods dominate with brilliant yellow leaves, but a healthy mix of red maples is thrown in for good measure. Off to the right, large decades-old maples, and a rare oak, bristle with dazzling burgundy and crimson colors. My favorite is the occasional maple that doesn't know what to do, so it plays safe with a mottled pastiche of red, green and yellow leaves.

There's so much color that a solitary russet brown maple rivets attention in this carnival of colors. Normally the rust color would seem drab but its distinctiveness shouts like a calliope.

A half-mile further along I catch a glimpse of a fly-fisher working a swimming pool-sized hole at the end of a long stretch of dancing riffles. Is there any other sport as elegant and graceful? Fluid casting motions are sensuous as line is stripped in an effort to reach farther into the pool's inflow. Through the shrubby screen of willows, his equipment looks to be pretty high-end with thick Orvis bib-style waders, a perfect vest and natty wool Stetson to cap it off.

He's focused on his cast and me on my stroll. We both want to be left alone to our thoughts and pleasures on this ice-cold morning.

The Boise River is an impressive fishery. Although fly-fishers routinely catch rainbow trout, there's also the special allure of landing elusive steelhead and salmon. Sadly, the Boise once ran full with both steelhead (the same species as rainbow trout) and salmon until dams along the Snake River in Hells Canyon stymied migration. The Idaho Department of Fish and Game now trucks returning steelhead from a trap at Hells Canyon Dam to Boise to replenish the river.

Steelhead leave the ocean and migrate back to the Snake River between May and October. They spawn in early spring helping to recreate the cycle of life. Steelhead begin their early lives in Idaho's rich river system before running to the sea where they generally grow to 5-10 pounds and occasionally up to 20 pounds eventually returning to their spawning grounds. On leaving the ocean they live off fat reserves accumulated at sea. Anglers obtain special permits to pursue these fish in the spring and fall.

Idaho can boast about the steelhead and salmon runs. Record salmon were observed in 2001. The largest salmon caught on an Idaho river was 54 pounds and the largest steelhead was just over 30 pounds. However, the state is infamous for its blue-ribbon trout waters such as the Henry's Fork and St. Joe. Warm water fish are also abundant including crappie, perch, bluegill and bass.

Sturgeons up to 10 feet in length and 1,000 pounds are found in the Snake River. These prehistoric fish are protected by law and must be released. For many fishers this is a dream of a lifetime. It takes stamina and skill to land a fish of this magnitude plus a huge bucket of plain old luck to hook one in the first place.

By the time I reach turnaround at Ann Morrison Park the whole world seems back in balance. Over another icy pedestrian bridge – summer's take-out when running the couple hour, six-mile rafting trip of the Boise from Barber Park – I have a chance to look back upstream at the fisher. It's a classic scene of yellow-leafed willows and cottonwoods bisected by a 100-160+ foot river rippling with a steady current over jillions of small round boulders. In the far background against a rose-tinged sky laden with high cirrus clouds the fly fisher stalks steelhead.

Life's good.

* * *

The following winter was extremely generous to Idaho with 150% above average snowfall reported throughout the state; in some locales even higher readings reached the Army Corps of Engineers.

The Corps was watching very carefully because it controls Lucky Peak Reservoir – perched precariously upstream of metropolitan Boise – which at normal full pool holds 300,000 acre feet of water, almost 1 acre foot for every Boise resident living downstream. The lake behind the reservoir stretches 12 miles long with 45 miles of shore. The dam begun in 1949, cost $19 million to build 2,340 feet of rolled earth fill embankment 340 feet high.

In mid-winter the Corps began releasing water in anticipation of run-off because the basin fueling Lucky Peak Reservoir had 130% of normal snow pack. Literally overnight the Boise started to rise. Gentle riffles and meanders that were so bucolic and characteristic of a watercourse at winter's rest disappeared. Deeper portions of the river that at low point run 1 ½ to 2 feet now counted 3+ feet of depth. Clarity was replaced by milky-gray coloration as the river's speed picked up; modest river rocks and sediment were swept downstream. Accumulated drift lost hold and began racing toward the Snake River.

It continued to rain at low elevations and snow in the high country so the Corps turned up the discharge another notch.

The river rose 3-4 feet. It was now an intimidating force rushing wildly downstream at a speed that can only be described as astonishing. In recorded history's worst flood on April 20, 1943, a reported 20,900 cubic feet per second (CFS) bullied its way through Boise – flood stage at the ragged edge of becoming uncontrolled.

Casual strolls along the greenbelt provided awesome entertainment. As willows and cottonwoods lost purchase they were swept into the seething, churning maelstrom. Soon stripped of protruding branches – even enormous limbs – and pounded from all sides, they emerged downstream as sleek racing torpedoes, similar to giant crude canoes participating in some wild race to oblivion.

Entire willow copses floated by; root masses pointed downstream fully catching the river's surge. Most were swept past occasional 2-4 foot falls of volcanic basalt erected by the Corps. Mother-loads of detritus catch on these barriers and remain, sinking roots into the riverbed and forming mini-islands – make-work for the Corps to scour out.

Although entertaining at first, it was easy to see how dangerous the situation had become. If someone fell into the river they would experience a shortened life expectancy. We continued walking the greenbelt with little concern until the Corps was forced to raise the river to flood stage. Now it was literally inches from our beloved footpaths and quickly portions of trail became submerged.

Homeowners along the river enjoyed the bittersweet romance of a river's roar lulling them to sleep while constantly contending with the nightmare that water would rise further to their foundations.

Late winter abruptly shifted to early spring.

For three weeks the Boise was running at full bore flood stage and then a spate of warm weather hit the Northwest. The Corps announced that everything was in control due to the wise early drawn-down of Luck Peak Reservoir. Nervous homeowners relaxed…for a day-or-two…until a Weather Service forecast indicated possible heavy thunderstorms. For a week Boise citizens walked a razor's edge. Above average temperatures coupled with a particularly nasty thunderstorm would tilt the tables in the river's favor. Massive flooding could occur.

Wildlife didn't know how to cope with this dilemma. Canada geese were the first to deliver broods of hatchlings in local ponds. Parents dared not take them to the river because they would be swept away by the aggressively rushing waters. This concentrated the geese population in small areas and created savage internecine warfare between broods.

Geese had it easy by comparison.

Ducks, especially mallards, were essentially kicked out from their normal breeding ground. Meanwhile all of the normal nesting sites directly bordering the Boise River were resting underwater. In surrounding ponds Canada geese claimed the entire territory as their own. Ducks received vicious retribution from the geese for even feeding on a pond that was considered home to a brood. By this time not only did they have to contend with outraged goose parents, but goslings had grown into giant sub-adults presenting a formidable threat themselves. The end result was a meager crop of ducklings. Only a couple mallard hens managed to raise more than 2-3 ducklings.

Running straight through a city doesn't do much to enhance the Boise River's image as an untamed watercourse brimming with life. However a closer look provides startling insight to exactly how wild the Boise is despite flowing through a major metropolitan city with 300,000+ people who dearly love this watercourse.

A river of life nurtures more than waterfowl.

The Boise Ridge — an undulating mountain ridge bracketing the Snake River and the southern-most portion of the Central Idaho mountain chain — offers extraordinary lift and replenishment for migrating raptors. West of the ridge are grass lands flowing off the mountainsides to river level. Raptors take full advantage of plentiful rodent and small mammal populations inhabiting these slopes. They rely on this ecosystem most intensively during winter months.

Some raptors also have their eyes focused squarely on abundant waterfowl living along the river. Watching an immature bald eagle lift off with a mallard hen in its talons is both inspiring for its graceful flight and terrifying to contemplate as far as the duck is concerned.

That's life as a mallard or for any of the dozens of other birds living on the Boise River: Canada Geese, American Widgeon, Hooded Mergansers, Common Mergansers, Wood Ducks, Double-crested Cormorant, American Coots, Spotted Sandpipers, Common Goldeneye, Pie-billed Grebes and various gulls.

Great Blue Herons prowl the wetlands. Golden Eagles, Bald Eagles, Swainsons Hawks, Red-tail Hawks, Kestrels, Ferruginous Hawks, Northern Harriers, Prairie Falcons, Gyrfalcon, Cooper's Hawks, Northern Goshawks, Peregrine Falcons, Rough-legged Hawks and Sharp-shinned Hawks are some of the raptors of note. Ospreys are seen along the river in warmer months. Owls (Barn Owls, Screech Owls, Burrowing Owls and Great Horned Owls, among other) round out phenomenally rich bird counts along the river of life.

Winter gradually petered out with sporadic rains of no consequence. This year the Boise had run full flood stage for weeks — a hissing dauntingly powerful snake. Kayakers, rafters, fishers and other recreationists watched longingly from the banks. Tackling these flood level waters would be insanity. Our river would drop in time, but only after nature had taken its course.

* * *

Spring literally exploded along the greenbelt and with it the Boise River gradually receded from flood stage. Winters can be cold, even harshly frigid, in Idaho with interminable darkness until the season turns. However, beginning in April this part of the world is distinctly electrifying. Leaves seemingly sprout overnight. Blossoms cover the river's crazy quilt of vegetation emitting intoxicating perfumes that drive hominoid nasal cavities insane. The fragrances are all so sweet, but hellish on swelling membranes dripping in allergic reaction to a flood of pollens.

Center stage in spring's fest of alluring scents is Idaho's state flower, Syringa (Philadelphus lewisii). Syringa is a member of the mock orange or lilac genus that consists of 20 species. It is a branching shrub that left uncultivated mimics climbing vines by sending upward long branches seeking glorious sunlight. Syringa produces 5-11 racemes, or flower clusters, capped by blossoms of four white petals with a pale-yellow center. This perennial native shrub can grow to 20 feet high, but typically tops out in the vicinity of 12 feet with a corresponding width.

Syringa's signature coyly sweet smell is intoxicating and fills the greenbelt with ambrosia that suggests greenbelt visitors have died and gone to Nirvana. Enjoy the unbridled burst of greenery because Black cottonwoods are gearing up to release their spore. Rafts of windborne cotton float across the sky making life unbearable to those with allergies and to fastidious homeowners fighting a losing battle with swirling balls of cotton.

As late spring matures into early summer forests come alive with avian residents who departed over the winter. Additionally, entire zoos of small mammals that call the river home appear often with young ones at their sides.

The river comes alive with magic.

Bailey, our trail dog, revels in walking with all of this life smothering the greenbelt. There are all sorts of critters to run into, not to mention legions of other dogs who are depositing scent for others to learn about — a constant grapple for territory.

Trail dog falls into a predictable routine of favorite places to mark and riverside beaches to cop a drink or two before carrying on with her rounds. Early one evening with her muzzle buried into the Boise I spot a sleek, broad and furry head surface 25 feet offshore. At first I'm convinced that it's a small beaver since it reacts by slapping the water and disappearing. Surfacing a bit closer to shore and swimming directly toward us I reassess my judgment call. The head is a bit too narrow to be a beaver.

Bailey is oblivious to it all. She raises her dripping chalky-white wet snout and gazes upstream while the mystery mammal cruises in a loping arc downstream. It's about the right size for a small beaver, but the head is a bit too pinched and the tail doesn't appear paddle-like. I'd like to conclude that this is an otter – that's what I want it to be since I've never seen one before. However I can't verify the sighting.

Goofus dog doesn't really care about what's out there. She's more interested in transporting all of that water just taken in to other beloved spots along the trail. We finish out a fine stroll. Next afternoon before leaving town, Bailey and I decide to do an express walk and repeat the previous night's route.

Halfway through our little jaunt we come upon Bailey's watering hole. That's when the mystery mammal strikes again in exactly the same spot.

Bailey's tongue is lapping up water a mile a minute. She's so focused that she doesn't see a two-foot trout – possibly a salmon – swim upriver right under her nose. But, the shape didn't seem quite right.

A few seconds later I hear a rustling thirty feel away on the riverbank. Trail dog hears it too and goes on alert. Then suddenly she's dashing toward the noise in dense foliage, rooting her way around rocks and branches only to flip 180 degrees and come back chasing a dark brown river otter.

They grind to a halt and the otter faces her. It is snout-to-snout as each sniffs the other. This looks like a pup or yearling that was fledged from its mother. Perhaps it's lonesome and that's why it was hanging out here on this beach looking for company.

Each nose is twitching, snout whiskers waving in the still air.

Otter figures it out – this isn't another otter, but something different – and spins on the run.

Bailey interprets it as play and chases the mischievous otter for forty feet before it dives into the water, resurfaces and then spins concise small circles checking us out and contemplating what to do next. Bailey lets out a diminutive woof to let the otter know that as far as she is concerned play should continue. Her companion isn't so confident about the intentions of the strange white fluff ball prancing along the muddy bank. Otter swims another revolution, takes one last look and porpoises under the surface – gone for good.

We're left scanning the river to see where the otter surfaces. A good 100 yards downstream a little head breaks the surface before diving again. As the otter slips away and we return to our walk I begin to add up the numerous animal encounters I've had along this river of life. It's quite a tally.

Very early one morning in predawn hours I drove to my office located yards from the river. From a huge metal trash bin along the road a skinny dark shape emerged and ran across the road to the river. Its arched back run was distinctive and a dead giveaway – this was a mink that had been feasting on garbage. Blacker than night and swift as can be, it avoided my headlights while sneaking into several bushes and the waiting river refuge.

A couple months later I was visiting an executive of a local corporation whose headquarters looked out on the Boise River. As I walked to the main entrance past a four-foot high row of sea green junipers, a black-brown torpedo ran from one clump to the next. This mink had a trash can by the corporation's entrance squarely in its sights. After I went inside, the mink became bolder and made a direct run up into the trash can looking for goodies.

Mink and otter are semi-aquatic, carnivorous mammals of the family Mustelidae which also includes marten, wolverine, polecat, badger, and weasels. Both mink and otter are found throughout most of North America especially areas with rivers, creeks, ponds and lakes that are surrounded by rocky or brushy cover. They have rich dark brown fur pelts with extraordinarily soft under-fur that are valued for clothing.

With long slender bodies, mink (Mustela vison) usually average two feet long (19-29 inches) with one-third to one-half of this body length formed by the tail. Mink have short legs and almost flat, boxy-pointed faces. They weight from three to five pounds and females tend to be smaller than males. In the wild they live for about three years and in captivity can live three times longer.

Mink breed after they are ten months old. Breeding usually occurs from March to April, and as late as June when days lengthen. Gestation periods vary considerably, from 40 to 75 days, since fertilized eggs may experience delayed implantation. Litter sizes also fluctuate from one to ten kits with the average being four to five.

Mink are highly creative in their diet. They eat fish, crayfish, birds' eggs, small mammals (such as shrews, voles mice, muskrats and rabbits), clams and crabs, frogs and ducks. In turn they are preyed on by owls, coyotes, falcons and hawks, snakes, bobcats, foxes and lynx.

Mink mark their territory with a repugnantly strong scent from anal glands. Similar to skunks, mink can discharge a putrid liquid when they are frightened.

Like mink, river otters (Lutra Canadensis) range over most of North America and they occupy many of the same habitats, especially those along rivers and streams. Otters have well-developed senses of smelling and hearing, but their eyesight is poor. Similar to mink, otters produce an alarmingly rank odor when excited.

Otters mimic the body structure of minks however they are considerably larger and muscular. Otters weigh from 15 to 35 pounds and range from 40 to 60 inches in length. One-third of this length may be tail. Otters have short stout legs with sharp claws, webbed hind feet and thick bodies with their necks usually no smaller than their heads.

Swimming is where otters excel. They are born blind and toothless in a burrow usually among two to three pups per litter (but ranging from one to six). They nurse until they are two months old. At that point their mothers entice them into the water where they will acclimate to solid food. They are weaned at 5 months.

Otters focus on fish for their diet but they will supplement this with crayfish, frogs, crabs, shellfish and other aquatic food sources such as snails and shrimp. Otters and mink are opportunists and will eat birds, small rodents and vegetable matter if they are hungry. Because they live in cold water they must consume huge volumes of food necessary to maintain their high metabolism.

Many of our animal encounters raise optimism about the ability of animals to live in parallel with us. Once when walking along a dirt trail undulating through dense riverine vegetation, I heard a splash coming from the river.

An adult doe stepped on the bank and shook herself after swimming across the Boise River. She began trotting upstream headed for who knows where? We went on stealth mode. For 75 yards we crept in silence but this effort went for naught – our scent had given us away. Clattering hooves on cobblestones was followed by a humongous splash as the deer leapt into the river and began swimming away.

Another evening several weeks later I was casually walking down the sidewalk mere yards from an access path to the greenbelt when a fox came trotting down the opposite sidewalk. Fully flush with a monstrous bristle-like tail, the fox merely went to ground head-first into a clump of bushes, disappearing in the process.

My office has a tiny little window looking out on the Boise River. One afternoon I rose from my chair in time to see a bald eagle slowly lumbering upward, every feather straining to grab air while launching upward with a dead duck in its talons.

What's a chance encounter with an otter, eagle, mink or a fox worth in a lifetime? These unanticipated run-ins enrich our lives and mold who we are.

* * *

For many Boiseans rafting is the closest they come to melding with the river. Normally our watercourse sits there slightly out of sight and out of mind; always at the periphery until summer's heat tempers chilly waters. When the river is finally opened for floating, kayaking and rafting, an endless procession of flotillas ensues.

Boise City's Parks and Recreation Department oversees the river's use through town and sponsors a six-mile float from Barber Park to Ann Morrison Park with four optional rest stops. Several modest falls have to be negotiated and rafters always have to be vigilantly on the lookout to avoid sweepers – fallen trees and branches projecting from the river bank – and shrubs along the shore that can capsize unwary craft. This pinch of lurking danger accentuates the whopping dollop of fun from rafting this undulating snake.

The river running season's initial weeks can be a bit intimidating if the water temperature hasn't moderated with summer's warmth. Add the prospects of a good stiff flow being released by the Corps of Engineers and it is easy to understand why so many Boiseites wait until July's dog days to make their voyages.

Our first float of a new season came in early July when the air temperature was predicted to warm to 97 degrees. All we had to do was show up at Barber Park with a credit card; the City's private contractor take cares of everything else. It provides inner tubes, 2-person kayaks, and 4-6 person rafts as well as life vests and paddles for a modest charge. Floaters are responsible for their own sun screen, non-alcoholic beverages and food. Everyone is encouraged to wear running/tennis shoes or sandals. Beyond that; bring the desire to have a great time. After rafting six miles the City will bus the equipment and you back to Barber Park. Set aside 3 hours for a fun ride.

Dropping some 40 bucks plus for equipment, we lug our bulbous blue four person raft, designer life vests, canary yellow paddles and assorted gear to launch point among yellow-green willow shrubs and overhanging cottonwoods. Nary a leaf is moving; it's as still as can be along the slightly gray-green Boise. The river is murky given a huge volume of snowmelt still being released at this time of year and moving downstream with purpose. Cool – but not cold – water temperature is perfect for a mid-afternoon float.

First order of business is squeezing Bailey into her stoplight-red doggy life vest. She will fight this tooth and nail until we've launched and new surroundings with their delectable scents take her mind off her restricting corset.

Sunglasses secure, straw sombrero pulled tight I'm set to push off. All that we need is for Valerie to finish loading the couple bags of drinks, food and extra clothing. Meanwhile Bailey is prancing nervously on the flexing waterbed-like floor desperate to understand what's going to happen next.

Pushing off, a Velcro-like current catches and gently spins us 180 degrees. Val chooses the right side of our raft, locking her foot under a flotation tube and scouting for pirates, debris or wildlife. For a mile we have nothing to worry about except becoming acclimated to the river's embrace. However, that's not exactly how Bailey sees it. She's as antsy as a cat on a hot tin roof and keeps fidgeting from one side to the next.

Bailey fidgets one too many times. That does it. She doesn't remember that her handy-dandy doggy vest has a strap handle. I pick her up like a fully-loaded six-pack, dropping her over the side. Reflexive dog-paddling kicks-in. I keep a hand directly behind her furry butt to make certain that we don't drift apart. She's cool now and stroking a mile a minute, blowing air out her snout, scared she's going to sink. A few more seconds and then I scoop her back into the raft, drenched, but cooled off.

For the next half mile we enjoy wild river banks slowly drifting by and an occasional house partially obscured among tall trees. If you didn't look above river level you'd have a difficult time telling that you're in the middle of a city.

There's something very elemental about being cast upon the water. Sights, sounds and scents take us back hundreds of years when we lived *within* the world rather than apart. Perpetually at the back of my mind is the possibility of rapids – concern for safety. How often do we live attuned to our very next step? Year-after-year layers of distance from nature pile on until we're estranged. It simply feels good to be back on the ragged edge where not every danger has been removed from a path we travel.

Down river is a faint low roar of falls looming above Baggley Park. Friends have assured us that none of the slight falls on the river are anything to worry about – we'll be able to maneuver without trouble. Others are paddling vigorously to set up for the falls, some steer right while others go left. From Valerie's eye the best line appears to be right where one monstrous floating hexagon-shaped raft is headed. The closer we get the more apparent it is that the raft isn't actually floating; it's hung up on rocks. Two guys standing in the middle of the rapids are trying to dislodge it.

Bad call – we've chosen a line with a narrow tongue of water. If we don't hit the tongue semi-head-on, we'll hang up as well.

Valerie barks out an order to paddle hard. Unfortunately my one paddle equals about three of her paddles so we spin at the worst possible moment. In two seconds we hit the falls. I drop my paddle and grab Bailey by her handle at the same second that we scrape backwards down a rocky chute bouncing our fannies over river rock.

We float free by the smallest of margins and drift back into the river's broad pool. Valerie shouts a few acid-laced instructions about proper paddling style and goof-proof tips on reading the proper line. In truth, I'm hopeless and focused on river fragrances and the sound of water gently lapping against the sides of our raft. Who cares if our form didn't meet guide-level standards?

Having negotiated these rapids, I now know what to expect. And, it's clear from watching several drenched water-rats who have crashed and burned that in most spots a normal adult can stand up and only be chest deep in the river.

For me the best parts of the float are moments when we enter serpentine channels. Adventure cloaks these unique sections of the river. It's like floating the Middle Fork of the Salmon or the Snake. Willow, cottonwood and maple drape shade along the river's bank, cooling things a good 5-10 degrees. At each curve a noticeable increase in current arises as the river swings back-and-forth. Each bend digs deeply into a cobblestone laden bank only to be followed by gentle riffles that sway us back-and-forth like a baby rocker. The life of a river guide looks pretty good.

Two-hours and six river miles after beginning we paddle toward shore. We're ready to finish after being French-fried in the sun, and we don't want to miss take-out because only an-eighth of a mile further are serious falls that rafts and tubes can't negotiate.

Once our bow strikes ground the magic evaporates. As we lug the awkward raft toward the city's waiting busses and trailers I cop a glance or two at those who have finished their float. A distinctive fuzziness commandeers their eyes and shadows their faces. For a few moments they'll still be connected to a wild river; unable to voluntarily let go. They're back out there in those shady curves enjoying a rocking sway of their rafts as they sweep toward a tinkling set of riffles. Some look like they are thinking about placid sections where sun bore delectably into their bones and a mother river cradled them like long lost children.

Everyone should have the opportunity to live intimately with a river of life. It can deliver startling revelations about the true worth of wildness and how such wildness adds demonstrable balance to life.

* * *

A year of seasons has passed and I'm one year older; a little wiser. The Boise River keeps on flowing regardless of life or death, unconcerned about whether I'm around or not. It simply fulfills its destiny as a river, rolling toward the sea.

Each day the river changes in some way. A side channel deepens siphoning off more flow and beginning diversion of the mother river until they become one. A stand of maples undercut by the river finally cannot hold to the bank any longer; it crashes into the current at midnight. No one is there to record the event, but the faithful like me register the change next morning as we go about our rounds taking the measure of the day and this river of life. Meanwhile a bald eagle passing through replenishes herself on rainbow trout in one of the huge pools by Morrison-Knudsen Nature Center. There's fewer trout but a healthier eagle as a result.

Many of these events go unnoticed as I saunter along the river each day. This doesn't lessen the connection I feel with Boise River. How many times have I seen sun glinting off its undulating surface at a series of riffles? Hundreds or thousands of times? Somehow it is never boring and I continue to find myself unconsciously sucking in a deep breath whenever these illuminating reflections happen along a stretch of river.

How many mink can I see scurrying across a path until I become jaded by their presence? When does the punky smell of decaying leaves go unnoticed instead of raising a smile on my face and emblazon a sharp reminder in my thick skull that fall is near? Is it possible to become so complacent with a mallard drake and hen swimming in file that they disappear from my field of vision?

When I live under a river's spell answers to questions such as these come easily. Over time I *become* the river and carry its precious set of memories with me wherever I go. The river shapes my identity, defining who I am. That's what it is like to live with a river running through my life, under a river's spell.

Venerating the Ineffable

12

Alpine Gardens

The high water mark in epiphanies I have enjoyed from tramping through wild lands is being able to appreciate their vibrant sacredness. How many splendid fields of wild flowers gone berserk does it take before someone awakes to the ringing spiritual overtones from walking through them? How many tiny babbling brooks with crystalline pure water weaving among gray-white-mica-speckled granite boulders beneath a sheltering overhang of prodigious Douglas fir limbs must a person enjoy before seeing the bigger picture?

Like many others I didn't get it – the epiphany of sacredness – right away. I was too immersed in the physical accomplishment side of backcountry adventuring to be bothered by the softer, visceral dimension right under my nose. However, my eyes did gradually open after a series of extraordinarily epic moments along a blossom-filled ridge below Glacier Peak, under a full-on confrontation with our galaxy from high on Mt. San Jacinto, and after being immersed in cathedral-like solitude by a Cascade lake. These instances, and many others like them, helped me develop a consciousness about the sanctity of wildness. To better understand, take a moment to become immersed in the riotous flower gardens flowing along Lost Creek Ridge.

A tiny, scarred and weather-worn wooden sign sits alongside a dusty gravel road almost hidden in flourishing head-high foliage. A feather could knock it down. However, the trail indicator's physical appearance only tells half of the story. Look more deeply; penetrate beneath the surface.

It's a sign pointing to a magical kingdom.

Leaning slightly toward the east, this beaten and bruised brown trailhead marker proclaims Round Lake some four miles in the distance. Just a lonely sign, just another trailhead, just another dense forest of premium Douglas fir, and just another sunny day in Glacier Peak Wilderness. Who could possibly envision the exciting moments this humble emblem holds for the next five days? Our journey will be spent largely above tree line in some of the Pacific Northwest's hyper-spectacular sub-alpine and alpine country.

We tumble out of the car stretching cramped muscles and gabbing away, chiding one another. Cooped up for several hours, endless energy pours out like a tsunami. Clio and his sons, Pete and Andy, are busy fussing with their packs. Me? I head for the heights. Our exuberance will settle in time – 3,550 feet of elevation gain up Lost Creek Ridge is the sadistic prescription.

After winter's prodigious snowfall and spring's buckets of rain, roadsides are bursting with vigorous life this summer. Wading through a dark green screen of shrubs, a low hillside bench is replaced by classic Northwest forest – tree upon repetitive tree with almost no underbrush. Looking up the mountainside, all that can be seen is an infinite stand of tree trunks capped by a crown of dark green needles.

At least it's cool inside this canopy; warming August sun will make this low 80-degree day pretty hot. I try to put the challenge looming overhead out of mind, focusing instead on the rarity of a Cascade forest wilting in heat while we chase adventure in the depths of an astonishing forest.

"Looks like another perfect day in God's country," Clio shouts to me as I rapidly cover ground — a disappearing bobble head.

Stopping mid-stride I spin to congratulate him on his prescient choice of August first for this hike, "We couldn't have timed it any better. But unlike the last trip you organized maybe this one will deliver a bit of sun."

"You're too easily discouraged. A few rainy days only invigorate the woods."

He seems to forget that we never took off our rainwear on that trip. This unending optimistic outlook is part of what makes my friend special and a joy to hike with in the Cascades.

"I'll wait for you guys on the ridge. Hope I don't have to wait in the rain very long." With that I dash uphill leaving Clio's crafty comeback bouncing off tree trunks like a pinball gone crazy.

The Douglas fir and hemlock screen may ruin stupendous views, but it's enchanting to hike through. Fallen needles carpet our pathway with a spongy step that almost resembles Jell-O. No matter how heavy a person walks, footfalls are silent. Eerie quiet commands the forest and tones down conversations. The only thing missing is water. Unfortunately our hillside is almost devoid of a small creek or stream, an anomaly in the Cascades.

Although springs and rivulets are few and far between, silence is not. Peace settles over the forest as we wind higher. Sometimes all you want is your iPod, Wii, Blackberry, Bluetooth, iPhone or the embracing banter of a favorite brew pub. On the other hand, there are moments like this when distractions can wait while a vacuum gobbles up any noise, even persistent whining from pesky mosquitoes. Sweat-wringing, calf-burning switchbacks climbing under a roof of towering trees form a perfect tonic for urban life left behind. It's back to basics with nature taking center-stage.

Anyone who has traipsed the Cascades' backcountry knows that faultless precipitation-free weather is as precious as an extremely expensive French wine; it deserves savoring. This explains my excitement when we pulled up to Round Lake's obscure trailhead. It seemed almost too good to be true. But, before we can lounge around camp it's time to focus on the doing of it; countless steps up a near-vertical hill under heavy pack.

After several switchbacks I'm losing sight and sound of Clio and his sons. Excess energy is burning off like a jet fighter at full throttle. Eventually elevation gain and oxygen deprivation combine to slow me down. I'm not trying to set a record; it simply feels great to be back in wilderness destined for spectacular country holding a promise of alpine rambles.

A niggling pain begins to accumulate with every step. Trace it to what were once well-worn boots that now are too tight at one heel. Dave Page, Seattle's infamous cobbler, recently replaced the Vibram soles on my leather Pivettas. Although he is a renowned craftsman, major boot surgery is always unpredictable. In the end about half a size was lost on the right boot. This is a battle my feet are bound to lose because heavy-duty hiking boots like these typically resist any sort of give. Perfectly suited to wet and slippery trails, downpours, icy snow banks and talus piles of the Northwest, they're definitely not fashionable for other parts of the country – too heavy and cumbersome. The Cascades demand a higher standard in footwear even for weekend warriors. From experience I know what awaits – an ugly blister-or-two are bound to pop up before reaching camp.

Our route to Round Lake climbs through a verdantly rich forest of never-ending trees. Who would not be captivated by the magnificence of a mature forest at its prime? Some may see this as monotonous, but infinite variations of hot-then-cool temperatures and micro climates surface along the path. From my perspective it's impossible to grow tired of perfection repeated endlessly.

With each step the surrounding forest wanes as large trees diminish and smaller ones dominate. Forest gradually yields to meadow until meadow gives way to rocky ridges.

Then the real adventure starts.

What looms above? This forest is full of sparkling mystery, reminiscent of Rick Bass' search for grizzly in the Southern San Juan Mountains of Colorado, a story told in *The Lost Grizzlies* (1997): "What lies out there just above our heads in the spirit world, and just around the corner in the dark woods? What thrumming powers murmur beneath our feet? If there are men and women whose hearts and minds fill with the nearly infinite systems of artificial intelligence, then surely there are woods savages who similarly indulge themselves by rooting among the infinite systems of natural intelligence. Today I feel like one of those savages." Like Bass, today we feel an enormous appetite for the wild. But, this doesn't answer the question of what lies above us on this trail.

Grizzly bears are part of the mystery and magic of these mountains. Ursus arctos horribilis has been migrating down from Canada. North Cascades National Park and Glacier Peak Wilderness offer a superbly wild environment for bears looking to conquer new territory. Less than a decade ago a bear biologist spotted a grizzly east of Round Lake over the Pacific Crest and north of Indian Head Peak. We'll be able to see this area once we're out of the trees. As a crow flies, that grizzly was little more than 5 miles away from where we're hiking.

Grizzly bears are occasionally sighted in the North Cascades Ecosystem (NCE), a vast area of 24,800 square kilometers centered around North Cascades National Park, Glacier Peak Wilderness and surrounding national forests. According to the *North Cascades Grizzly Bear Ecosystem Evaluation: Final Report* by J.A. Almack and colleagues for the Interagency Grizzly Bear Committee (Denver, 1993), a population of 10-20 bears inhabits the ecosystem. The Sierra Club acknowledges the possibility of 5-20 bears in line with Fish and Wildlife Service estimates.

The Grizzly Bear Outreach Project (http://www.bearinfo. org) (GBOP) was initiated in April 2002 as a means of providing education about grizzly bear recovery. Two non-governmental conservation organizations and 5 governmental agencies offered seed funding. The project approach of GBOP includes community perceptions analyses, one-on-one meetings, small focus group meetings, a coalition of community members, a brochure, a website and a modular slideshow.

The GBOP indicates that between 1983 and 1991 20 confirmed sightings of grizzly bears have occurred in the NCE with 82 high reliability sightings. Recent observations include a photograph of a grizzly bear track on Bacon Peak in Whatcom County (1983), a front track in the Thunder Creek drainage of North Cascades National Park (1991), a bear biologist sighting of a grizzly on the south side of Glacier Peak (1996), video tapes of a grizzly bear in Canada's Manning Provincial Park (adjacent to the United States' Cascades National Park) (2002), and sighting, tracks and scat of a bear near Chesaw, Washington.

Insight Wildlife Management, a non-governmental research and education group that facilitates GBOP indicates that 200 to 400 bears are needed to create a viable population. Ironically, Hudson Bay Company records suggest that 3,788 grizzly bear hides were shipped from the North Cascades between 1827 and 1859. That's roughly 118 grizzlies harvested every year. Consequently, the NCE appears capable of supporting a viable population over the long-run.

Not everyone is in favor of a vibrant grizzly bear population in the NCE. This became readily apparent when Canada established the North Cascades Grizzly Bear Recovery Plan. Local U.S. communities near the border became agitated about Canada's intention to reintroduce grizzly bears. Augmentation by reintroduction is viewed as the best means for reestablishing a viable population – a process that could take at least 30 years.

A sunny clearing sits at a switchback hinting about a transition in scenery. Raising my pace in anticipation, I quickly cop a glance below to see how everyone is progressing, but not a soul is in sight. Their voices, laughter and banter that softened as the way grew strenuous, has simply disappeared. I'm not worried about them; *yet*. However, the avalanche path at my side is flush with greenery – perfect fodder and edible tidbits for endangered grizzly bears drifting south.

This massive avalanche slide is overgrown with a wild mix of grasses, flowers and mountain shrubs. Moving silently to its edge, I'm uncertain of what this window may reveal. Like Bass I'm naturally curious about grizzly bear possibilities around this corner. Pulse rising with anticipation, I sidle up to a spectacular view; a classic Washington calendar shot. Across the valley Sloan Peak's northern slope is awash in shining glaciers and vast snowfields. Like a hitchhiker's crooked thumb, it juts skyward begging me to stop.

Pausing in the forest's shadows I've gone on stealth mode hoping to mask my intrusion on this deadly silent avalanche chute. It's preternaturally quiet; almost uncommonly so. Not even a bird is pecking around among the bushes. A brief zephyr rises from below filling my nostrils with rich fragrances of summer flowers, shrubs and baking earth – but no hint of musty bears rummaging for supper. Nothing seems to be moving either above or below this steep defile's sweet spot.

To the east Glacier Peak's rocky summit resembles a warning beacon on the cab of a construction pick-up. Summer has taken a toll on its brilliance. Snowfields and rock intertwine leaving a less than majestic filthy appearance. By contrast, most of the Northwest's famous glaciated volcanoes show off pristine white spires and dazzling glaciers. The difference is altitude. At 10,541 feet, Glacier Peak is the lowest among Mt. Baker, Mt. Rainier and Mt. Adams whose distant summits stand Empire State Building tall and brilliantly white. The Cascade Crest and interminable mountain peaks curve to the south while to the southwest prominent pinnacles rocky spires like Bedal Peak, Mt. Dickerman and Mt. Forgotten hover over verdant valleys.

Fabulous weather may not seem like such a big deal to those from dry climates, but it's all a matter of viewpoint. Remember the Pacific Northwest's well-earned reputation – opportunities to enjoy the backcountry without dripping cloud cover or some maelstrom sweeping menacingly down the Pacific Coast are few and far between. A perfectly sunny day at Glacier Peak *is* cause to celebrate most righteously.

For perspective, consider Bruce Barcott's (2007) testimony in *The Measure of a Mountain*: "The Pacific Northwest boasts a long and honorable tradition of rain-soaked misery. One of its earliest and perhaps best descriptions was recorded nearly two centuries ago by the great American explorer and abysmal speller William Clark. Clark spent a winter on the Oregon-Washington coast, which is to rain what the Antarctic is to snow. 'Rained all the after part of last night, rain continues this morning,' he wrote in late 1805. 'We are all wet cold and disagreeable.' During their coastal wintering, Lewis and Clark's Corps of Discovery enjoyed a total of twelve days without rain. At one point it poured for eleven days straight 'without a longer intermission than 2 hours at a time.'"

Not surprisingly when sun finally breaks cloud cover and spreads glorious warmth into every nook and cranny, it's difficult not to feel infectious good cheer. During these special moments the Cascades radiate life; sun dancing on fir and hemlock needles; reflecting off lakes, streams and glacial ice.

Such a moment unfolded for me three seasons before on the Stillaguamish River roughly seven miles distant from Round Lake. About to set off from the trailhead to Alp-like backcountry above Monte Cristo, I waited at riverside with sun bouncing off multi-hued river rocks in a jumbled mosaic of brown, gray, white, black and yellow. The roiling current reflected back a-thousand-and-one sparkles, diamonds floating on the river's surface while sun warmed me to the marrow. It was a moment of such profound contentment that I had difficulty leaving when our group was finally ready; I had already been to the wilderness and back. This is how powerful a sunny morning can be in the Cascades' magical mountains.

Evidence of former logging is visible down along the Sauk River Valley. Like spokes of a wheel, clear-cut paths radiate from the former location of a spar pole. From up here it's obvious where huge trees fell before being transported down the river to Darrington. If there's any good news about intensive logging from decades past it's that Pacific Northwest forests are able to regenerate almost as quickly as a fraternity consumes a keg of beer. Seedlings, moss, fern and other voracious guests consume nutrients in sodden bark of nurse logs and stumps. Inferior trees that were not worth taking flourish robustly in added sunlight producing incredible growth.

Stretching toward the sky, they soon cover the remains of virgin forest reduced to lumber.

It's still difficult for me to see above the avalanche chute, but smaller firs text-message that the end is near — mileage and elevation have accumulated. Like a young child on Christmas Eve, there's no end to my impatience. I'm thirsty for an alpine world under a blanket of sun and my overwhelming goal is to reach the ridge before weather gnomes steal this gift.

A few minor switchbacks and then I break free into sub-alpine country. Now it's possible to gawk at Lost Creek Ridge's long undulating spine; a ridge we'll be negotiating over the next two days. Passage should be unhindered; only a few remnants of last winter's snow hide in depressions and gullies. All of the right ingredients — snowmelt, blazing sun, fertile soil and determined plant life on an unstoppable mission — coalesce to create a flower garden gone wild. Lost Creek Ridge wears a verdant green cloak signifying that summer is peaking and with it a tantalizing profusion of flower-filled meadows.

Several ecosystems are found in the vicinity of Lost Creek Ridge. Round Lake Trail begins in montane forest that is prevalent throughout the western Cascades. River valleys nurture profuse stands of western hemlock, western red cedar and Douglas fir. These splendid forests lie between 1,500 and 3,000 feet in elevation. Cedars tend to dominate in moist habitats while Douglas fir prefers sun. Both cedar and hemlock are shade tolerant which enables them to out-compete Douglas fir in climax, or mature, forest communities.

The Sauk River Valley found at the base of Lost Creek Ridge offers ideal habitat for old-growth western red cedar given generous precipitation and cool temperatures. In places that escaped early logging, ancient trees can still be found that are 1,000 years old.

It is not uncommon for wizened western red cedar to have base trunk circumferences of 10+ feet and crowns topping at 200 feet.

Interspersed in sunnier, yet moist, open areas of montane forests are big-leaf maples, black cottonwoods and alders. These deciduous trees are found along streams and bogs that are too damp for evergreens. Typically these trees are the first to reclaim areas of blow-downs or other natural disturbances that open the forest canopy to sunlight.

Vine maples also inhabit montane communities particularly in avalanche slopes. Routine sloughing of snow in these steep alleyways prevents evergreens from becoming established. Vine maples combine with slide alders and other montane-loving shrubs to create almost impenetrable tangles of woody braches on avalanche slopes. Although this may restrict our ability to navigate these areas, they help to stabilize soil in zones prone to landslides.

The sub-alpine ecosystem is found from 3,000 to 5,500 feet in elevation. Pacific silver firs and Mountain hemlock begin to progressively dominate over western red hemlock and Douglas fir above 3,000 feet. Engelmann spruce, western larch and lodgepole pine are also found in drier sub-alpine conditions.

Sub-alpine climates imply colder temperatures, more wind and generally harsher conditions (in precipitation, soil and sunlight exposure). Consequently viable tree communities tend to thrive as groups or copses. These clumps are surrounded by expansive meadows with a plethora of shrubs (e.g., mountain heather, juniper, huckleberry, serviceberry and boxwood) and wildflowers (e.g., glacier lilies, marsh marigolds, lupine, pasqueflower, western anemone, yarrow and phlox).

Above 5,500 feet in elevation the North Cascades ecosystem typically represents alpine conditions. Ultraviolet exposure as well as vulnerability to wind, snow and rain limits plant diversity. Trees such as fir, cedar and hemlock are stunted if they are able to establish footholds. Shrubs are also low-lying including willow, heather, spirea and huckleberry. Flowering plants tend to grow in clumps or mats. Common examples include mosses, grasses, phlox, cinquefoil and saxifrages.

We've fortunately chosen a week where wildflowers are at their apex creating a multi-color spectacle resembling a box of vivid crayons standing at attention. So much depends on timing, luck and just the right mixture of sun, snow melt, rain, and growth to create a bounty of blossoms like that washing over this ridge's rough spine. Flowers rarely retain vibrant colors for more than two weeks, and it's virtually impossible to predict when a crescendo will occur. We've unknowingly planned this trip for an encore moment.

Purple and white lupine swirl with red, magenta and lavender Indian paintbrush in vales, draws and hollows. Lost Creek Ridge's massive slopes are smothered in a kaleidoscope of hues. Old men of the mountains – pasqueflowers – stand like miniature sentinels with ZZ Top beards waving gracefully in a soft, gentle breeze. The garden appears to go on forever, it's that expansive. In many respects it's like catching a concert by a world-class entertainer at the absolute epitome of a rich and maturing career.

Stunted copses of fir punctuate flowered coulees that offer sheltered unique microclimates and nurturing perfect conditions for rare blossoms. I'm speechless amid these waves of Technicolor, transfixed, anchored in place. Pete, Andy and Clio finally catch up with me because I'm so busy dawdling through the flower gardens.

Everyone is at a loss for words. Terms like "spectacular," "beautiful" and "stunning" hardly capture what our eyes behold. We stumble along with heads flipping from side-to-side like a dog's tail, awe-struck by an intoxicating combination of silence, visual excess and warmth.

Nearing a weather-worn cedar trail sign staked into a saddle of the ridge, Glacier Peak levitates on the eastern horizon. Trouble is brewing. Some bear has taken a few bites out of the sign and used it as a convenient rubbing post. No one else seems to notice it so I keep my big mouth shut. We're about to descend into a supremely wild basin that offers perfect seclusion for an itinerant bear who has fled from Canada without a proper passport.

Beyond this sign Lost Creek Ridge is cloaked with an almost incomprehensible medley of color. Clio is stunned. Mouth agape he mutters, "Is it possible for the Cascades to get any better than this?" Our supreme mountain meadow moment personifies the very essence of what inexorably draws people to the outdoors like hummingbirds to a perfect flower. And, having sipped this nectar it will be difficult to go back to more mundane, relatively pedestrian mountain scenery.

Clio is wearing a broad beatific smile on his face; radiant with joy. Not a word passes between us for several minutes. Scanning the view in a full 360 degree pirouette, Clio turns to me and says sparingly, "This is truly a magnificent world."

Gary Snyder, poet, shaman, philosopher and wilderness guru argues that it is essential to do more than merely enjoy a great experience such as we are witnessing along Lost Creek Ridge. In *The Practice of the Wild*, Snyder (1990) states: "The point is to make intimate contact with the real world, real self....The best purpose of such studies and hikes is to be able to come back to the lowlands and see the land about us, agricultural, suburban, urban, as a part of the same territory — never totally ruined, never completely unnatural. It can be restored, and humans could live in considerable numbers on much of it. Great Brown Bear is walking with us, Salmon swimming upstream with us, as we stroll a city street."

We're standing up to our knees awash in a quilt of wildflowers with the crushing splendor of the Cascades. These mountains are famous for rough weather, dark mystery, physical challenges and rampant life. For all intents and purposes we're naïve students learning about Earth's unmatched beauty on an undulating wilderness ridge. In comparison, Snyder's admonition to appreciate the beauty of city streets is a challenge of a higher magnitude. For the moment we will try to take it one class at a time.

Huddling like a covey of quail at the 5,550-foot saddle, we set sight on our home for the night. Nestled next to a side trail down to Round Lake, a tiny blue gem sits 450 feet below in a rocky and desolate-looking basin.

Our reward for struggling up a nearly vertical hillside is this glorious moment when there's no more up to go. Now we can coast without brakes dropping to a little jewel living off snowmelt in what must be a frigid basin for much of the year. The trail winds below Round Lake for several hundred feet before doubling back toward a roaring outlet stream. Splashing some thirty feet down to the trail, a glorious modest brook burbles with fresh water; curling in and out of gray-green moss shrouded stones; festooned with white and yellow marsh marigolds and magenta flowers. Several copses of fir act as sentinels guarding the lake. Behind them Pete and Andy have located prime camping spots – a backcountry home where for once a rain fly is superfluous in view of incredible weather.

That evening sharing side-splitting stories around the campfire, coals start to slowly wink out of existence. Soft half light of purple-blue dusk descends over the Cascades. Yet, we're reluctant to head to bed. It's as though we're seeing the planet through a new set of spectacles; a perspective that was alien only twelve hours earlier. Unbeknownst to us, the show isn't over. Lingering moments of deep rosy alpenglow wash over trees, scree and rock slides sloping into Round Lake. The entire basin is richly bathed in a warm rose-transitioning-to-yellow glow as a magnificent sun settles in cloudless skies.

Alpenglow is an optical phenomenon occurring before sunrise and sunset when a reddish, whitish or golden glow bathes the mountains. However, mountains are not an essential factor for observing alpenglow. In many cases the sky and high clouds will take on a rosy glow as daylight changes to night. This is termed "afterglow" since it is associated with the sky instead of mountains.

Alpenglow derives its name from twilight's mellowing light reflected off snow, ice, moisture, or glaciers in the Alps. As the setting sun sends its final rays of scattered red light, mountains provide a convenient backdrop accentuating the color.

The same phenomenon occurs for afterglow and nighttime's approaching darkness. A rosy band of color rises above the oncoming black of night. Dust particles suspended high in the atmosphere create perfect conditions for afterglow. Major volcanic eruptions spew out dust that can create vivid sunsets. As long as this dust remains floating in the atmosphere, the probabilities are good that vivid sunsets will ensue.

Some regions, such as the Alps, are particularly conducive to alpenglow. The Sandia Mountains above Albuquerque, New Mexico are named for the watermelon ("sandia" in Spanish) color they acquire in winter at sunset. The Sierra Mountains in California are also famous for their alpenglow and remarkable ability to reflect light at sunrise and sunset.

Enveloped in the warm embrace of alpenglow, Round Lake's and Lost Creek Ridge's absolute wildness floods over us. These are the ultimate moments we seek in this backcountry — precious minutes that stand out above the rest of the day; the remainder of our lives. This rich light is so comforting that it's easy to forget how far away from civilization we've trekked. Yet, for this brief period all we know are a deep sense of peace and unbridled elation about being disconnected from society. We've become an integral part of this untamed land where glaciers robe precipitous flanks of soaring peaks and alpine country holds sway.

* * *

Next morning I'm first up to stoke the fire and heat water for hot chocolate. A few dry twigs and then an optimistic blaze flickers to life, growing as finger-sized branches add meat to this inferno. Popping and crackling its warmth takes a chill off this early morning sequestered deep beneath the looming crest of Lost Creek Ridge. Eventually Clio climbs out of his tent with an "oof" before walking over to join the dancing flames.

"I see it's sunny again this morning," he gloats with a twinkle in his eye.

"Did you hear the rain squall blow by in the middle of the night?" I lie to test his convictions. Clio is a notoriously sound sleeper so this catches him off guard a bit.

With a furrowed brow he continues: "If a storm came through it was intended to freshen those fields for our benefit."

Can't argue with that logic. I stir the coals and with pot in hand lean over to pour him a cup of hot water. His laughing eyes tell me he caught the ribbing.

My heart wells with fondness for this dear friend. Camaraderie is all part and parcel of enjoying wild country around smoking campfires. Friendships send down deep roots under these conditions. Although campfires may be ecologically detrimental, they hold inestimable value for creating lasting affections such as Clio and I enjoy.

Prior to climbing out of Round Lake's basin, I pick my way west from camp, going off trail, plunging into a thriving forest of Douglas fir and cedar on the ridge's shaded north-slope. The reward is a picture-perfect view of heavily glaciated Pugh Mountain and a valley twisting and turning down into the dark bowels of Pugh Creek drainage. No official trail navigates Pugh Creek and looking out on the watershed all that comes to mind is how utterly untamed this wilderness canyon appears compared to other countless gullies spiraling off surrounding peaks.

Precipitous walls covered in thick fir with impenetrable brush like a mangy dog's hide close the valley to casual exploration. A sudden breeze whisks past carrying the scent of wild land and hidden critters. It's the sort of magical Shangri-La that could easily host grizzlies migrating down from Canada – one more intriguing cul-de-sac to explore in the future; one more hidden enclave for stealth-like grizzlies.

Rocking on my haunches, lost in thought, a revelation begins to shroud over me in a mesmerizing embrace. I'm finally wandering the Cascades' alpine country at the very peak of blossoming; a wildflower extravaganza. It is doubtful that alpine gardens can be more profuse or poised at their apex. Twelve-some hours ago we walked through every conceivable color and discernible permutation.

Yet despite yesterday's perfection, I marvel that this ultimate moment is not what's tugging at my heartstrings. It's a confusing contradiction. I longed for a chance, just once in my lifetime, to go on a demanding trek that would give me the chance to wade through fields of wildflowers gone berserk. Now that I've wallowed in those Elysian Fields I'm somehow refocused on what most would consider par-for-the-course-forest.

Don't get me wrong; I feel exceptionally lucky to finally have seen what so many jealously want to enjoy – alpine gardens ablaze.

In this slightly chilly morning moment, reflection raises deeper thoughts and understanding. It isn't the tough hike or wildflowers, but the *wild* in the flowers – and especially the *wildness* in Pugh Creek drainage – that command attention. Prospects for a wayward grizzly to come lumbering up this fern-dominated hillside personify what sets my soul on fire. It's an intuitive realization that scenic beauty is valuable – extremely prized – but so much less than this mountain's surrounding montage.

For a single infinitesimal moment, *five minutes…that's all*, I'm bathed in wildness; totally immersed in this little grotto overlooking a seldom violated drainage. Any human dent on the steeply descending hillside is virtually nonexistent. Only the mountain can speak for certain about how many and what species of bears have gone over Lost Creek Ridge to see what they could see. This mountainside is as pristinely wild as any spot can be in the Lower 48.

Three hundred seconds devoted to a complete reversal in thinking. When I started this multi-day trek I was focused on the adventure of an arduous backpack deep in a flower garden wilderness. Now I'm startled, positively shaken, by a new insight: adventure on this trip isn't about our physical challenge or what many would consider exquisite beauty; it's all about an intrinsically introspective moment. Here in the middle of nowhere my thinking changes forever in a fundamentally significant way; a paradigm shift of appreciation.

I'm not chasing adventure by notching a strenuous backpack on my life list or chalking up a ramble through blissful meadows. My actual adventure is realizing that I desperately crave wildness and for a few precious minutes I essentially meld as completely as one can with the surrounding forest. It's an adventure in mindset that neither the incredible flowers nor the grueling trail will ever hope to match.

Breaking this magic moment I rise and set off for camp giving one last longing glance following this lost creek flowing toward massive underbrush of clubfoot and alder. Absolutely nothing is stirring; not bird, squirrel nor grizzly. But it doesn't matter that such critters remain hidden. What's more important is the possibility that at any given second they *could* materialize. That's pure unadulterated wildness and as about as BIG an adventure as they come.

After breakfast Clio leads us up and over Lost Creek Ridge out of Round Lake's basin. Broaching ridgeline, we're greeted by dazzling sun and cloudless skies – a miracle of two nice days in a row. From here we'll traverse the ridge's south side in transect toward Kennedy Hot Springs – an overly popular destination on the headwaters of White Chuck River.

There's only one problem.

The trail immediately grows sketchy. We slice through meadows redolent with the bouquet of damp earth, wildflowers in bloom and vegetation released from decaying snowdrifts. Confusion rises from small paths wandering back-and-forth across the ridgeline like veins on the back of an old man's hands. Which should we choose?

Any semblance of a single well-defined trail peters out very quickly. Barely decipherable paths hunt around ridge-top depressions that up until two weeks ago were covered in snow. Now they overflow with a profusion of wildflowers whose fragile existence is belied by bold colors shouting for attention. Do they know that the end of summer is nearing? It's only three weeks until both the high country and these blossom bowls succumb to fall's chilly bite.

Andy and Pete are out front sniffing for the best path like Springer Spaniels ready to point. Despite their sharp eyes, we take several dead-end routes through the brush leading to precipitous knife-edge cliffs falling 700-800 feet to rubble of chalk-white boulders. There's neither rhyme nor reason for this spider-web lacing along Lost Creek Ridge. Those exploring before us tried their best to find a way around these snow-filled depressions. So we resign ourselves to hunting and pecking for an easy way, certain of the general route, but not always the next twenty yards.

Over the next four hours we'll trek several miles enjoying a 360-degree view. To the east Glacier Peak commands the eastern skyline with impressive gray-white glaciers flowing from its peak. To the north at 10,778 feet, Mount Baker, an active volcano, squats robed in white splendor. Receiving heavier snowfall than Glacier Peak, it stands out in sharp relief – only 70 miles away. Mt. Baker is flanked to the east by Mount Shuksan and Mount Challenger in North Cascades National Park, two significant peaks with a bit more heft and elevation than other snow-covered and glaciated peaks in this area.

Snowcapped peaks resemble tips of waves. Estimates suggest that 40 percent of all active glaciers in the United States are found in Mount Baker National Forest and North Cascades National Park. On south-facing slopes stretching toward Canada, sun has melted much of last winter's accumulation leaving precipitous mountainsides a startling fluorescent green as vegetation goes cosmic. Avalanche chutes slide thousands of feet into invitingly lush valleys burgeoning with life. This view changes when flip-flopping 180 degrees and looking south. North slopes of distant ridges and summits hidden in shadows are accumulating massive snowfields and mini-glaciers. It looks like someone dropped huge buckets of vanilla ice cream on the ridges.

Andy and Pete are dashing about 100 yards ahead of us trying to break the silent code of this complex maze. They have their work cut out for them because as far as we can see, alpine country stretches like an octopus' tentacles. I'm following in Clio's boot steps half asleep as mind-numbing sun penetrates to my core. In my deep contentment and cozy stupor, it's the small things along this ridge that magnify to enormous proportions.

A miniature spring sounds a barely audible gurgle as it nearly drowns a patch of richly profuse yellow flowers. The slight swirl of a gentle breeze moves like a wave along Lost Creek Ridge making everything dance to its cadence. We try to balance the perceptual disconformities of our vague pathway with the vacuous void of a precipitous drop below this knife-edge ridge.

Clio finally breaks the silence. "I can't remember when the flowers were so abundant. They're energetically sparkling, vibrantly alive. It warms my heart to know that Andy and Pete have this opportunity to see them at their best."

I'm at a loss for words. Clio's comments embody that remarkable love between father and sons. Here in the middle of splendor, he's thinking about them first and foremost. There are times to chat and times to remain silent; and this is one of those moments to say something by not saying anything at all.

Ten minutes later Clio hesitates slightly before taking a couple steps up a slick snowdrift. As I grind to a halt behind him the time is ripe to share my thoughts, "What do they enjoy most – the flowers or ferreting out our route?"

He lets out a sigh after negotiating the snow bank and then muses, "It's hard to say. Do you and I fully appreciate these moments? Or, is this just another pretty picture notched on our backpacks?"

Love for the land has to start somewhere, sometime. This may be that special moment for Pete and Andy. That's how an appreciation for wilderness begins; by being out there.

Tom Brown, Jr. (1980) offered a bit of good advice about how to appreciate beauty of this magnitude: "When most of us are taught to look at nature, we are taught to observe it from a certain perspective. We view it for its beauty or its oddness. We look at it through microscopes or field glasses or single-lens reflex cameras. I was taught to flow with my surroundings and discover the purpose of something through being as close to that object or animal as the spirit would allow. I was a part of the mist being blown through the forest on a gentle breeze. I touched everything with my spirit and tasted its sweetness as I flowed in and through the undergrowth." Our challenge is to flow in, through and along with this ridge – becoming one with the ridge – in Brown's analogy, becoming one with the massive North Cascades.

During the early afternoon our skills are honed in observing nature and flowing in and through meadow upon meadow. As the afternoon turns toward evening we drop to Camp Lake, a diminutive jewel hunkered down in the western lee of the Cascade crest. Occasionally a lake will be distinguished by its dazzling color. Such is the case for Camp Lake, an extraordinary example; a sapphire beauty with the deepest blue imaginable.

The size of a football field, steep cliffs ring the lake. Who knows to what great depth this lake reaches in purchasing its distinctive color? A practical yardstick for measuring this lake's volume is small gray submarines slowly swimming around its perimeter. Like so many magical things about the Cascades, a sweet surprise unveils itself. Huge trout, on order of eighteen inches and higher, float near the surface, grazing for insects.

Clio and I scramble 70-80 feet up a little fir-covered knoll to get a better read. Trout methodically wheel around the basin, some clock-wise, others counter-clock-wise, patrolling for goodies. Without fishing tackle, there's no hope of catching one of these giants.

Not a problem.

Keeping with the positive juju of this adventure, our quandary is answered shortly thereafter by sharp eyes. Andy spies a fifteen inch monster trapped in grassy channels of the outlet stream. He literally corrals the fish by hand and leaps up triumphantly, the fat fish oozing out of his hands; soon destined for dinner.

A fish is especially welcomed on this trip because Clio planned all of our breakfasts and dinners. He's the not the least bit apologetic about going with freeze-dried fare. That way the meal manufacturer does all of the heavy lifting in menu planning. He only wants to open a packet and have everything there with no fuss or muss. The downside is taste and texture. As a result we crave fresh food and the trout is a little gift from Heaven after a couple days of cardboard meals.

Freeze-dried fare also has an advantage of preparation. Only one stove is needed to heat water or in worst cases, such as dinner tonight, to prepare pasta and other ingredients that need a long time to cook. We tend to supplement the stove with a small campfire to heat water in a coffee pot or to fry unlucky trout. A fire does double duty in drawing our little community together.

Purists recoil at the thought of having a campfire; particularly the thought of a campfire in sub-alpine country. A solid argument can be made that campfires in sub-alpine country are extremely extravagant and ecologically adverse. At or above tree line there is limited wood to burn. Fires encourage the wanton destruction of trees as campers hack off live branches because dead timber, branches and logs have already been consumed long before. Campfires also concentrate use in a limited area resulting in devastation of habitat as people shuffle around in the same spot killing grasses and flowering plants.

Campfire rings are an ugly eyesore to many purists. Soot and ashes blow out of campfire pits spreading a repulsive charcoal-colored patina to fragile sub-alpine soil. As campers tramp down and compact the soil around fire pits, prospects for rehabilitation diminish. Little paths radiate from campfire pits like spokes from a wheel due to people repeatedly walking in the same place. Especially in sub-alpine conditions, the growing season is too short for vegetation to recover from concentrated use. In short order campsites become an indelible mark of human incursion.

Yes, campfires are undeniably destructive. Although I have never created a new fire pit, I am guilty of using existing campsites and adding to the wear and tear of these formerly attractive spots.

I should be ashamed.

But, I'm not.

Is a campfire essential? Absolutely not, except when weather is so harsh that it threatens survival to forego a roaring blaze. Some of my friends refuse to have a fire regardless of whether we set up camp in the forest or sub-alpine country. They don't want to add to the degradation of habitat. I respect that opinion and try to go without a fire when camping together.

But there is a rub. A campfire is very symbolic of wilderness adventuring. The smell of campfire smoke is intoxicating; the flicker of yellow-red flames along burning logs mesmerizing. Nothing draws people together like a campfire. Somewhere deep in the recesses of our brains we are hardwired to those ancient bygone days when a fire represented security, safety and camaraderie. My friends tend to parcel out the very best of themselves – the essence of their souls – around campfires. We open the pages of our lives and peel back the covers to share in intimate ways that are unthinkable even around the best cup of latté at a local Starbucks.

Most of the trails I follow penetrate wilderness areas that see few people. Frankly, my impact from a little fire is seldom significant in these unused areas – at least that's how I rationalize things.

Yet, in my heart I know that any campfire, even in the most remote and seldom visited areas, means human impact. So I try to keep it toned down. I'll go without when near or above timberline or in places that see heavy use. That's the price we all have to pay for too many people and too little wilderness.

The time is coming when authorities could essentially ban all campfires. It's happening in most of our charismatic national parks or high profile wilderness areas. It's sad for me to think that young folk may never know the joy of sharing around a campfire. Life will be less when you can't get smoke in your eyes, roast marshmallows over an open flame, or take the early morning chill off by a bright dancing blaze.

Exhausted from trail miles – probably 3 times more than necessary with a snow-free path – and sensory overload from alpine splendor, we're ready to hit the sack. Andy plays with a stick jabbing hot coals to break them down. Pete gazes pensively into a few meager flickering flames. Clio and I say nothing, silently nursing muscles that have been taxed to the limit.

In the campfire's final moments conversation focuses on tomorrow. We'll drop off this alpine ridge into a forested canyon holding Kennedy Hot Springs. These vomit-orange colored hot springs are bound to exponentially increase the number of people encountered – a depressing thought since to this point we've seen no one else. A strategy surfaces. We'll camp well away from the hot springs to maintain Glacier Peak's magical spell.

With a warm breeze blowing over the camp nary a sound is heard as red-hot coals of the campfire crackle out of existence. Backing into my tent I kneel down as though praying, pulling the rest of my gear inside. As I reach up to close the mosquito netting a comet shoots across the darkening sky briefly illuminating the night. Seconds later an icefall reverberates from high above on Glacier Peak. Perfect way to end another glorious day.

It's the lullaby of pristine land; a comforting melody etched into our genes. How lucky can I get? To be outside and alive; our sleep is sweeter for these gifts.

* * *

Next morning our first challenge is crossing Little Siberia, an area of stark plant-deprived tundra and fields of dome-shaped boulders like a pod of porpoises breaking the ocean surface. Heather is starting to blossom in this high mountain park where snow frequently never melts. Delicate alpine vegetation struggles valiantly to survive; to chalk up another summer before winter's onslaught slams down on the Cascades. In less than a week Little Siberia will transform into a polka-dot mixture of pink flowers on sea-green shrubs. However, having been spoiled by Lost Creek Ridge's inestimable grandeur, Little Siberia seems almost barren by comparison.

We pick our way across the half-mile long park before beginning a free-fall descent into Lake Byrne followed by steep switchbacks into Kennedy Hot Springs. In many respects Lost Creek Ridge's world-class splendor is underscored when we drop down into Lake Byrne — *drop down into*. Coming up the other direction from the White Chuck River most people never reach Lake Byrne. They generally struggle to get to Kennedy Hot Springs, a good bit of mileage from trailhead parking. Those who want to avoid multitudes drawn to the hot springs continue climbing to Lake Byrne. Once at this sub-alpine lake few make the additional effort to plod on to Little Siberia.

As we reenter forest, Lake Byrne's spectacular views evaporate, replaced by a tedium of trees. Sparkling mountain meadows are exchanged for a well-defined rut winding through a forest of look-a-like Douglas firs. Thin cloudiness substitutes for blue sky as the weather begins to change. Looking back on the pinnacle we experienced to reach Little Siberia, it will take some substantial effort to flow through Glacier Peak's forest with the same spirit as we did along Lost Creek Ridge.

Heads bent with eyes focusing on the trail, we spread out as our individual paces vary. These are moments when I retreat within myself. Who knows what others are thinking? I'm replaying in my mind the infinity of mountain flowers gone berserk and that supremely special moment of wildness captured in Mt. Pugh's drainage. Eventually a nondescript camp appears a mile above the busy trail junction with Kennedy Hot Springs. Our base lies alongside a richly flush, rushing stream that is picking up volume as it feeds White Chuck River. Compared to our sub-alpine campsites this forest feels claustrophobic. We're penned in with few majestic views or attention-grabbing attractions. Having been spoiled by supernatural alpine country, these lowlands lack charm and sparkle. It was easy to flow with and through our surroundings in the high country. Now Tom Brown's admonition for melding with the land presents a difficult challenge.

An opaque sky darkens into the dismal gray of an oncoming storm. It's time to set up the rain-fly as a preventative measure because certainly it will rain tonight. In summer it's rare that an entire week goes by unblemished. A day or two of rain is par for the course. Rummaging through my pack trying to find the fly, I'm in for a surprise. Much to my chagrin, I used the rain-fly to cover my pack in the car. This was extremely effective in hiding it from would-be thieves, but not so brilliant now that I need it. Somehow

I didn't stuff the fly in with the rest of the gear when we left the cars.

This little lapse in negligence could cost me plenty. Although there have been no errant storms the last two nights, it's unrealistic to expect a full week of rain-free weather in the Pacific Northwest. Now we're smack dab in the middle of Glacier Peak Wilderness. We're as close to flowing in and through the mountain as we possibly can be. A sinking feeling sweeps over me. Rain, any rain, could be quite uncomfortable, a recipe for disaster.

Clio comes to my rescue. "Cheer up. It's not going to rain. I have that on good authority. Besides, if it does you can simply move in with me."

I fret and fume about this lapse for an hour and then give up the vigil as darkness steals over our camp. A few irregular low-volume snores drift over from Clio. Pete and Andy appear to be dead to the world since they zipped up their tent 20 minutes ago. Another night begins to unfold in glacier country. With a soft breeze gently caressing trees and shrubs, my eyes grow heavy. Only one pestering thought disintegrates as sleep approaches.

If the weather will just hold....

* * *

Morning dawns gray and damp. Humidity drips off anything that's standing still while occasional sprinkles fall in gentle waves. It's not enough to soak through my tent yet, but it definitely looks like the Pacific Northwest is about to live down to its reputation. I hastily stow my down sleeping bag to keep it somewhat dry and step outside to a world of water. The only consolation is knowing that persistent precipitation nurtures the wildflower gardens we enjoyed along Lost Creek Ridge.

We're on the final leg of the trek traveling a couple miles up to White Pass before switch-backing down into the Sauk River drainage. Flanking the White Chuck River, we hike progressively toward Red Pass and its twin, White Pass. Sub-alpine country around the passes seems rather mundane compared to the undulating sides of Lost Creek Ridge. Even Glacier Peak has lost its sparkle and visibility, hidden in the midst of a concave cloud cap.

Few flowers dot high meadows and bowls forming the north face of Red Pass. Grass is reluctant to grow in this park. Any number of reasons is at play here – soil, exposure to sun, gray of a cloudy day, or the refrigerating effect of nearby glaciers – that spell the difference in the timing and depth of blossoming. Whatever the specific cause, Red Pass lacks the dancing sun, exuberant blooms and singing creeks several miles distant along Lost Creek Ridge.

It isn't until after we finally haul our sorry tired-out bodies to the top of Red Pass that the world begins singing vibrantly again. At the back of my mind is realization that the worst day hiking is better than the best day at work. But, after having been overwhelmed with Lost Creek Ridge, the bar for appreciating this world has been raised just a bit too high.

Things change at Red Pass. Even though slight rain showers mingle with sun, grand views of sub-alpine and alpine country overwhelm our funk – a marvelous world spreads out into distant horizons beneath our boots.

Drawing a map with his hand in the air Clio points out our destination a couple miles down the mountainside – the Sauk River. The best news is the direction. It's down – down never up – from this point to the trailhead. The physical challenge of climbing mountains with an enormous pack is over. Peter and Andy race off in search of camp, smelling nearness of the barn, kidding and shouting to each other down the trail.

As we cross the west face of Red Creek's drainage magenta monkey flowers grow exuberantly down the sides of springs and streams; flowing like water toward the lowlands. Both flowers and rivulets are fed by pockets of snow melting fast to beat the end of summer. Along the slopes of Red Pass, the land undulates in small waves resembling a sea of miniature rolling hills with occasional pockets still gripping sun-resistant snow. The stunning voice of alpine scenery calls; bountiful with flowers, rivulets, grassy slopes and endless vistas.

Thousands of feet we climbed up to the passes and ridges are ours to lose. Long steep switchbacks take us from our aerie to soft valley floor in seemingly no time at all. Clio's wisdom in following this loop clock-wise is immediately apparent. The trail is exposed to the full brunt of sun in contrast to the almost impenetrable canopy shading us on the way to Round Lake. It would have been one hot hike out of the Sauk Valley if we had gone counter-clock-wise.

Avalanches have raked the entire south-facing slope of this immense drainage. In spots a few stunted trees grow well below the glide path of those winter freight trains. What an exhilarating sight to see a slab avalanche a half-mile or more across launch off this ridge. But, that's another season in what seems to be another world. For now where there have been avalanches an abundance of bushes flourishes; bushes that at this time of year offer nutritious feed and berries — just the sort that ravenous black and grizzly bears love to consume.

Bears are anticipated at every corner. We compensate by serving up obnoxiously loud conversation intended to scare the critters off. We're probably too far south and west to position ourselves in true grizzly country, but infrequent sightings indicate Ursus arctos horribilis is out there waiting for the unwary. Does it really matter that the biggest threat may only be black bears rather than grizz? Black bears living here are huge and reason enough to be on alert.

As afternoon gives ground and dusk begins to lie over the land, we've traded Glacier Peak's high drainages for stands of old growth forest that miraculously avoided lumberjacks' saws. A remarkably peaceful walk ensues as time begins to slow down. Those pesky clouds that bothered us at Red Pass have passed over leaving the sky bright blue and pure. Swaddled in shade we glide several miles toward what will be our last camp.

Few environmental issues have become as controversial a lightning rod as that of old growth forests. Those who favor logging old growth forests point to economic benefits local communities reap from lumber harvesting and to the suspect logic of allowing large, mature trees to naturally die and decay thereby providing limited use to society. These arguments are countered by those who question placing monetary values on ancient life and healthy ecosystems. With so little remaining acreage in old growth available, these opponents suggest that the logging and lumber industry turn elsewhere for natural resources.

The debate about old growth forests continues to rage. Some see the "best management" as doing nothing at all. Others perceive that enlightened intervention can make ancient forests better. It is unlikely that both sides will inadvertently reach common ground.

It only takes an innocent walk through primary woodlands or old growth forests for me to understand the treasure of these forests. In my mind old growth forest is simply what forests resembled before Euro-Americans arrived on this continent. These are woods that have remained untouched, untrammeled and inviolate by humans.

It's easy to appreciate the centerpiece of old growth forests – huge towering trees dominate. In the Northwest this often means trees that have lived from 200 to 1,000 years. Douglas fir, western red cedar and western hemlock achieve gigantic proportions in the temperate climate. I find myself overwhelmed by awe, staring up into the canopy trying to figure out where these mammoth specimens end. Their girth is astounding adding to their mystery and magic. I usually try to envision moments throughout the hundreds of years – the freezing winters, unchecked gales, periodic droughts, and endless rains – that they have endured.

After becoming accustomed to coexisting with extraordinarily large trees, my attention focuses on the under story and ingredients giving rise to photosynthesis gone wild. Water is usually readily available. Old growth communities are typically sheltered from fierce winds. But, there is also a less tangible ingredient that I believe contributes to the nurturing environment they inhabit. Inevitably these groves are deadly quiet. A reverence surrounds them; a regal characteristic that ultimately marks each tree as a distinctive individual, one that is an integral part of a noble community.

Whether you support cutting down old growth forests or leaving them standing we ultimately all share one common thought. Ancient forests are unique compared to other woods. To some, like me, this is treasure enough to leave them alone. To others, the treasure is in harvesting the lumber.

I would hate for our children and their children to miss the opportunity of observing the palpable spirit of old growth forests firsthand. But, that is the legacy if ancient trees in old growth forests are harvested.

Once the final tent site is selected our group grows a bit melancholy. For Clio it might be recognition that this will be his last night to share with his boys; for Andy and Pete it might be realization that home will have to wait for another night to pass. For me, sorrow is knowing that one of the world's most captivating treks ends tomorrow; Glacier Peak's ridge of wonder is falling from our grasp.

That evening clustering close to a blazing campfire, Clio shares his thoughts about the circles of life we experience over the years compared to the circle of adventure we've just completed. It's akin to the following conversation Elizabeth Gilbert recorded with neo-mountain man Eustace Conway in *The Last American Man*: "'I live,' Eustace said, 'in nature, where everything is connected, circular. The seasons are circular. The planet is circular, and so is its passage around the sun. The course of water over the earth is circular, coming down from the sky and circulating through the world to spread life and then evaporating up again...The ancient people understood that our world is a circle, but we modern people have lost sight of that.'"

Clio believes that we have completed an epic circle, each day a circle unto itself. What we saw, breathed, felt, smelled, heard and anticipated is beautiful because it relates to the circular beauty of a near perfect world. His talk is powerful and I want to think that we will understand and retain this lesson in a way that affects us long into the future; and that we will influence others as a result. Clio has some help from Glacier Peak. It takes a pretty shallow person to not be affected by this week we've experienced, by Lost Creek Ridge.

* * *

On that fateful final morning we rise to a deep, almost freezing, chill. It's a sign of clear skies. Inexplicably today is cloud-free and sunny despite my continuing worry about impending rain. Leaving a rain fly in the car will do that to you in the Cascades. You'll always be looking over your shoulder anticipating the worst. Clio's sixth sense told him all along how the weather on this trip would turn out. I just needed to trust his intuition.

After a calorie-starved breakfast everyone is packed and ready to go. We rejoice in loads that are like feathers since most of our food has disappeared over the course of this hike. Our passion for wilderness isn't any less despite the fact that we're looking toward home. Wilderness and civilization tend to balance each other this way. Each makes the other valuable until we're filled to the brim and ready for the scales to tip back in the opposite direction.

Perhaps ten minutes from camp we wind through truly ancient old growth forest. Douglas fir and hemlock dominate this valley like so many other drainages in the Cascades.

There's magic in the air once again.

Wildness comes slamming back, reluctant to let go. An added measure of moisture drains off Red Mountain upping the ante for something special along the Sauk River. In a small hidden glen, the largesse of land well-watered nurtures a stand of towering western red cedar. Their trunks are gargantuan and their tops beyond sight. We pass in awe, in reverent silence. Sacred groves such as these can only be found out here surrounded by the circular beauty of wildness.

A bit of sadness accompanies the majesty of this old growth. When these mammoth legacy trees fall in good time due to natural causes, the circle is completed. They will rest peacefully below Lost Creek Ridge surrounded by Glacier Peak's wildness and waiting for those joyous moments when a grizzly bear tiptoes past. Like us, the bear might be an itinerant walker who marvels at what a wonderful world we enjoy.

13

Solitude

Todd Tanner was out in the north woods of Montana as a hunting guide when he experienced a revelation about the crush of civilization. His client that day was hyper-nervous about being in grizzly bear and mountain lion country and continued to jabber on childishly about his fears. Tanner thought the guy would never shut up. An impressive buck came into view. Terrified of the unknown and distracted by the threatening peace and quiet of the forest, Tanner's client missed his first rifle shot at the trophy buck. Disgusted, Tanner left the frightened hunter seated on a rock as he silently tracked the large buck, trying to herd it back.

Tanner (2002) recounts his inner struggle: "Twenty minutes later, just over the crest of the ridge, I sat down with my back against the larch....It is never silent in the deep woods, but it is often quiet, and if you allow that quiet to seep inside yourself, you might even find a moment of tranquility, of real peace. I luxuriated in the stillness – and the heady smell of the November forest, and the warmth of the afternoon sun – for a few precious minutes and then, with great effort I contemplated my hunter, sitting alone on his rock. Sitting there alone and afraid. As I stood up to walk back, I wondered what it tells us about ourselves when we need noise (and bustle, and roads, and telephones, and televisions, and buildings, and crowds of people who look, walk, talk, and act just like we do) to feel at ease? What, in our pride and arrogance, have we allowed ourselves to become?"

Many who recreate in the outdoors can sympathize with Tanner's appreciation for a forest's serenity as well as his disdain for a client's urban-centric fears. And so, it's sometimes necessary — essential — to go alone deeply into the wild, far from the noise, press of humanity and clutter of our lives in order to seek an adventure filled with solitude.

* * *

Whining like a worn-out food blender whirling at fever pitch, the 1100 cc Opel engine thrashes wildly as I expertly weave the diminutive red car through one tight turn after another. It's approaching late afternoon this mid-December and I'm trying to beat a soon-to-be setting fuzzy yellow sun. Carving a vicious line through a roller coaster curve, down to the right and back up to the left, I cop a blurry glance west, in the direction of the Pacific Ocean, to gauge just how much time is left in this early winter's day. Gears grinding like a speed drill plowing through thick aluminum within a fragile transmission not at all designed for these artful speed shifts, the Opel gives me everything that it has and then some. A sick thought floats through my muddled mind that this is a very weird way to begin a trip — racing like the wind to reach a Forest Service trailhead. My actions are bizarrely antithetical to my goals, but who cares? Nothing like a spirited drive up the mountain.

Although Los Angeles presents the perfect concoction of commercialization, intrusive noise and wearying press of human flesh, it also offers a surprising bonus. Ringed by lofty mountains that are gorgeous with a winter mantle of fresh snow, quick retreat is possible almost any day. The Southern Sierras – San Gabriel, San Bernardino and San Jacinto Mountains – offer many excellent spots in which to escape and in the process to access lonesome wilderness.

Boulder-laden Mt. San Jacinto towers over lower foothills through which I'm speeding. At 10,804 feet, it's a significant peak and essentially the last massif in the Southern Sierras. Lofty elevation nurtures a dense ponderosa pine forest and relatively prolific growth for this climate. Surrounded by coastal plains and a dead straight drop-off to Palm Springs below, the mountain is very much a sky island of life jutting up toward the sun. Rocky ramparts offer infinite possibilities for those interested in bouldering and Spiderman-like rock climbing. Nestled among granite-infested forested slopes are hundreds of summer homes. Center attention focuses on Idyllwild with style-conscious shops offering amusement to Southern California's hordes seeking Mt. San Jacinto's cool summer climate.

Cheap bias ply tires squeal as another turn falls to the master. Imagine what would be possible with a proper vehicle befitting my skill? The little Opel continues to give it her all as I slash through hills carved deep with road cuts tempting idiots like me to vastly exceed their ability and that of their vehicles. I whip recklessly around a curve and came face to ass-end with a large delivery truck crawling slowly up this sinuous road. Double yellow lines halt my revelry and I revert back to sanity.

The first vestiges of Idyllwild begin to appear along the side of the road – tightly clustered homes and then commercial buildings. I keep an eye out for official signs indicating the route to the U.S.

Forest Service. A backcountry permit is needed to camp overnight – all in the name of bureaucracy. However, past experience suggests that this is one Forest Service arm that seriously enforces the permit system. Once on a weekend hike I trudged with hundreds of others up an almost two thousand foot set of switchbacks only to find San Bernardino National Forest rangers at the top checking permits. If you didn't have one, you were sent down. Imagine, investing all that effort to reach the mother country only to be turned back at the final threshold leading to gorgeous forest, meadows and wildness.

A small, but visible sign, points the way to a dark brown office. The Forest Service's usual light green color has been sacrificed for something that blends with the woods. As I pull into a nearly empty parking lot at 4:00 p.m., a Forest Service truck is the only other vehicle around. Sprinting to the door, I can't see any lights on within this bastion of officialdom sequestered in a dark grove of trees. Wonder where everyone is? Much to my chagrin, the door is locked and there are no directions for obtaining a permit after hours. Well, I will just take a chance that Smokey is not on patrol. More than likely few others will be sharing the wilderness with me this evening.

Tahquitz Peak's trailhead in Humber Park is deserted. Poor little Opel will spend the night alone at 6,400 feet in the darkening forest lot shaded by enormous pine and fir. A thought crosses my mind about antifreeze – did we put fresh liquid in the radiator to handle tonight's freezing temperatures? In reality it's too late to do anything about it now. Wrangling my forest green pack out of the back seat, I go through the time-honored ritual of lacing up scruffy hiking boots before setting off across the parking lot at a brisk pace.

A light wool shirt feels just perfect beginning the switch-backing climb up Devil's Slide Trail. This heavily-used path reaches a pine and oak forested saddle providing unrestricted access to expansive meadows and relatively flat forested benches on the mountain's southern shoulder. My pack feels just right although loaded with extra expedition-weight gear to handle a winter camp. I'm fairly light on food since this is only a one-night ramble. By mid-morning the next day I expect to be well on my way back to the trailhead and a pleasant lunch in Idyllwild before racing the red Opel down the mountain.

Up the gravelly trail I run with Tahquitz Peak atop Lilly Rock, one of the southern sentinels at San Jacinto, acting as a barometer on progress. Tahquitz sports a lookout tower with fabulous views into the Southern California haze. Prominent throughout my final drive to Idyllwild, it is comforting to see the granite spire and face. Climbers generally test their mettle on cracks and crevices over the broad gray face and it's a little surprising that none are on belay today.

Within no time I'm rounding a final switchback to the pass. Topping the final rise, dirty white snow banks linger here and there among the trees – an expansive forest after the chaparral-laden lower slopes. Heavy accumulations of dark brown pine needles soften forest floor while oak and other native bushes stand as gray skeletons waiting patiently, slumbering until next spring. Manzanita is profuse in sunny spots and adds a bit of color to this forest's otherwise bleak winter harshness.

Philip Caputo published an insightful article entitled "Alone" in *Men's Journal* (2002) that replayed a trip he took deep within the Gila National Forest of southwestern New Mexico. Caputo eloquently captures what visits to the wild are all about: "I have come this way to take a kind of American walkabout. My reasons are contained in a remark Theodore Roosevelt Jr. made to one of his brothers, expressing his loathing for the sort of holiday we would call a 'family vacation.' 'When I go,' he said, 'I go hard and I go alone.' That should be every backpacker's motto. I am going hard because I think it's important to test yourself. I am going alone because I wish to follow my own agenda, not a guide's; and because I don't want to deal with the needs, wishes, and complaints of a companion. I am seeking more than escape from the toe-jam of contemporary American society." Wildness delivers solitude and a chance to test yourself in the most gentle, and ferocious ways. Winter is also the ultimate season for hard core adventure in exceptionally remote country.

Like Caputo and Roosevelt before him, many people find that ventures to wild country, *alone*, can be very invigorating. Such trips are also made that much better when balanced by a sufficient number of adventures in which you share wilderness with people that you enjoy. But, they do not serve as a substitute for "escaping from the toe-jam of contemporary American society" as a solitary individual. When alone in the wilds – immersed in solitude – you have a better opportunity for adventure. This is highly accentuated when deep into winter.

No one, absolutely no one, is around at this pass making my transition from civilization to the wild an easy leap. The climb to Saddle Junction has worked its magic and I finally get it – this is pure, unadulterated solitude. Time slows down and my obsessive ways come to a screeching halt. No longer in a hurry to beat the approaching night, I revel in a forest that is mine; all mine. I don't have to think about the feelings, needs or cares of others. I don't have to worry about which campsite I select in case other campers locate nearby. There will be no intrusions tonight – no loud conversations, no kids fooling around camp, no unexpected encounters when deep in thought, no racket from scouts trying to gather firewood for an illegal fire – just solitude.

Glancing down on a tiny trickle of snowmelt reality hits squarely home. Finally I am alone in the wild on an enticing adventure. Meditating on this wondrous thought for a few moments, a little seed of doubt begins to sprout as I pick up my pack, ready to move on to an eastern campsite almost two miles distant. What if I need help? What if a storm comes in and snows to great depths? What if the night turns cold – ugly cold? What if a bear raids my camp?

What if?

What if?

Anxiety such as this is something to be toned down; untold catastrophes wait – and an equal number of untold magical moments. I've had more than a long apprenticeship of day hiking and backpacking; enough to be considered very well experienced. Admittedly most of my backpacking trips have been with friends; while day trips have been a mixture. It's those solo trips that add a sharp edge of wariness to my trip this afternoon. I have dodged many bullets when hiking alone that I had no right to escape other than from plain dumb luck. This is not the kind of country that a sensible person wants to rely on luck. It's all too easy to end up dead when your luck runs out.

These small, but important, discoveries learned when hiking alone craft a knowledge base about survival. As these lessons accumulate an interesting phenomenon also occurs: a platform is created from which deeper, richer epiphanies emerge. It is this base that makes my solo trek into San Jacinto thinkable at a time of the year when two-foot snows can happen any day; any night. Given all the backcountry excursions I've experienced I'm now willing to test my pluck and the collective wisdom from previous treks under this evening's big time circumstances.

Heading east from Saddle Junction, I begin walking a little more carefully down the trail, cognizant of my exposure, confident in my abilities, and hungry for solitude.

With darkness descending, the path winds through several meadows alive with dazzling dark green ferns and jade colored skunk cabbage in summer. Throughout these very meadows I've seen mustard-yellow leopard lilies standing tall among the fern's heavy undergrowth. By this time of year, however, brittle cold has robbed all vegetation, except the evergreens, of living color; the forest is dourly robed in dismal brown. Following the dusty trail through these russet fields alternating with groves of tall Jeffrey pine and cedar, the way rises slightly toward the eastern edge of San Jacinto's shoulder. Night is coming all too quickly and I'm beginning to get desperate about finding a suitable campsite.

Half a mile later in an obscure ravine, a cozy hide-away appears that others have used for their nest. I'm home for the night, in solitude but not alone. My friends include an old time-worn tent, parka and extreme conditions sleeping bag. The tent goes up in seconds flat – a reliable home in a lost corner of wilderness squatting securely among sheltering oak and pine. Firing up the stove, the precise amount of water that will be used for dinner is meted out very carefully. This is a dry camp and I won't be able to access water until tomorrow at Round Valley several miles to the north. While macaroni and cheese are bubbling away my hefty sleeping bag is spread out to loft – my guess is that I'll need its entire volume tonight – while body heat begins to inflate a luxurious down parka that chases away the enveloping chill.

Chores such as these that normally seem to take a long time when chatting with friends around a campfire are over in minutes when surrounded by solitude. Before I know it, all camping details are out of the way. Macaroni and cheese serve as a great reminder that some years ago I took my very first overnight backpack with my brother-in-law to Round Valley – next morning's destination.

What a difference a few years make. Our naiveté was legendary; our luck extraordinary. We didn't know what we were doing. One thing was certain; we didn't want to schlep a bunch of gear up this mountain. I didn't bring a tent or sleeping pad because I didn't own them – a poncho would do double duty for rain and for a ground cloth. My sleeping bag was down filled, but it didn't have a mummy shape – there was no insulation for my head. I rationalized that a wool cap would keep me warm. Besides, it was California, and as they say, it never rains in California. A gargantuan aluminum external frame pack that I used was rented from a local backpacking store. It was comfortable but weighed a ton.

The image that remains emblazoned in my brain is that of my brother-in-law standing with two arms outstretched against a VW-sized boulder enveloping the stove and its bubbling treasure. Beneath his protective embrace our macaroni and cheese was cooking over a Svea stove. Mind you, Jon is built – a former linebacker for San Diego State University and a pro football candidate. Why did I ever think that one serving of mac-n-cheese would cover two famished hikers?

Water was another matter. I brought one quart and somehow managed to hike miles in brutal summer heat up thousands of feet without succumbing to dehydration. I had no idea that our first available water source was some ten miles distant. Filtration? I simply assumed that there would be a spigot at the Forest Service campground. Fool.

Conditions were ripe for disaster – a scorching afternoon instead of a cool, cloudy day; atypical freezing temperatures; clouds of mosquitoes or horseflies; any significant rain shower, much less a deluge or even a hail storm; or getting lost – we had no map. We could survive without food despite being a bit uncomfortable, but other than that almost any little glitch could spell big time trouble.

Shaking my head at the almost comical predicament I felt grateful for how far I had come. We didn't know any better that first trip. Nonetheless we were none the worse for wear and in fact reveled in our little circuit walk because our packs were so light. Sometimes ignorance is truly bliss; and Jon and I were most righteously blissful dudes on that journey.

Snapping back to the present it all seems like some strange Stanley Kubrick dream. Cuddled in the forest's stillness on the edge of slumber, I empty my mind of all thoughts except awareness of this wild place. It's moments like these that draw me to the outdoors; moments of great rarity. With nowhere to go, no one to interact with and no trivial chores to perform I am able to focus squarely on the magnificence of wildness. For the most part the vacuum of sound is complete except for gentle sighing of the wind through pines and rustle of leaves as gusts penetrate oak thickets. Amid this quiet I'm alone with the mountain.

Ultimately a fast moving frigid river of air drives me to tent and sleeping bag. It's only slightly after 6:00 p.m., but glacial air moves relentlessly off San Jacinto's heights toward desert trophy mansions below. Snuggling into my bag and waiting the requisite twenty minutes until full loft is attained, I'm eventually able to remove my furnace-masquerading-as-down jacket. Lying in near perfect darkness, a long wait for morning commences and I begin to reconcile the person that I have become with the person that I want to be – connected to the wild.

In due time, I drift off to a deeply satisfying sleep. The lights have literally gone out and I have no recollection of anything except loss of total consciousness.

That all changes somewhere about midnight.

What's up?

Where am I?

Why am I shivering?

I awake with a start – freezing to death. Adrenaline drives me into action. Even with mummy bag zipped up, my cold body sends warning signals to my brain. I reach for my trusty parka and quickly slither it into the bag with as little loss of heat as can be managed. Then begins a struggle of putting on this bulky jacket in extremely tight quarters; there's plenty of motivation to get the job done quickly.

Trying to gain control of the situation, I patiently wait for down to loft and equanimity to return within my nylon tent. Gradually warmth rises and I know that trouble has been averted, but for how long? Frigid morning light is still hours distant. I had expected it to be this cold at 4:00 a.m., not at 1:00 a.m. And I know which direction the temperature will go over the course of the next three hours. Still, I have my gloves and wool cap to add as things go from bad to worse and if push comes to shove, I can always start a fire.

Humbled, I settle back having come to terms with the mountain; warmed to the core once again. But another problem arises. I'm unable to sleep having been in bed for almost eight hours. At the same time I'm curious about how visible the stars might be this night. Putting on a wool cap and toasty gloves I zip open the tent door and feel a rush of brittle night air flood into my tent. Bones creaking, my body fights gravity as I seek an open view of the night sky.

Down the trail a few yards, a car-sized boulder offers an excellent perch for night viewing. Despite a slight haze the sky explodes in white diamonds sprinkled across a velvety black canvas. My effort in getting here and weathering the risks and discomfort are repaid by a precious revelation.

What a phenomenal universe. Galaxies shower their light upon me, even though I can only see neighboring stars and planets with much clarity or comprehension. This fantastic display meshes so well with the heavenly solitude and quiet of Mt. San Jacinto. Our little urban worlds and lives focused on trivial material things and conspicuous consumption seem so insignificant compared to the spectacle above. In near total quiet I absorb the wonder of our magnificent Earth – only one of uncountable celestial bodies.

This is a defining moment for how I will henceforth look at my life and our planet. I may be without company on this mountain – on this spot of our globe – but I understand instinctively that I'm never truly alone – merely surrounded by solitude.

Feeling completely spent, but more alive than I can ever remember, I head back to my little cocoon and the little death we seem to die every time we go to sleep.

Along about 4:30 a.m. I rise, pull on gloves and cap, and leave the cocoon of warmth. On the distant eastern skyline night begins to fade into black-gray dawn. It will still be another half an hour until birds stir. But, the change in light on the horizon is discernible. Glad to be free of the tent, willing to sacrifice a little cold for the opportunity to watch a new day dawn, I hunker down on the hillside. Fast moving cloud cover extends well over the eastern California and western Arizona deserts – I can almost see that far. Nonetheless, a sliver of radiant red soon fills a narrow slit on the horizon – the sun is gradually rising on a new day. I watch as its radiance beats back the clouds and its brightness beams if only for brief seconds from the distant horizon to my mountain.

Breakfast is very brief, but hot chocolate instills warmth necessary to last those few rough moments when all gear is packed and down coat is stuffed in anticipation of a brisk walk to generate heat. Water is now a serious concern and I desperately hope that my planned source will deliver. Walking in the totally silent and calm morning, breath blowing out in clouds of fog, my extremities gradually begin to return to their senses. Within the hour I arrive at shallow Hidden Lake – a rarity in these mountains. It's nothing but a gigantic plate of ice sitting there cold, unfriendly and uninviting, a perfect rink for anyone with ice skates.

A side trail to the tram into Palm Springs comes up rather quickly but I don't harbor any illusions that anyone will be operating the beast at this hour. Besides trailside views to the east are sufficient for my needs. I want to get to water and then up San Jacinto peak as quickly as I can. Thus, begins a fast plod through scrawny pine forest on the north slope of Mt. San Jacinto's ridge. Given the modest moisture that these trees have to draw from it's amazing they hold on. Nonetheless, the forest seems monochromatic. Perhaps this is due to coming off my high the night before; perhaps it's the gray and dismal cloud cover. How can this forest possibly compare to the dazzling display of swirling stars?

The sometimes-rocky trail weaves through round moss covered boulders and spindly trees before reaching luxuriant Round Valley. All hopes for water are quickly dashed as I see the brown grasses. My memory saw them as a flourishing green carpet in summer; I have forgotten that winter will change the complexion entirely. And, as I process thoughts about the iced over lake and the dead meadow at my feet, I know with certainty the Forest Service spigot will not be working. Why in the world did I think that in these frigid temperatures it would be working? The Forest Service drained it months ago. Next opportunity for water will be a cienega down from Wellman's Divide on the south-facing slope of Mt. San Jacinto.

There are times when you simply have to hunker down and slog it out, and now is one of those moments. I concentrate sharply on the task and take it steady climbing up out of Round Valley and its deserted campground. Before long I reach the divide leading down to Saddle Junction where the trail levels out after climbing up Devil's Slide Trail.

A side route snakes 800 feet up through rock, snow and ice to the summit of Mt. San Jacinto. I think about breaking out my stove and melting snow to replenish my water supply, but it just doesn't seem worth the trouble at this point. Skies are overcast. A sharp wind blows down the mountain and I don't relish the thought of visiting loftier heights under a significant wind-chill.

On the south-facing slope feeble sun provides a sparse measure of comfort. I have had enough of frigid temperatures last night and early this morning. No reason to press my luck. Looking south over undulating ridges festooned with lodgepole pine, cedar and shiny granite boulders, patches of snow offer some relief from winter's gray. Wellman's Divide offers one last opportunity to savor the solitude I've enjoyed these brief two days where the only sounds reaching my ears are those made by this majestic mountain. Things that in the city seemed so important have been reduced to their true value out here amid nature. Refreshed and ready to enter back into the fray, I pull pack straps tight and drop down the trail.

Ten minutes later I come upon a small creek dribbling water on the trail beneath a twisted pine. Most of the spring's flow is petrified into ice. Long icicles hang over rocks down which the water courses. No wonder the other minute springs and flows typically encountered in summer are nowhere to be found. They're frozen solid.

Turning to continue, I see a young fellow several switchbacks below hiking to the peak. And, as he passes, my moments of solitude on this most southern of the Sierra mountains crystallize into memories.

* * *

In *The Quest*, Tom Brown, Jr. (1991) recounted his reactions after returning from a vision quest that was especially rich in insights and understanding. He noted: "I don't think that I can remember a day before this one where I felt more alive or where Nature was more real and intense. I was in a world so different than I had ever known. It was a world full of beauty, rapture, and a sense of expansion. A pure world untainted by the things of man, my analysis, or my thoughts. All through the day I could sense so much more."

In many respects this is precisely how I felt upon reaching the trusty red Opel sitting desolately in the trailhead parking lot. My winter adventure left me sensing things far outside my normal realm of perception.

Driving more slowly, more deliberately, into Idyllwild and down the flanks of Mt. San Jacinto, I maintain a deep sense of peace about life and wild places. Like Tom Brown Jr., this winter backpack trip served as a sort of mini-vision quest. It helped me know at least a brief moment when rational humans did not hold sway and where the magic of a mountain, its spirit and the universe held court. Insignificant distractions and the minutiae of life that have driven me to this adventure are exactly that — trivial. But, I'm very thankful that they led me to this backcountry adventure in the Southern Sierra.

14

Sacred Ground

Olympic National Park in Washington state; yesterday was inarguably glacial. An early June day where temperatures never exceeded 46 degrees and rain showers pelted everyone into seclusion, today I'm anxious to stretch my legs and blend back into the land. Camped at the base of Storm King Mountain on Lake Crescent's shores, intriguing possibilities abound. Barnes Creek flows serenely into the lake while offering not-so-subtle hints of captivating water draining from sub-alpine country of Happy Lake Ridge and Baldy Ridge. A trail ambles up Barnes Creek toward Baldy Ridge and possibilities for Storm King Mountain. This neglected path isn't listed on any list of top 40 hikes of the Olympics – a perfect reason to see what it has to offer.

Walking along a verdant, sodden trail at Lake Crescent, spongy tread provides bounce to my step and hints at powerful volumes of water this area receives. The way threads through a hushed grove of immense cedar and fir all dark, peaceful and cool. Thick emerald-like moss grows on ancient fallen trees now serving as nurse logs to incubate a future forest. Impenetrable clumps of salmon berry and

salah form a twisting green corridor bracketing the path and creating inviting habitat for birds and chipmunks flitting about. Veiled
by lacy canopy overhead, a brief moment of sweet sun streams
through this forest cathedral and adds an undeniably reverent tone
to this morning. All is right in the world.

Such sacred moments fill me with inexplicable joy. I'm much
less apologetic these days about how astonishing discoveries like this
influence my pace. In younger years when all I could think about
was the final destination, I wouldn't have been caught dead dawdling
to caress a stunning downed cedar with an appreciative once-over
whose bark resembles a luxurious green fur coat. Formerly when
summiting a peak I was known as five-minute-Howard... there
were zillions of miles of trail to be covered. I wanted to impress
others with those long marches for which Bob Marshall developed
a legendary reputation. Five minutes was all that I could spare in my
zeal to cover every single mile of terra firma.

Admittedly a good long hike that makes my rear-end drag still
remains a special tonic to soothe my weary soul. However, lately
I've found that a continuous diet of physical exertion is made much
better by sublime moments of contemplation about the larger
scheme of things. This will sound like pure heresy to young folks
whose peak-bagging flames still burn brightly within. After all, they
rationalize, who is to say that they aren't appreciating wild country
as well as us old slugs?

An answer lies within the depth of concentration required to
shift from mere appreciation to recognition of a special sacredness associated with any wild setting. Few people can calm their
minds sufficiently in a brief respite lasting a few minutes to think
at a higher level. Five-minute-Wonder-Boy certainly failed. He was
typically too busy sucking air and rummaging through his pack
looking for a sugary snack, wadded-up map, tepid quart of water

or long-sleeved shirt to invest more than a nano-second in thinking higher thoughts.

In my case the cost of idolizing the physical side of adventure wasn't too high. Over time I managed to reach the point that I appreciate both – physical exertion associated with a BIG undeniably impressive goal such as a peak, forest glen or alpine lake, *and* reflective recognition that many things merit extra attention along the path to whatever objective I am pursuing. That something special deserving a meritorious break in physical activity is the hallowed aura associated with wild places; where the sum of the parts – forest, stream, rocks, meadows and other unique constituent parts forming the whole – leave me absolutely spell-bound and at a loss for words.

That the journey is more important than the destination is hardly an inimitable discovery. But it does have heft in a world where too many wilderness voyagers – young and old alike – get caught up with the doing of it to appreciate the more subtle, even divine, undertones. That's when wilderness is reduced to nothing more than a form of Disneyland entertainment and recreation only totals to a shallow take-away. Perhaps this is an inevitable downside of adventure; its physical demands tend to override the rich enjoyment from melding with the land waiting patiently along a trail, single-track, frothing rapid, snow-bound slope or rocky cove.

Curving around a monster of a fallen western red cedar, my trail ambles south toward Barnes Creek. This is one time that a direct route is not necessarily the best route. On mornings like this it pays to explore every nook and cranny as life reemerges after days of blustery and sopping weather.

Perhaps it is the juxtaposition of the Olympic Peninsula's rainforest with high desert characterizing my home that enables me to better appreciate the finer details and plethora of small, but fascinating, stories bracketing this walk. Back home I have deep respect for scraggly vegetation — sage, chamisa, bitterbrush, sumac — that is able to withstand excruciatingly prolonged drought. Even in their desiccated state I still admire these plants because I simultaneously see them in my mind as flush after monsoon rains have transformed them; the fleeting Jekyll phase of their Jekyll-and-Hyde existence.

Surrounded by this world-class rainforest I'm bowled-over because almost no soil is untouched by vegetation. What a definitive contrast to high desert where plants have lots of breathing space around them and any out-of-the-ordinary collection of moisture due to a fortuitous depression, fledgling arroyo, or overturned rock spells vigorous life. Except for the path I'm walking, it is near impossible to find a square-inch of naked soil. This great disconformity drops me down a couple of gears when that macho adventurer part of me wants to get up the mountain to see what I can see. All these plants and so little time — so little understanding of what they are and how they survive when jam-packed together like peas in a pod.

This profusion of life inevitably reins in that deep-seated drive to blast right through these lowlands. The remarkable greenest — plants, shrubs and trees everywhere I turn — combined with looming forest canopy instill a silence that is definitely hallowed. All is hush as cool zephyrs gently shake a few branches. I could no more power walk through this glen than I could a synagogue, church or mosque. And, such a captivating setting inevitably leaves me thankful that the Maker of Life could shower us with such inordinate blessings.

Wwwwhhhooosssshhhhhhhhh.

From somewhere above a large mysterious form drops to forest floor on a fallen cedar's southern exposure. It's time to go into stealth mode to check out the action. Creeping silently and crouching as low to the ground as possible to hide my presence, grateful that whatever critter dropped to the ground hasn't run off; I carefully approach a turn in the trail hidden by the fallen cedar's gargantuan root mass. Without a second thought I've switched from worshiping this lush forest primeval back to full adventure mode.

On the other side of this rough-barked cedar and teetering next to a well-ventilated, hollowed-out log is an owl with a discouraged, angry look. It must have missed a chipmunk at the very last moment. Turning to look at me, a new intruder, the owl pauses briefly and then soars upward to a large branch in a distant cedar. Hooting to let the lucky chipmunk know that it will eventually have the last say in the matter, wise old owl ruffles its feathers and hunkers down waiting for the next unwary morsel that, like me, thought this would be a great day to get outside.

I can't quite tell what type of owl this is. It doesn't have ear tuffs so characteristic of a great horned owl, long-eared owl, or short-eared owl nor the bulk of those species. That leaves either the rare spotted owl or the barred owl. It's impossible for me to tell the difference because the primary distinguishing factor is size — the spotted owl is smaller — and arcane markings on the breast or flanks. Whichever species it is, I'm happy that it dropped down to see me.

The northern spotted owl is infamous for disrupting timber harvesting in the Pacific Northwest. More than a few families lost their livelihood due to this endangered species — some in the vicinity of Lake Crescent. The spotted owl typically nests in old growth forest, a predilection that stymies lumber companies intent on cutting down choice trees with huge payoff.

Recently lumberjacks may be inadvertently receiving a boost due to an ongoing battle of the species. As nature takes its course northern spotted owls may inevitably disappear despite the protection afforded threatened or endangered species. The lumberjacks' ally is none other than barred owls.

Spotted owls (Strix occidentalis) are represented by three subspecies: Strix occidentalis caurina (Northern spotted owl found in habitats like Olympic National Park), Strix occidentalis occidentalis, and Strix occidentalis lucida (Mexican Spotted Owl). Their average length is 17-18 inches with a wingspan of 40-42 inches and weight of 1-1.25 pounds. Spotted owls have brown plumage with abundantly white spotted breasts or flanks, dark eyes and gray beaks. They have a propensity for nesting in tree cavities and abandoned nests of raptors.

Barred owls (Strix varia) are gray in color compared to the brownish spotted owl and tend to have white horizontal bars on their chest in addition to white vertical streaks on their bellies. Their beaks are usually yellow and their eyes are brown.

Barred owls are typically 21 inches long with a wingspan of 40+ inches and weight of 1.5 pounds. Barred owls also rely on tree cavities and they are not hesitant to commandeer abandoned raptor nests.

The barred owl is geographically widespread across North America, but particularly dominant east of the Mississippi. In contrast, spotted owls are found primarily along the Pacific coast from California to Washington. A third member of the owl family, the Mexican spotted owl, can be found throughout Arizona and New Mexico as well as into Colorado and Arizona.

In Olympic National Park barred owls were relatively rare until about 15 years ago. Since then they have been progressively displacing northern spotted owls. Barred owls display greater aggressiveness and adaptability. Northern spotted owls are vacating their nests, but they haven't entirely moved back to the mainland. They are believed to be relocating somewhere in the same vicinity as their original nesting sites. Increased avian competition for prime nesting sites and scarce food could eventually tip the scales in favor of the barred owl thus undermining human efforts to maintain this endangered species.

With friend owl hunkered down for the moment I drift back to my passion. Sunlight breaks through the canopy in a most stunning display of light and shadow. Twenty yards ahead golden glowing shafts penetrate to forest floor intensifying the woods and its gift to walkers: a palpable sense of being lavishly bathed in emeralds. Bird magic may be over for the day, but not the incomparable embroidery of greenery that has delayed my progress toward a waiting mountainside. Time to get up that hillside; I'm yearning for views over the Strait of Juan de Fuca and Vancouver Island in the far distance.

My trail seeks Barnes Creek's valley opening through a broad, vast meadow with thick waist-level lime-green grass – remnants of a pioneer's homestead – and into another stand of majestic western red cedar. Jumping over muddy pools of standing water, I'm beginning to wonder whether it ever really dries out here where the northwestern tip of the continent slams up against the Pacific Ocean. This forest thrives on all of the excess rain; trees literally soar showing the land's vitality. It's made all that much more inviting by Barnes Creek's rushing pure waters that are spilling, foaming, dancing, and plowing headlong toward Lake Crescent and soon the arms of the sea. Who couldn't be more than a little enchanted by this rollicking pristine creek?

A trail junction offers two equally attractive possibilities – continue along Barnes Creek or head almost straight up toward the mountaintop. This is a more difficult decision than it might otherwise appear. To this point my walk has been richly satisfying. Why give up perfection and the pervading holiness shrouding this creek? I could stay in this cathedral forever, but adventure tugs at my shirtsleeve.

Choosing the unknown above me, it only takes several minutes on a switch-backing trail before dense foliage is left behind along the creek. Looking down onto the green mass nurtured by Barnes Creek, it's easy to see a distinct shift in vegetation from valley to mountain-side. On these drier hills Douglas fir replaces western red cedar as the dominant tree. It's a sharp transition that occurs like a snap of the fingers, seemingly akin to a cloud suddenly blocking out the sun.

I'm ready for trees that don't humiliate a human. A blanket-like forest of dense Douglas fir typical for the Northwest would certainly speed up my progress. I'm ready to break a big-time sweat getting to the high reaches of this peninsula. Sometimes there is nothing like a good stiff climb. Given all of the introspection I've been through in the last half hour, now is as good a time as any to shift back to power mode.

Two swift switchbacks in succession reaching for the sky force me to crank up my exertion output two levels. Once again I return to that warm-and-fuzzy comfort zone of blistering pace and deep mea-sured breathing. All other deeper thoughts quickly evaporate leaving me totally focused on climbing and the adventure of penetrating country that judging by this diminishing trail sees few visitors.

Good ideas can come crashing down without a moment's notice. By the time I reach the fourth switchback a radical change boggles my mind. I've left the huge western red cedar behind only to be replaced by supremely gigantic Douglas fir. I screech to a halt and crane my neck backward to take in this unanticipated anomaly. These colossal trees make Barnes Creek's cedar forest seem mun-dane by comparison.

Astounding!

How in the world do trees grow this tall and thick? I feel like I've shrunk down to nothing. Surrounded by immeasurably soaring giants I'm very, very insignificant in a forest of spectacular beauty. These Douglas fir are massive with five-to-six foot trunks standing well over one hundred feet tall and much more. The scale is almost incomprehensible in this inspirational shrine of giants. Mossy strands like full-grown beards smother gray-black trunks of the fir. Old men at a troll convention would be righteously jealous.

Among sword fern, Oregon grape and moss covered trunks in this magnificent hall I marvel that it can all fit together so perfectly. Wildness on the grandest scale tucked secretly away on this hillside leads to one irrefutable conclusion: *I'm walking on sacred ground.*

Pack off of my back, perspiration cooling in a slight breeze of the morning; I am absolutely alone, not lonesome; standing in silence and solemn adoration as sunlight gently filters down from the skyscraper canopy. Tops of these mutant trees are lost in the stratosphere beyond my reach. But somewhere in the pit of my soul I know that it doesn't matter that I'm six feet tall and my companions twenty or twenty-five times higher. As amazement smothers me I realize that we fit in equally and play an important role within something of cosmic significance.

These superlatively wild moments at Barnes Creek began with an unanticipated visit from a wise old owl. Its presence should have given me a premonition that today was going to be a very special day – one filled with sparkling wildness and soul-altering insights. Seldom does a little hike offer up such an unanticipated mega dose of both physical and spiritual adventure. In the end owl's drop-in was wholly prophetic, despite the fact that I initially saw it as just a bird. That swooshing apparition was symbolic of the special – to me, holy – ground I was about to trod.

* * *

Mammoth trees, unforeseen visitors, church-like quiet, steep mountain terrain and unique rainforest combine in a mosaic where adventure plays out perfectly on both physical and spiritual dimensions. Yet, it is more often the exception than the rule that these two dimensions (or others such as the emotional side) will surface on any outdoor adventure. For the most part it is fairly easy to predict situations where physical adventures have an opportunity to speak the loudest. That's the advantage of word-of-mouth yarns, topographical maps, trail guides, and vast media accessible today. The epiphany-side of adventure is an entirely different matter.

I have discovered that one sure-fire way of increasing the odds that my adventures will be multi-dimensional is to begin slightly before daybreak. As black of night eases into those fleeting moments of gray before sun claims the day, starting a journey at that moment seems to be a requisite for a day marked by fortuitous revelations. Once the sun is fully up, wildness retreats back a notch or two.

A decrepit avocado green backpack settles snugly as sweat-stained shoulder straps and frayed waist belt tighten. Who doesn't feel the marvelous thrill of a looming journey race down their spine at moments like this? I'm optimistic that this trip will turn out exactly as planned but also bothered by nuisance little details cluttering my mind. Did I turn off the stove at home? Was the back door locked? Did I bring insect repellant? Should I have brought a heavier fleece jacket? Once I start walking, all that garbage evaporates leaving high spirits about my jolly passion.

Worn-out leather boots with stiff Vibram soles launch dust squalls calf-high before dissipating into ethereal clouds of the finest tan-brown powder. A short jog in the trail and then I enter dense forest upon a fir and hemlock needle cushion. Shimmering light reflects off a distant tiny ribbon of creek that dances in a brushy ravine. Overhead a few sunny rays flitter down through a mosaic of random breaks in the brooding canopy. Morning's refrigerator freeze is all gone with the sun; a victim of summer's force. It will be back if I climb high enough to distant snow fields.

Cascade trails seem like they seldom follow river valleys. They are perpetually switch-backing, and more often scrambling their way, toward rocky summits, along undulating ridgelines, and destined for blue-green lakes spare as can be hunkered down in talus-laced basins. It's this prospect of honest hard work that draws me here. After interminable hours of earning a livelihood, I return to life, resurrected by progressively narrowing contour intervals.

I'm weaving in and out among a maze of trees reaching to the sky, a muddle of uniform trunks all brown-black and deeply incised with convoluted canyons. My mind empties while putting one foot in front of the other. Ten minutes later, it's time to shed a long sleeve shirt which means the stone on my back must also be cantilevered down, a nagging in-law who just won't go away.

Evaporating perspiration steams in the cool air nudging me toward filtered sun, a meager commodity down here on the forest floor. Muscles warmed and ready for the task ahead, I finally feel normal after attending to business this past week. Seattle is sweet, but urban life's relentless press gnaws away at my pathetic soul. Memories of my last outing seem eons away, fuzzy at the edges.

Higher on the mountain brief openings suggest a possible crest and prospects of Lake Dorothy at 3,058 feet. In a few stubborn places the trail is spongy and damp, but as I climb toward a rounded ridge, roots serve as stairway with dry tread. Loved to death, this trail is pounded from innumerable visitors eager to gaze on Lake Dorothy's splendor. A very early morning departure has me well ahead of the hordes, but I'm still concerned about the prospects for Bear and Deer Lakes. Who will be going far and deep this afternoon, intruding on those higher lakes? With luck, Lake Dorothy will be so alluring that greedy old me may have them all to myself.

This trail bobbles up and down, skating the eastern shoreline, climbing over and around gray-brown boulders protruding from the water's depths. Nine mystical tree-covered islands seem to float like Spanish galleons on the Lake Dorothy's surface. Two of them anchored about forty feet from shore, each the size of a small house, call guests to drop in. It's tempting until you test the glacial water. A short swim seems harmless but inserting my arm to the elbow settles the question. A dip would be more enticing in the afternoon.

At Lake Dorothy's southern end black-green waters fade into lighter shades of cobalt and emerald. That's my reference point and I continue in glowing sun after stopping to remove my sopping t-shirt. Then it's in and out, jogging to evade various tree and rock obstacles before running back to forest edge in bypassing a slight cove or rocky promontory. Meanwhile the trail's width diminishes; funny how a half-mile along this almost mile-and-a-half-plus lake can make such a difference in use. People stop on the edge of adventure, just at the threshold where uncertainty kicks in; the path less distinct, the physical challenge invigorating, and the scene otherworldly.

A little-known secret about enjoying pristine wilderness without accompanying hordes of people is to exploit The Law of Insurmountable Obstacles. According to this rule, any significant wilderness impediment is sufficient to stop 80 percent of backcountry travelers.

The vast majority of people will stop and turn around rather than tackle a difficult natural obstacle. Most people simply give up when confronted by a roaring stream; steep canyon requiring an elevation loss of 400 feet followed by a commensurate 400 foot climb out; an eighth-mile of blow-downs blocking the trail; a sharply steep climb that materializes out of nowhere along a path with modest vertical rise; a 65-yard perpetual snowfield; rocky scree where vestiges of trail are lost and ducks (hand stacked rock columns) show the way; or any other unusual conundrum.

This phenomenon is evident at any trailhead where the trail starts and stays steep. Width of the trail may be four feet at the beginning. Walk a half-mile higher and the path has narrowed to three feet. Go another half mile and a narrow two-foot walkway remains. People lose momentum at the slightest drop of a mosquito's wing on the trail.

It's not as though I haven't succumbed to The Law of Insurmountable Obstacles many times myself. One of my routine walking paths becomes heavily snowbound in winter. Despite climbing 4 miles and some 2,500 feet, I can never seem to rationalize finishing the last quarter mile over a 2-3 foot base of snow. I convince myself that it's too icy or that the snow is rotten and I may twist an ankle if I break through a hole. At most it may take an extra 5-10 minutes to finish the walk, but my mind plays tricks by making the obstacle seem larger than it really is.

In the final analysis wildness wins. The Law of Insurmountable Obstacles ensures that fewer people penetrate deeply into the backcountry. Over a gushing stream before climbing upward almost eight hundred feet, Lake Dorothy and its islands fall away beneath my boots. I've adopted a methodical cadence balancing progress and breath. Except for four modest switchbacks, the trail definitely heads up. In several places the path is virtually obscure; a limited number of hikers make the effort to come this far. Not many want to make the sacrifice needed to reach the upper lakes, especially with snow waiting above.

One hundred feet from what appears to be ridge top, a foot-and-a-half high jagged snowline abruptly appears. Hidden in lingering dark shadows on this northeastern slope, last winter's snow cover remains well into summer. Hopefully I'll be able to find a bare spot for my tent, but if not, an insulated pad should do the trick. After all, this backcountry foray will only last one night. There's plenty of time back in Seattle to sleep in a bed.

Cresting the ridge's rounded shoulder snow briefly disappears in the sunny warmth of a clearing. Marsh anemones sprout optimistically in a damp sink. Fir needles, saturated by water and simultaneously baked by sun, send up ambrosia and memories of other trails, other adventures in the wild. From here splotches of foot-deep snow cover the ground. Twenty-foot high conifers work hard to survive. Their sub-alpine environment eventually runs to the ragged edge of alpine territory higher on the mountain's spine.

One last glance back to Lake Dorothy provides all the incentive I need to keep going. Today's hikers have arrived and small groups with brightly colored t-shirts are spread along the shoreline whiling away time before lunch. Thank goodness for seven hundred feet. It's only six or so mature Douglas fir standing end to end, but more than most folk want to tackle after reaching the main attraction of Lake Dorothy.

Bear Lake lies ahead at 3,610 feet after a modest drop from a saddle. Portions of the trail are partially free from snow so it's hunt-and-peck along the northern shore looking for a dry spot. Eventually one appears that isn't serving as a holding pond for melting snow. Here's where I'll spend the night; my tent mere feet from the shore looking out on sheets of ice still floating around Bear Lake.

The remainder of the afternoon unfolds pretty predictably due to mellow conditions. Home goes up fast with rain-fly erected in case the weather gods decide to change their minds. Domestic chores out of the way, I head west to circumambulate Deer Lake that is 27 feet lower than Bear Lake and fed by a gushing stream from its twin. Surprisingly Deer Lake is ice-free. Since each lake is about one-tenth of a square mile in size, perhaps depth explains the difference in ice. On Deer Lake's western shoulder a path weaves a hundred yards toward a sharp plummet of four hundred feet to Snoqualmie Lake.

An old trail switch backs to this once accessible lake. It subsequently became remote when a road washed out. The Forest Service left things the way they were and in the process promoted wildness. It doesn't take very long for the Earth to reclaim land when vehicle access is limited. Foot travel is now the primary mode for reaching this special spot folded into the Alpine Lakes Wilderness. I follow this old trail down to see what Snoqualmie Lake is all about. Ice free, it's an impressively large lake compared to Deer and Bear Lakes and about half as large as Lake Dorothy.

* * *

Next morning, clambering out of my tent with down jacket as a barrier against enveloping chill, I head toward soft golden-yellow sunshine on the western snow-covered shore cleaving Bear and Deer Lakes. Those first steps out of a tent always bristle with sensory overload. Cold muscles groan as I struggle to stand upright while assessing a new day's beauty. Flexing my stiff back, the price for not doing this often enough is driven painfully home. Momentary grogginess holds sway while I try to take it all in: crisp fir-scented air, cloudless baby blue sky, nary a breeze, and vast stillness. No diminutive curling waves are lapping the shore this morning.

Hunger throws a tantrum in my stomach's rumbling pit but I'm being gently called to something more meaningful than pandering to that unquenchable machine. A few stiff steps and I spin around taking a measure of this wilderness. There's no deep decision to make, no earth-shattering issues to contemplate. The outlet stream where Bear and Deer Lakes kiss exerts a magnetic pull that cannot be denied. Its energy is over-powering, leaving no choice. I give in and stumble over snow-slick mossy rocks and assorted shrubs, over fallen fir limbs toward this single illuminated spot chosen by the sun.

Stepping down a couple of feet at the stream's edge to accommodate a pesky deadfall poking me in the legs, only the merry gurgling sound of water rolling from one basin to the next breaks this morning's total silence. Amazing how it all fits together. Snow gradually melting in perfect proportion after a half-year's steady accumulation fills Bear Lake to overflowing so that the gift can be shared with Deer Lake. It is passed on down the line to Snoqualmie Lake and then to the Taylor River and Puget Sound. An endless circle unfolding precisely as it has since time immemorial.

Sun penetrates my exposed skin while also fluffing the down parka; it's one of those very special moments that mark the high point of immersion in the wild. According to an early Hasidic saying, "When you walk across the fields with your mind pure and holy, then from all the stones, and all growing things, and all animals, the sparks of their soul come out and cling to you, and then they are purified and become a holy fire in you." My mind is an empty vessel uncontaminated with concerns of the day or even recollections of my other life expensed in earning a living. I'm living life right now at its ultimate level; completely consumed; totally focused on the present.

For a few brief moments I rise to a spiritual level that's elusive in outdoor adventuring. It isn't just the embracing penetrating warmth of sun on body after eight hours of a little death in a down-filled mummy coffin. It's more — I'm walking on sacred ground.

I'm literally part of all that exists. I've gone from a physical plane of existence to a higher spiritual one. All that's asked is for me to stand there with mind empty of its normal clutter, receptive to the sparks of tiny stream, brimming lakes, picturesque basins, shadowing firs and fresh breezes as sun lights the chill air on fire. And that moment epitomizes what it means to savor the last best adventure – a moment of sacred epiphany.

15

Epiphany's Postlude

High on Cuyamaca Peak in parched, rugged coastal mountains near San Diego a captivating spring gushes steadily, discharging icy-cold water, a legacy from sporadic winter snow and occasional monsoon rain. Resting at almost 6,000 feet, this spring commands a lofty height for these Sierra-wannabe mountains. Surrounded by thickets of mountain mahogany, glossy green fern, evergreen ceanothus (California lilac), gray-tinged manzanita on drier exposed slopes, and scattered cedar sheltered from rushing ocean winds, this precious water source has an imposing view over a striking spine of mountains. They rise dramatically from scorching desert floor some sixty miles distant.

In such a serene spot it seems ludicrous that a massive infusion of adrenaline is driving me crazy this spring afternoon. I'm anxious beyond belief with pulse racing; gasping for air like a serial smoker chained to a decades-old habit. My senses are wide open, attenuated. I hear, smell, see and feel the wildness. Seems silly to be in such distress on this mellow hillside in an overused – many would say abused – forest of Southern California.

Fear this: several weeks ago, mere yards from this spring a cougar methodically stalked and killed a middle-aged woman innocently out birding.

Seemed like no big deal when I was driving up to the trailhead. With an enormous ration of bravado I speculated that a cougar wouldn't tangle with someone of my size. Now that I'm out here all alone that macho spin just doesn't quite cut it. Deafening silence is eerie; it never seemed this quiet before on Cuyamaca Peak.

Lull before the storm?

What's over in the cedars there among the rustling ferns?

Can lightning strike twice?

My mind tries to assemble some order; to answer these questions systematically and to turn off the faucet of adrenaline starting to overwhelm rational thought – the logic of wishful thinking.

It's fascinating that even in humble Cleveland National Forest where the most menacing confrontations are normally with illegal aliens and angry rattlesnakes, deadly efficient predators are a life-threatening consideration. Walks in Cuyamaca Rancho State Park are now writ large with adventure.

Most travelers appreciatively stop to taste this spring's sparkling water and then lose themselves to big views eastward. Topped with huge granite boulders piled like so many loose marbles, Stonewall Peak juts defiantly skyward while shallow blue-green Lake Cuyamaca rests at its base – a precious treasure in this Mediterranean climate. Farther south rolling amber meadows festooned with squat gray Gambel oaks invite speculation about life of early settlers and Native tribes in this sky island.

Gazing out on nearby forest, meadows and lake, my sight is inevitably drawn to distant gray haze and a discernible transition to desert. Lower mountain ridges are completely smothered with Roma tomato-shaped brown boulders and virtually no trees. This is the beginning of the end to a magical anomaly – semi-lush growth of chaparral forest in a waterless ocean of land. Nonetheless, a compelling beauty, and spirit, dwells in this place. A red-tail hawk soars searchingly overhead while nagging chilled breezes subside momentarily allowing warmth of golden sun to penetrate. Perfume of chaparral mixed with high pine forest overwhelms my senses; it's easy to see that this inspiring vista captures the essence of something larger, something grander, at work.

While admiring this miraculous world spread before me, the modest spring continues its chore behind my back – nourishing a verdant fern garden, refreshing flitting birds seeking a bit of moisture in the warming sun, and gathering in diminutive pools for larger mammals, such as mountain lions, biding their time before stepping to the fount of life.

Most people easily recognize the distinctiveness of this special place, but they typically attribute it to the vast view of a water-challenged ecosystem – mountains and desert sprawling to the eastern horizon-line. Few probably think about merely turning around and focusing on this fascinating micro world surrounding spring and glen; a paradigm shift in perspective would enable them to capture the same tangible essence of something grander.

Cuyamaca Peak's spring radiates a palpable spirit of the backcountry. This mojo is what draws many people to the natural world. It's more than the sum of impressive visual geography, abundant flora and unusual dollop of moisture. It's more than just the beauty of the earth or the opportunity for adventure. This spirit is the intuitive feeling in my gut that something larger than humans has been at work in the landscape and in my life. Now that pumas are added to this equation, the wildness of Cuyamaca Peak increases exponentially.

Turning from the spring toward the final sweaty summit ascent, I'm thankful for this rich intoxicating summit quest and my rising adrenaline. Certainly I don't want someone else to lose their life at the hands of a mountain lion just to give my backcountry adventure a heightened rush; that's not the point. The uncomplicated intrinsic beauty of the spring has always been sufficient to raise a persistent trickle of appreciation in my veins. What's different after the puma attack is an undeniably clear understanding about why my adrenaline used to simultaneously spike in direct proportion with my pleasure when visiting this little enclave.

Danger was quietly lurking in the cedars, under the manzanita and amidst the ferns. Ancient wisdom stored in my genes informed me subconsciously. On this fine spring day, that wisdom also commands my consciousness. Intuitively I know that I need to be more cautious. Now that knowledge is laid bare; it's a revelation that will forever change how I walk this mountainside. But it took something much larger than me – a chance attack by a native predator – to open my eyes to the full breadth of wildness embracing Cuyamaca Peak.

That there is something grander in the wild is a central tenant in the belief systems of many indigenous people. Joseph Marshall, III explains the Lakota perspective: "All living things are related because we are all children of the Earth. And everything we do affects the Earth and everything on it, including the human race. The more water we pollute, the less there is for us to drink. The more land we contaminate, the less we have to grow crops. The more forest we cut down, the less oxygen there is for us to breathe. We humans have made the Earth needy by our greed and selfishness, both rooted in the idea that the Earth was created for us."

Marshall suggests that the Earth is part of something much larger, of a grand design. Unable to accept this notion, our society has tended to adopt a worldview – a view of the universe – of human centrality. But, it only takes a close look at a humble spring on the brushy side of Cuyamaca Peak, or a sudden rustling of dense foliage above the spring, to dash this fallacy into a million pieces.

* * *

October 29, 2003.

That date is forever etched into the history of Cuyamaca Rancho State Park and Cleveland National Forest in the hills outside San Diego. The Cedar Fire, started that day by a lost hunter, burned 100% of the park, completely devastating a wonderful gem of nature. Six hundred year old sugar pines were torched in the process, some almost vaporized. Ancient oaks were rendered to charcoal. A heritage of Civilian Conservation Corps construction went up in smoke. It all burned; totally black. Gone forever.

Cuyamaca Peak is vastly altered. Anyone who drives through the park can immediately see the widespread habitat destruction and an incinerated ecosystem. My sweet spring near Cuyamaca Peak still flows. In those first years following the fire it continued to dribble, but not to welcoming pools within a special glen. All the charming spring could do was create a messy mixture of gray ash, blackened soil and mucky water.

Don't count nature out. Powerful forces are at play here; cosmic pressures far exceeding what most of us could ever imagine possible.

Almost a decade later, this glen struggles to rejuvenate itself. Charming water rushes from the earth to tumble down a rocky channel some forty feet long before coalescing in a gravel-strewn bowl on the side of the trail. Where spring waters overwhelm the bowl a slick mossy stain wets Lookout Trail's asphalt. The fire may have won a brief battle, but nature is focused on setting things right. In another 50 years with abundant moisture it's possible that reclamation will take place. If drought years pile up it could be a couple of centuries before all is well. For some, this horrible desecration is too much to bear and by necessity they seek precious wildness elsewhere.

Many grieve the infinite losses at Cuyamaca Peak or any wild habitat succumbing to human frailty. But, with each new spring season comes rebirth. Snow and rain from winter nurture seeds and plants that somehow escaped an inferno's wrath. Throughout the ancient rancho ceanothus has literally exploded. This lilac family member loves drought and nutrients provided in the massive fire. Vegetation has been reestablished around the spring. Luminescent green sprouts of manzanita reach skyward, and vivid mixture of ceanothus, ferns, grasses and Gambel oak capture the spring's lifeblood. Cedar seedlings are trying to break through the claustrophobia. In time lonely puma will return as other life reestablishes itself – squirrels, rabbits, lizards, rattlesnakes and all other life that called Cuyamaca Peak home.

And, in good measure I'll return with the seasons to enjoy the passing of years, the rise of adrenaline and the spirit of wildness.

Cuyamaca's spring is supremely emblematic of epiphanies I've been lucky to enjoy in my wilderness ramblings. It always seems that when something most compelling – a dramatic vista, unusual rock formations or towering peaks, charismatic wildlife, or, raging whitewater – commandeers attention, I discover a totally unique and completely unanticipated little gift off to the side or right under my nose. The sum of these revelations is simultaneously intoxicating and baffling; paradoxical in a world where there is continual pressure to reject wildness as one of, if not *the*, imperatives essential to life lived well.

Realizing that I need to look more intently for things unique personifies this contradiction. Reflecting back over zillions of trail miles hiked; uncountable smoky campfires embraced; and, thousands of days spent chasing wild country; the ultimate last best adventure for me has been a methodical transformation of how I think about, perceive and appreciate wildness.

In a world where conventional wisdom tends to squash more enlightened views of backcountry adventuring, simple lessons learned in looking unconventionally at wildness and adventure appear to be particularly meritorious. It is precisely this reversed algorithm, a contrarian way of looking at things, which may ultimately spell salvation for our ravaged planet as well as for wilderness that lifts our spirits and lives.

Sources for Additional Reading

Chapter 1: The End of Adventure

Bangs, Richard. *Adventure without End*, Mountaineer Books, Seattle, WA, 2002, pp.212-221.

Chouinard, Yvon. *Let My People Go Surfing: The Education of a Reluctant Businessman*, Penguin Press, New York, 2005, pp. 159.

Jenkins, Mark. *A Man's Life: Dispatches from Dangerous Places*, Rodale Press, Emmaus, PA, 2007, pp. 82-90.

Leopold, Aldo. *A Sand County Almanac*, Oxford University Press, New York, 1949, 139.

Chapter 4: They're in There Somewhere

Armstrong, S. "Backstory: In the Tetons with grizzly bear researchers." *The Christian Science Monitor.* http://www.usatoday.com/tech/science/2005-11-16-bear-trail_x.htm.

Armstrong, S. "Backstory: On the trail of an icon." *The Christian Science Monitor.* http://www.csmonitor.com/2005/1116/p20s01-sten.html.

"Communication and social order within a wolf pack." http://www.ualberta.ca/~jzgurski/wcomm.html.

Fox, D. "More than meets the eye: Behavior and conservation." Conservation Biology. Summer 2003, Vol. 4, No. 3.

"Grand Teton Lodge Company." http://www.vailresorts.com/ourcompany.

Harrington, F.H. "What's in a howl?" NOVA Online. http://www.pbs.org/wgbh/nova/wolves/howl.html.

"Jackson Lake Lodge." http://www.Gtlc.com/lodgeJac.aspx.

Khltkbr. "What moose need." http://www.xyz.net/~khltkbr/projects/moose/needs.html.

"National Elk Refuge in Grand Teton and Jackson Hole Wyoming." http://www.jacksonholewy.net/attractions/jh_elk_refuge.php.

Runtz, M.W.P. "Moose behavior." http://www.mooseworld.com/behavior.htm.

Sloan, M. "Wolf sounds." Wolf Park, Battle Ground, IN. http://www.wolfpark.org/wolfsounds.html.

Chapter 5: Comfort Zone

"Spatial changes in alpine treeline vegetation patterns, Glacier National Park, Montana." Northern Rocky Mountain Science Center. http://www.nrmsc.usgs.gov/research/treeline_rsrch.htm.

"Sub-alpine ecosystem." http://www.wnps.org/ecosystems/sub_alpine_eco/sub_alpine.htm

Wilson, E.O. The Future of Life. Knopf: NY. 2002.

Chapter 6: Winter Revelation

"About us." http://www.redfeather.com.

Associated Press. "Body found in 2nd Mount Hood snow cave." MSNBC. http://www.msnbc.msn.com/id/16220398.

Associated Press. "Fallen climber was no stranger to risk." MSNBC. http://www.msnbc.msn.com/id/16272081/?displaymode=1006.

Associated Press. "Officials call off Mount Hood search." MSNBC. http://www.msnbc.msn.com/id/16296529/print/1/displaymode/1098/.

Fought, T. "Small teams look for clues on Mt. Hood. *Chicago Tribune Online Edition*. December 22, 2006.
.

"Innovation: Tubbs celebrates 100 years of explorations and innovation launching snowshoes into the next century!" http://www.tubbssnowshoes.com/innovation/.

"Oregon: Search for climbers end." *The New York Times*. Nytimes.com. December 21, 2006.

Milton, P. "Friend hopes for New York man as Oregon mountain search continues." http://www.boston.com/news/local/new_hampshire/articles/2006/12/18/friend_hopes_for_....

Stengle, J. "Killed climber had a passion for adventure." http://www.katu.com/news/4951417.html.

Tucker, J. "Snowshoeing." http://www.snowshoeracing.com/history.htm.

United State Snowshoe Association. http://www.snowshoeracing.com/home.htm.

Chapter 10: A Spirit of Adventureousness

Flores, D. "Karl Bodmer's gift." *Big Sky Journal.* Vol. 9, no. 5, p. 36

Chapter 12: Alpine Gardens

Almack, J.A. North Cascades grizzly bear ecosystem evaluation. Final report. 1993. http://www.nps.gov/noca/adhi-12f.htm

Barcott, B. *The Measure of a Mountain.* Sasquatch Books, Seattle. 2007.

Bass, R. *The Lost Grizzlies.* Mariner Books: New York. 1997.

Brown, T. *The Search.* Berkley Publishing Group, New York. 1980. p.46.

Cohen, S.L. "Rightful place?" *The Planet Online Edition.* http://planet.wwu.edu/oldsite/fall02/fall02_rightful.htm.

Friederich, S. "Keep Canadian grizzly bears north of border, lawmakers say." *Seattle Post Intelligencer*, April 10, 2003.

Grizzly Bear Outreach Project. http://www.bearinfo.org/abstract.htm.

"North Cascades. The diversity of life and its processes." http://www.nps.gov/noca/biodiversity.htm.

Snyder, G. *The Practice of the Wild.* North Point Press. 1990

Chapter 13: Solitude

Brown, T. *The Quest.* The Berkley publishing Group: New York. 1991, p. 91.

Caputo, P. "Alone." Wild Stories: The Best of Men's Journal. Crown Publishers: New York, 2002.

Todd Tanner. "Afraid," in Rick Bass (ed.) *The Roadless Yaak.* Guilford, Connecticut: The Lyons Press. 2002, p. 38-39.

Chapter 14: Sacred Ground

Marcot, B.G. and J.W. Thomas. "Of spotted owls, old growth and new policies: A history since the Interagency Scientific Committee Report." General Technical Report PNW-GTR-408, September, 1997.